AMERICAN CATHOLICISM
AND SOCIAL ACTION

American Catholicism
and Social Action:
A Search for Social Justice
1865-1950

AARON I. ABELL
Professor of History
University of Notre Dame

UNIVERSITY OF NOTRE DAME PRESS · 1963

Nihil Obstat: Edward D. Head, M.S.S.W.
Censor Deputatus

Imprimatur: ✠ Francis Cardinal Spellman
Archbishop of New York
July 13, 1960

The nihil obstat and imprimatur are official declarations that a book or pamphlet is free of doctrinal or moral error. No implication is contained therein that those who have granted the nihil obstat and imprimatur agree with the contents, opinions or statements expressed.

First Paperback Edition

University of Notre Dame Press
Notre Dame, Indiana

Library of Congress Catalog Card Number 60-15164

For
Frank and Sophia Schell

CONTENTS

PREFACE

The pages that follow present the Roman Catholic contribution to the social justice movement in the United States. Since by common consent the contribution has been an impressive one, especially in recent years, the time has come to recount the story of its genesis and development. No study to date has attempted to give a general description or interpretative synthesis of the Catholic social movement in its entirety. Although a few excellent monographs have been written on various phases of Catholic social thought and action, these studies cover only a small part of the field and, with an exception or two, do not employ the social justice approach; that is, they do not view human welfare in its social aspects as a mutual sharing of burdens and benefits by interrelated persons, groups, and public authorities.

I have endeavored to tell the story of Catholic social reform in its integral fullness, somewhat on the model of my study, *The Urban Impact on American Protestantism, 1865–1900*, Harvard Historical Studies, LIV (Cambridge, 1943). As in that book, so also in the present volume, I try to make the reader constantly aware of the dynamic interplay of "charity" or social service, labor association, and state action as the great propulsive influences in social reform. As chiefly wage-earning immigrants, American Catholics displayed many radical tendencies on the industrial front. This fact presented the Church with a double problem: how, on the one hand, to champion the cause of the poor without endangering the public interest or the common good, and, on the other, how to oppose socialism without negating or ignoring the claims of social reform. The ways in which Catholicism attempted to meet this ever present challenge form the major theme of this essay. Only less important is the theme of Americanization in Catholic thought and action. As a religious minority against which opposition was easily aroused, American Catholics were ever obliged to appease public opinion. To this end, Catholic social liberals insisted that immigrants speedily conform to American customs and ways and that the Church itself accommodate its ideal of authoritarian inclusiveness to the realities of the American "sect" system. As the reader will discover, I have throughout most of the book discussed the Church's charity and social service in the context of Americanization. Only with the advent of drastic restriction of immigration in the mid-1920s did this phase of Catholic social history become of relatively minor importance.

In the preparation of this study I have become indebted to many persons and institutions. In more ways than note taking my wife, Elizabeth Schell Abell, lent support and encouragement. A grant-in-aid from the Social Science Research Council accelerated my work in its early stages. From time to time the University of Notre Dame lessened my teaching load and provided student assistants. The Reverend Bartholomew F. Fair of St. Charles Seminary, Overbrook, Pennsylvania, placed at my disposal the rich pamphlet and newspaper collection of the American Catholic Historical Society of Philadelphia. To all these kindly helpers I am genuinely grateful. I owe most, however, to the distinguished historian and archivist Thomas T. McAvoy, C.S.C. As colleague and department head, Father McAvoy has shown continuous interest in the progress of this work, and I have immensely profited from his wise counsel and vast knowledge of American Catholic history.

AMERICAN CATHOLICISM
AND SOCIAL ACTION

CHAPTER I

The Formation of the Catholic Minority: Early Social Patterns

The Catholic Church in America and the economic foundations of the social justice movement took shape simultaneously, each with unanticipated rapidity. Until the closing decades of the nineteenth century the national myth proclaimed that Old World social conditions did not — and could not — exist in the United States, that in this land of liberty and unparalleled opportunity every person of energy, character, and foresight could escape want and enjoy the adornments of life. Yet the misery present in the rapidly growing cities — containing one sixth of the population by 1860 — was clearly irremovable without recourse to concerted effort. As urban industrialism strode speedily to dominance after 1865, controversy flared between individualists on the one hand and the advocates of full or mitigated socialization on the other.[1]

In this contest the country's religious forces, including the Catholic Church, actively and creatively participated. Apart from its urban environment, the Catholic Church would, in fact, have lacked numerical influence. At the end of the American Revolution, American Catholics numbered less than twenty-five thousand, the Holy See was informed by John Carroll, soon to be designated Bishop of Baltimore, the first in the new nation. Centered in Maryland and eastern Pennsylvania, these Catholics were planters and farmers, Carroll reported, "except the merchants and mechanics living in Philadelphia."[2] While all could see that, like other religious bodies, Catholicism under Carroll, his associates, and immediate successors profited from the religious freedom guaranteed in the new Constitu-

[1] See especially Sidney Fine, *Laissez Faire and the General Welfare State; A Study of Conflict in American Thought, 1865–1900* (Ann Arbor, 1954).

[2] John Gilmary Shea, *History of the Catholic Church in the United States,* II, 258.

tion, the assumption persisted that it could not gain a real foothold in the country. By intermingling with Protestants on the expanding frontier where priests were few, the scattered Catholic immigrants were expected to lose their faith. Only in part were these hopes or fears to be realized. Largely through financial inability to reach the receding frontier and take up farming, Catholic newcomers, especially the Irish, settled in the seaboard cities more numerously than did the immigrant adherents of most other faiths. Well over a half million by 1840, engaged "in the humble, laborious, but useful occupations of life," [3] Catholic communicants reached the three-million mark in the next two decades,[4] the accessions stemming chiefly from poverty-stricken peasants fleeing famine and pestilence in Ireland and in lesser degree from displaced farmers and craftsmen in German lands feeling the first impacts of the Industrial Revolution.

Not all Catholic immigrants congregated in cities. Here and there on the frontier Irish Catholics founded agricultural settlements, while the major part of German Catholics until 1860 and many thereafter occupied large rural areas, chiefly in the states of the Old Northwest.[5] Never more than fifteen per cent of the total Catholic population, these farmers maintained a vigorous religious life which in the twentieth century developed an articulate awareness of rural claims on social justice. No immigrant Catholic community rivaled the sizable exodus of Maryland Catholics into central Kentucky in the late eighteenth century. Planned by a "league" of about sixty families, the migration was in some respects a colonization venture.[6] Given diocesan organization in 1808, these Anglo-American Catho-

---

[3] Peter Guilday, *The National Pastorals of the American Hierarchy* (1792–1919), p. 85.

[4] *Dunigan's American Catholic Almanac* (New York, 1860), pp. 297–341; *The American Christian Record* (New York, 1860), p. 382; Thomas O'Gorman, *A History of the Catholic Church in the United States* (New York, 1895), p. 496.

[5] Mary Gilbert Kelly, O.P., *Catholic Immigrant Colonization Projects in the United States, 1815–1860* (New York, 1939); Emmet H. Rothan, O. F. M., *The German Catholic Immigrant in the United States (1830–1860)* (Washington, D.C., 1946). For some later developments, see Mary Evangela Henthorne, B.V.M., *The Irish Catholic Colonization Association of the United States* (Champaign, 1932), and James P. Shannon, *Catholic Colonization on the Western Frontier* (New Haven, 1957).

[6] Sr. M. Ramona Mattingly, *The Catholic Church on the Kentucky Frontiers* (1785–1812), p. 8.

lics of the frontier besides supplying their own religious needs nurtured ecclesiastics of national reputation, among them Martin John Spalding, Archbishop of Baltimore in Reconstruction days, and his nephew, John Lancaster Spalding, famed educator and social critic, who presided over the Diocese of Peoria as its first bishop (1877–1916).

The few rural Catholics served only to underscore the observations of Philip Schaff, the Swiss-American ecclesiastical historian, that

> On the proper body of the American nation, the substantial middle class, if such we may speak of in a republic (and such one must find after all) the Roman Church has very slight hold. As in England and Scotland, so in America, it meets only the extremes of society, especially the lowest, poorest and most uncultivated class of emigrants, who form, so to speak, its flesh and blood; embracing also, almost everywhere a larger or smaller number of influential families of the higher and educated order, including many converts from the different Protestant denominations, especially the Episcopal.[7]

Schaff's mid-century words became even more aptly descriptive in later decades when to the Irish and German immigrants were added millions more, predominantly Catholic, from French Canada, southern and eastern Europe, and in lesser degree from neighboring parts of Latin America. Only among English and Scandinavian Christians were Catholics of negligible importance.

Converts to Catholicism were relatively few, with their descendants until 1860 less than three per cent of the total Catholic population.[8] Not numbers but leadership was the esteemed contribution of these accessions, mostly religious intellectuals. In conspicuous degree they helped their newly discovered Church to establish and maintain desperately needed charitable institutions. "Not only have we to erect and maintain the Church, the Seminary and the Schoolhouse," explained the bishops at their First Plenary Council of Baltimore in 1852, "but we have to found Hospitals, establish orphanages, and provide for every want of suffering humanity, which Religion forbids us to neglect."[9] Beginning with Elizabeth Bayley Seton,

---

[7] *America: Political, Social and Religious* (New York, 1855), p. 226.

[8] Edward G. Mannix, *The American Convert Movement* (New York, 1923), pp. 12, 107–10.

[9] "Pastoral Letter of 1852," in Guilday, op. cit., p. 187.

socially prominent New York widow, who founded in 1808 the American branch of the Sisters of Charity,[10] converts increasingly specialized in institutional works of mercy of which slightly more than a hundred were operating under Catholic auspices by 1860.

More than for their social service, the converts were prized in Catholic circles for apologetical reasons, chiefly in the area of civil-ecclesiastical relations. No Catholic wrote more clearly or candidly in this field than Archbishop John Hughes of New York, the most powerful figure among mid-century American prelates. He pointed out that, in all the generations before the Declaration of Independence was announced, the Catholic Church had "never found herself face to face with the civil government of any country except as its favorite or its foe." This fact had nourished the widespread assumption not only among Protestants but among many Catholics as well that Catholicity might flourish only in lands where it enjoyed state support or suffered persecution, "like certain weeds, growing and producing the most vegetation when trampled on." Actually, however, Catholic growth since Carroll's day, chiefly from immigration, had amply demonstrated that the Church could "win its own battles" and "meet the steady gaze of a free people and an enlightened age." Hughes was not in the least inclined to minimize Catholic losses, stating that "hundreds of thousands of the descendants of Catholic immigrants" had "fallen away from their religion." He did not attribute their alienation, however, to the impact of American liberty. In his phraseology the immigrants had not "examined their religion in the light of the age or in the presence of equality." [11] On this issue the archbishop's views recalled the widely known pronouncements of Alexis de Tocqueville that Catholics, "the most republican and democratic class in the United States," were "at the same time the most submissive believers and the most independent citizens." [12]

---

[10] Annabelle M. Melville, *Elizabeth Bayley Seton, 1774–1821* (New York, 1951), pp. 153–83; Peter Guilday, *The Life and Times of John Carroll* (New York, 1922), p. 500.

[11] "Lecture on the Present Condition and Prospects of the Catholic Church in the United States" (1856), in Lawrence Kehoe, editor, *Complete Works of the Most Rev. John Hughes*, II, 122–32.

[12] *Democracy in America* (Phillips Bradley edition; New York, 1945), I, 300–2.

If in "lamentable degree" immigrants had abandoned Catholicism,[13] their defection, insisted the ever realistic Hughes, stemmed from social disorders and the lack of adequate missionary means in the way of priestly personnel and material resources. Immigrants died "at the rate of one in three," he pointed out, because in addition to their susceptibility to cholera and yellow fever epidemics "they are especially exposed to the accidents of life, to sickness, hardships of every kind, and toilsome poverty." "Calamities of one kind and another," he summarized, "the death or ignorance of their parents, it may be, or their remote situation from the opportunities of practicing and learning their religion, account sufficiently for the falling away of those who are acknowledged to have been lost to the Catholic Church." The archbishop regretted that the converts, men and women of high character impelled by truth, not worldly advantage, to enter the Church, compensated for less than a third of the apostate immigrants. Yet they were numerous enough to provide a "true test" of Catholicism's compatibility with intelligence and liberty, to make pulp of the familiar charge that, while Catholicity might be embraced by men in "despair and darkness," it had no attractions for people of education and refinement. Nor would these men "of American birth, freemen who love freedom," he observed, "sacrifice legitimate freedom while embracing Catholicism...."[14]

As a group, the converts were at great pains to swell their ranks from fellow Americans of native stock. They reasoned that if Catholicism satisfied their own existing requirements it had the power to realize the aspirations of all religiously minded people. Most articulate were the philosopher-publicist Orestes A. Brownson

[13] See Daniel Dorchester, *Problems of Religious Progress* (rev. ed.; New York, 1900), pp. 584–92, for a long list of estimated losses by Catholic authorities beginning with Bishop John England of Charleston, who stated in 1837 that nearly four million Catholic immigrants had deserted the Church. For a more recent view that the Church has suffered only nominal defections see Bishop J. F. Regis Canevin, "The Rise and Progress of the Catholic Church in the United States," American Federation of Catholic Societies, *Bulletin*, VI (July 1912), 1; same author, "Loss and Gain in the Catholic Church in the United States (1810–1916), *Catholic Historical Review*, II (January 1917), 377–85; and Bishop Gerald Shaughnessy, *Has the Immigrant Kept the Faith? A Study of Immigration and Catholic Growth in the United States, 1770–1920* (New York, 1925).

[14] Op. cit.

(1803–76) and the missionary priest Isaac T. Hecker (1819–88).[15] Lifelong friends, Brownson and Hecker entered the Church in 1844, sobered but not disillusioned by their active careers in the social and intellectual upheavals of the day. Both men harbored the conviction that the claims of the Catholic Church, properly presented, must prove irresistible to the great body of Americans, however diverse their religious and social backgrounds. The conversion of America to Catholicism polarized Hecker's thought and action. Year in and year out, first as a Redemptorist and after 1858 as head of his own society, the Missionary Priests of St. Paul the Apostle, Hecker audaciously contended that the Catholic faith met all the needs of the soul, was grounded on reason, made room for the natural virtues of the robust American, and accepted and guaranteed the cherished American liberties, not excluding religious liberty. He correctly observed that countless Protestants, in their enthusiasm for liberty and democracy, had rejected predestination, human inability, and similar theological tenets. In the hope of making Catholicism attractive to these people, Hecker pleaded for more individuality in Catholic teaching, pointing out that the Church had followed this practice in the Middle Ages. Only when challenged by the Protestant Reformation had Catholicism been obliged to stress its divine authority at the expense in some degree of individual freedom and the manly virtues. Having finally vindicated its divine authority through acts and measures culminating in the decrees of the Vatican Council, the Church should return to its older humanism.[16]

As anxious as Hecker to win converts, Brownson did not view the task as one of harmonizing individuality and authority in the theological field. The problem was one rather of modernizing Catholic attitudes on Church-State relations. When not in a despairing mood Brownson believed that American progressives, "the living portion of the Protestant world," numerous in his day and "the

[15] Arthur M. Schlesinger, Jr., *Orestes A. Brownson; A Pilgrim's Progress* (Boston, 1939); Theodore Maynard, *Orestes A. Brownson, Yankee, Radical, Catholic* (New York, 1943); Vincent F. Holden, C.S.P., *The Early Years of Isaac Hecker (1819–1844)*, Washington, D.C., 1939; Walter Elliott, C.S.P., *The Life of Father Hecker* (New York, 1891).

[16] *Questions of the Soul* (New York, 1855); *Aspirations of Nature* (New York, 1857); and *The Church and the Age* (New York, 1887), esp. pp. 64–114.

majority tomorrow," [17] will "readily accept the Church, if they only find that she requires no change in our institutions," and that "they owe, as they do, to her and the teachings of her doctors the principles which they most highly prize in them." [18] He defended doctrinal intolerance, approved the mixed civil and ecclesiastical regimes of the Middle Ages which had suppressed infidel, heretical, and schismatic sects as anti-social conspiracies, but repeatedly insisted that "in a normal or civilized state of society, Catholicity is perfectly compatible with political toleration, and concedes at least as extensive toleration as is professed, and for the most part honorably maintained, by our American government." In the event of a majority of Americans becoming Catholics, the constitutional provisions respecting religious freedom need not be altered. Not on grounds of expediency but as a matter of principle, he emphasized, Catholics must repudiate religious persecution. Knowing full well that Catholics as a weak minority found toleration to their advantage, Protestants and unbelievers "place no confidence in our preaching," he warned, "unless we show clearly and undeniably that it is in harmony with the principles of our Church, where she is strong as well as where she is apparently weak." [19]

As if to reassure his fellow Catholics, Brownson insisted that America provided a fit environment in which to build a great Catholic civilization.[20] Only the methods and arguments of the Church, not her doctrines or traditions, need undergo Americanization. Specifically, Brownson suggested that Catholics retain their composure in the presence of the Know-Nothing movement which proposed to bar immigrants from officeholding and to extend the period required for their naturalization. In his Americanizing zeal Brownson intimated that if Catholics should openly support these proposals, which were after all designed rather to safeguard Anglo-American

[17] "The Great Question," *Brownson's Quarterly Review*, New Series, I (October 1847), 419.

[18] "The Constitution of the Church," ibid., Third Series, IV (January 1856), 20.

[19] "Civil and Religious Toleration," ibid., New Series, III (July 1849), 308–9; see also "The Church and the Republic," in Henry F. Brownson, editor, *The Works of Orestes A. Brownson*, XII, 20–32; "Separation of Church and State," ibid., 406–38; *The American Republic* (Detroit, 1895), pp. 199–222.

[20] "Mission of America," in Henry F. Brownson, editor, op. cit., XI, 551–84; "The Church and Modern Civilization," ibid., XII, 135–36.

culture than to stamp out Catholicism, they would thereby allay
Protestant apprehensions and win additional converts.[21] Deeming
the suggestion an insult, his fellow Catholics launched instead a
program of combative benevolence. Among the first to act were
the German Catholics whose faith was ridiculed by free-thinking
German immigrants as well as by American nativists.[22] In self-
defense a few recently founded German Catholic beneficial societies
federated in 1855 into the Central Verein. Growing steadily in the
years that followed, the Verein from the outset fought secret societies, provided sickness benefits, and aided education and charity.[23]
In later years it offered life insurance, befriended immigrants,
and furthered the cause of Catholic sociology and the labor movement.[24]

By other methods Irish Catholics were impelled to forge even
stronger weapons against nativist wrath. Owing to their large numbers and extreme poverty, they were by many deemed responsible
for major urban evils, including corrupt politics, swollen relief rolls,
and crowded jails and almshouses. More favor for the Irish in the
public eye seemed to depend on their attaining an economic level
equal to that of other immigrant groups. Journalists and Western
bishops dinned on Irish ears the apparently obvious remedy, namely,
a mass movement from the life-destroying cities to the salubrious
and cheap lands on the public domain. This was the constant
theme of the Irish revolutionist, Thomas D'Arcy McGee, whose
letters and speeches induced a considerable number of his fellow
immigrants, individually and in groups, to settle in the West.[25]
Largely at his behest the Catholic Convention to Promote Colonization in North America assembled at Buffalo early in 1856. This

21 Philip J. Mitchell, C.S.C., "A Study of Orestes A. Brownson's views on
the Know-Nothing Movement," (Master's thesis, University of Notre Dame,
1945), pp. 31–36, 38–41, 48–51, 75–76, 79–80; "The Church and the Republic,"
loc. cit., 3–4; "Catholic Schools and Education," ibid., 510–11.

22 Rothan, op. cit., pp. 108–22.

23 Alfred Steckel, "The Roman Catholic Central Society of the United States
of North America," *Records of the American Catholic Historical Society*, VI
(1895), 250–60.

24 Joseph Matt, *Deutscher Romisch-Katholischer Central-Verein* (St. Louis,
1893), pp. 40–46; Mary Liguori Brophy, B.V.M., *The Social Thought of the
German Roman Catholic Central Verein* (Washington, D.C., 1941), pp. 1–14.

25 William J. Onahan, "Irish Settlements in Illinois," *Catholic World*,
XXXIII (May 1881), 157–62.

widely heralded meeting — "the first practical movement for the benefit of our race on this side of the Atlantic," editorialized the *Pilot* of Boston [26] — deplored the wretched condition of Irish immigrants and hoped for their speedy improvement in America. In Europe, the convention recalled, "the social fabric is menaced" by the landless "who have no hopes of permanently improving the condition of themselves or their posterity. Such a class in such a country as this," the assembly insisted, "ought to be for ages to come unknown." [27]

Although the convention drew up a plan of colonization based on the joint-stock principle, Irish people with savings refused to invest in the enterprise, noting that its intended beneficiaries — the victims of urban poverty — showed little interest. Moreover, Archbishop Hughes denounced "directed" colonization which he believed would encourage and perpetuate Irish clannishness, and thus inflame rather than assuage nativist feeling.[28] His opinion would have been more plausible had the Church's drive to expand Catholic charities in cities met with hearty public approval. But state and local governments only grudgingly extended to Catholics the generous aid long proffered private benevolence — land on which to erect hospitals, orphanages, and homes for the helpless and the erring, and grants of money for building funds and the partial support of inmates.[29] Nor would the public authorities except in isolated instances permit priests to read mass and administer the sacraments in jails and almshouses filled to overflowing with professing Catholics.

From private philanthropy, however, the Church scented the major danger. Newer forms of charity organization — for example, associations for improving the condition of the poor and children's aid societies — emerged during the 1840s and 1850s as did also a significant number of Protestant city missions. These agencies wisely focused attention on the potentially "dangerous classes," notably

[26] February 23, 1856.

[27] "Address of the Catholic Convention to Promote Colonization in North America to the Friends of Catholic Settlements," *Pilot*, March 1, 1856.

[28] Henry J. Browne, "Archbishop Hughes and Western Colonization," *Catholic Historical Review*, XXXVI (October 1950), 267, 274–75, 284–85.

[29] Rev. John C. Lord and Rev. Bernard O'Reilly, *Discussion Relative to the Buffalo Hospital of the Sisters of Charity* (Buffalo, 1850).

neglected children, the destitute and often vicious victims of wretched family life. As they carried on their work they proselyted Catholics with frenzied zeal from motives that were quite as much political and social as religious. Not sure that any Catholic children could grow up to be good citizens, the societies and missions, the better to isolate the destitute ones from the Church's influence, scurried off thousands of them to Protestant homes in the West.[30]

Numerous Catholics in positions of responsibility determined to meet this serious challenge by providing exposed youth with special religious training and thorough and prolonged instruction in the useful arts. The initiative was taken by the Brothers and the Sisters of Holy Cross,[31] whose activities centered around the University of Notre Dame, founded in 1842 by the Reverend Edward Sorin of the Congregation of Holy Cross. In 1846 the Brothers, with funds supplied by the Reverend Stephen T. Badin, established "a supplement" to the "male orphan asylums of the country," namely, "a manual labor school" where boys between the ages of twelve and twenty-one were taught trades "suited to their talents and inclinations, to fit them for usefulness in society." [32] The Sisters opened a similar school for girls in nearby Bertrand, Michigan, repeating the performance in later years in Philadelphia, Baltimore, and New Orleans.[33] By 1860 the Brothers had also founded additional manual labor schools near Vincennes, in Baltimore, and in New Orleans where on a model farm they instructed "the grown up boys in the knowledge of Agriculture. . . ." [34]

In his attempt at St. Patrick's Orphanage in Baltimore to emulate the Brothers of Holy Cross, the Reverend James Dolan failed for lack of sufficient support. But the less ambitious project, the Home of the Angel Guardian, opened in Boston in 1851 by the convert-priest George Foxcroft Haskins, continuously provided desti-

[30] Francis E. Lane, *American Charities and the Child of the Immigrant* (Washington, D.C., 1932), pp. 45–97.

[31] John O'Grady, *Catholic Charities in the United States; History and Problems* (Washington, D.C., 1931), p. 108.

[32] *Metropolitan Catholic Almanac and Laity's Directory, 1846* (Baltimore, 1845).

[33] Ibid., 1856, p. 184; ibid., 1857, p. 153; ibid., 1861, pp. 110–11.

[34] Ibid., 1857, p. 235; ibid., 1861, pp. 57, 110–11.

tute and wayward boys with two years' religious training along with a bit of preparation for practical life.[35] In some of the leading cities, beginning in Pittsburgh after 1843, the Sisters of Mercy established houses of protection for working girls of unblemished character. To these institutions, their main social interest, they were wont to attach houses of industry or industrial schools to the end that "the children of the poor may be fitted to become useful and virtuous members of society." [36] A similar course was followed by the Sisters of Charity to the extent permitted by their preoccupation as the leading American sisterhood with hospitals, orphanages, and parochial schools.[37]

Most prominent in the industrial school movement was the distinguished ex-Bishop of the Protestant Episcopal Church, Levi Silliman Ives, who entered the Catholic Church in 1852, partly because he admired its attitude toward the poor. From the day of his conversion until his death in 1867 Ives made use of his unique position to impress upon Catholics the country over the importance of dealing properly with neglected youth.[38] Aside from speechmaking, his efforts were confined to the New York area where for a time he and his associates, after the example of Protestant institutions, placed destitute children in rural Catholic homes. The work failed to accomplish its purpose: "I can call to mind only a single instance," the noted convert later wrote, "where the child either did not abscond or prove utterly ungovernable and worthless." [39] Bitter over the non-access of priests to Catholic inmates of public reformatories, Ives urged Catholics to erect their own institutions in which the requisite training, both spiritual and industrial, could be given.[40] These schools should have the right, he contended, to ingather

[35] John O'Grady, *Levi Silliman Ives, Pioneer Leader in Catholic Charities* (New York, 1933), pp. 57–61.

[36] *Metropolitan Catholic Almanac and Laity's Directory, 1849*, pp. 165–66; Mary E. Herron, *The Sisters of Mercy in the United States* (New York, 1929), pp. 11, 32–33, 43, 89–90, 92, 129, 132, 153–54, 179–81, 198–200.

[37] *Metropolitan Catholic Almanac and Laity's Directory, 1857*, p. 185; ibid. (1858), pp. 42, 157; ibid. (1861), p. 124; Elinor Tong Dehey, *Religious Orders of Women in the United States* (rev. ed.; Cleveland, 1930), pp. 69–100.

[38] John O'Grady, op. cit., pp. 1–51, passim.

[39] *The Protection of Destitute Catholic Children* (New York, 1864), p. 18.

[40] *Church and State Charities Compared* (New York, 1857), pp. 33–49, 53–68.

children, of Catholic parentage, who ran afoul of the law. To these ends, Ives persuaded Catholics of means and influence to organize the Society for the Protection of Destitute Catholic Children which in the face of strong opposition secured a charter from the New York legislature in 1863. With Ives as its president the society established in 1865 the New York Catholic Protectory which with public as well as private support soon made a creditable record in reforming the viciously destitute of both sexes. Located on a 114-acre plot in Westchester County, the Protectory instructed in both agriculture and the various trades.[41]

Realizing the importance for social work of sustained interest on the part of the laity, Ives was notably successful in securing it. He made use of lay organizations, mainly the Society of St. Vincent de Paul, the international missionary and charitable association which Frédéric Ozanam, the French social philosopher, had established in 1833.[42] Bryan Mullanphy, whose family set up an Irish Fund for Western Immigrants, organized the first American conference of the society in 1845 at the Cathedral Church in St. Louis. Designed primarily for poor relief, the society soon supplanted the older benevolent associations (excepting the racial ones) which had well served Catholic needs in the earlier part of the century. As immigration increased the newer society grew steadily, having by 1865 some seventy-five conferences,[43] with nearly four thousand members in "55 different localities. . . ."[44] Excepting the societies of Brooklyn, New Orleans, and St. Louis, which reported directly to Paris, the scattered conferences in 1860 federated in the Superior Council of New York. Such growth as the society experienced in its earlier days owed most to Ives, whose lecture tours communicated his infectious enthusiasm for the welfare of neglected children, leading to the formation of conferences and, more important still, inspiring them all to make child care a "special work." The New York conferences, twenty in number by 1864, assumed responsibility for the

[41] Lane, op. cit., pp. 120–124.

[42] Daniel T. McColgan, *A Century of Charity*, I, 1–52.

[43] L. T. Jamme, "The Society in America," *St. Vincent de Paul Quarterly*, II (May 1897), 97.

[44] *Report of the Superior Council of New York to the Council General of the Society of St. Vincent de Paul* (New York, 1865), pp. 42–43.

maintenance of the Catholic Protectory, and in the society's first
two national conventions, in 1864 and 1865, the problem of destitute children was thoroughly discussed.[45]

In other fields of social action the results attained before 1865
were much less impressive. Among the better-educated young men
numerous literary societies arose during the 1850s. They were relatively powerless, however, to counteract the attractions of saloons,
casinos, and gambling dens since as a rule they lacked club and
recreational features. The exception was the Newark Young Men's
Catholic Association whose Institute, erected in 1857 by the Reverend Bernard J. McQuaid, later Bishop of Rochester, comprised
reading, music, and billiard rooms along with a gymnasium and a
lecture hall.[46]

As for intemperance, the Church authorities and many lay folk
were alive to the moral and physical misery caused by its widespread virulence. From 1840 date the Catholic temperance societies [47] and their first official endorsement — by the Fourth Pro-
vincial Council of Baltimore. In a diocesan visitation the following
year Bishop Hughes found in the congregations "with only one or
two exceptions" temperance associations which included "nearly
the whole of the Catholic population." [48] The same trend appeared
in other dioceses. After losing its momentum, the movement was
revived temporarily by Ireland's great apostle of temperance, the
Capuchin Theobald Mathew, who administered the pledge to over
a half million people during his extended American tour at mid-
century. The great friar's crusade was more humanitarian than
Catholic, appealing to Americans irrespective of religious belief. A
pledge-taker rather than an organizer, he nevertheless inspired the
formation of many "Father Mathew societies" which not only urged
their members to be temperate but aided them in a material way

[45] O'Grady, op. cit., pp. 64–65, 73–78.
[46] Frederick J. Zwierlein, *The Life and Letters of Bishop McQuaid* (Rochester,
1925–27), I, 343–44; *Metropolitan Catholic Almanac and Laity's Directory,
1859*, p. 88.
[47] Ibid., 1841, pp. 98, 112–13; ibid., 1842, p. 135; ibid., 1843, pp. 81, 119;
ibid., 1845, pp. 86, 95; ibid., 1845, p. 97.
[48] "State of the Diocese of New York in 1841," in Kehoe, editor, op. cit.,
I, 438.

with sickness and other benefits. Inasmuch as they lacked a firm religious basis, few survived the decade of the 1850s.[49]

Although Catholic social work stemmed directly from the crying need to protect poor, helpless immigrants, other motives entered indirectly into its genesis and continuing development. Thus the core idea in Americanism, namely, the desire to win recruits from the non-Catholic population and to make the Church an integral and vitally important aspect of American civilization, was an ever present factor. In 1857, when the Church's benevolence was still in its infancy, Brownson, reviewing somewhat critically Father Hecker's book, *Aspirations of Nature,* made clear the connection between social work and Catholic influence on the cultivated classes. In a notable passage he reminded his friend that

> The conversion of bad Catholics, the proper training of Catholic children, the correction of the vice of intemperance, and other immoralities prevalent in a portion of our Catholic population — would do more for the conversion of non-Catholics than all the books and reviews we can write, all the journals we can edit, or efforts we can expressly make for their conversion, for it would prove to them, what they now doubt, the practical moral efficiency of our religion. We must provide first for our own spiritual wants, get our own population all right, and then we may turn our attention with confidence and success to those who are without.[50]

Father Hecker, on his part, was ready by this date to conjoin the two objectives of convert-making and social service. With four companions, all native American converts and ex-members of the Redemptorist order, he organized in 1858 the afore-mentioned community, the Missionary Priests of St. Paul the Apostle. Its formation occasioned by Redemptorist refusal to open an American mission house, the new society attempted with papal approval to develop a profounder synthesis of Catholicism, reason, and liberty.[51] If the Paul-

---

[49] Sr. Joan Bland, *Hibernian Crusade. The Story of the Catholic Total Abstinence Union of America* (Washington, D.C., 1951), pp. 21–42; John Francis Maguire, *Father Mathew; A Biography* (New York, 1887), pp. 488–89, 514, 517.

[50] *Brownson's Quarterly Review,* New York Series, II (October 1857), 495–96.

[51] Elliott, op. cit., pp. 251–301, 332–47; Alphonse Lugan, *The Paulists: An American Community* (New York, 1925); James M. Gillis, *The Paulists* (New York, 1932).

ists stressed this philosophy because of its likely appeal to Protestants, they did not propose to preach only to "heretics and unbelievers," as Brownson pointed out, "but to all the faithful and the unfaithful. . . ." [52] Thus in a poor suburb of New York City — "Shantyopolis," Hecker called it — they developed the great parish of St. Paul the Apostle whose social agencies, beginning with a conference of the St. Vincent de Paul Society, exemplified in the years that followed every aspect of progressive Church work. [53] "Think of it," exclaimed James Parton, the free religionist, "a movement designed to convert Mr. Emerson and the educated people of America was made, *first of all*, to minister to the spiritual wants of the poorest and most ignorant people living in the Northern States!" [54] In sermons "rough but hearty," the Paulists preached a truly "muscular" Christianity not only to their own but to Catholic congregations throughout the country. Laying stress on the practice of the everyday virtues, these missions, eighty-one in number by 1865, waged unrelenting war on social evils, especially intemperance and its saloonkeeping abettors. [55] "The only people that looked sad at this mission," a pastor wrote, "are the first men in my parish, the rumsellers." [56]

Through publication rather than preaching the Paulists were destined to make their most fruitful contribution to the Catholic social movement. By drawing freely on the family fortune Hecker was able to launch a distinguished monthly journal, the *Catholic World*, in 1865, and the Catholic Publication House the following year. The magazine was particularly important for the thoroughness with which it explored the whole field of benevolence and charity in its

[52] *Brownson's Quarterly Review*, Third New York Series, I (April 1860), 247–48.

[53] Lida Rose McCabe, "Progressive Methods of Church Work: a Roman Catholic Parish," *Christian Union*, January 7, 1893.

[54] "Our Roman Catholic Brethren," *Atlantic Monthly*, XXI (May 1868), 565.

[55] Social reform was one fulfillment of the Paulist view "that practical religion consists in the sanctification of everyday life." In a book long planned but never written, on *Perfect Life in Common Ways*, Hecker intended to show "that the ordinary duties of life are the high-roads to sanctity. There is no other way of perfection for the great mass of Christians than in the performance of the common duties of life with an eye to God." Father Hecker to George Simpson, February 22, 1861, in Abbot Gasquet, editor, "Some Letters of Father Hecker," *Catholic World*, LXXXIII (June 1906), 356–57.

[56] Elliott, op. cit., p. 327.

relationship to the Church's progress in the postwar years.[57] In so well performing this task of research and informational diffusion, the *Catholic World* helped Catholics play their full part in the great crusade for urban welfare which engaged the humanitarian movement in the new era that dawned at the end of the Civil War.

Only indirectly or negatively did a few leading Catholics before 1865 and for some years thereafter express dissatisfaction with *laissez-faire* social policy. Brownson feared that the interest of many immigrants in radical democracy would plunge them into socialism, which in his view was as useless and futile as it was erroneous and wicked. "All that is in any sense good or worth having," he wrote, "the individual can always, under any political or social order, secure by a simple effort of his will." [58] This social individualism stemmed in part from his conviction, voiced also by the elder Spalding and possibly others, that poverty and self-denial, not wealth, were the truly Christian ideals.[59] Practically considered, the Catholic leadership believed, no doubt, that adherence to a *laissez-faire* policy would perpetuate the reasonably satisfactory existing system of agriculture, small business, and the handicrafts.

[57] "Religion in New York," III (June 1866), 381–89; "The Sanitary and Moral Condition of New York City," VII (July, August 1868), 553–66, 712–14; "The Charities of New York," VIII (November 1868), 279–85; "Who Shall Take Care of Our Sick?" VIII (October 1868), 42–55; "Who Shall Take Care of the Poor?" VIII (February, March, 1869), 703–15, 734–40; "The Little Sisters of the Poor," VIII (October 1868), 110–16; "The Duties of the Rich in Christian Society," XIV (February, March 1872), 577–81, 753–57; ibid., XV (April, May, June, July 1872), 37–41, 145–49, 289–94, 510–18; "The Homeless Poor of New York City," XVI (November 1872), 206–12.

[58] "Socialism and the Church," *Brownson's Quarterly Review*, New Series, III (January 1849), 116; for an extended discussion of Brownson's views on the social implications of democracy, see Lawrence Roemer, *Brownson on Democracy and the Trend Toward Socialism* (New York, 1953).

[59] M.J.S., "Mammonism and the Poor," *Brownson's Quarterly Review*, New York Series, III (April 1858), 144–71.

CHAPTER II

The Urban Welfare Crusade:
Charity Phase, 1865–85

Slowed down but not interrupted by the Civil War, the Catholic social movement gained the momentum of a veritable crusade in the aftermath of the great fratricidal struggle. Catholic social effort, as it intensified in the early postwar period, did not wander far from its freshly traced paths: it continued to combat misery and vice along the prewar lines of moral exhortation, almsgiving, and the works of mercy. Catholics as a body, even during the depression of 1873–78, devoted only passing attention to the economic or industrial causes of moral degradation. A few Catholics, it is true, acidly proclaimed that the rising order of *laissez-faire* industrialism was inherently evil,[1] and the Church itself did not oppose trade unionism or labor legislation provided these methods of reform were properly used.[2] For the time being, however, Catholics were content, for the most part, to seek social improvement within the framework of existing arrangements.

This attitude was in no sense peculiar to Catholics. With the battle against human bondage seemingly won, humanitarian leadership in the country at large now focused its attention on the larger cities whose unsolved problems grew in complexity and magnitude with each passing year. The moral crisis in cities acquired peremptory urgency from the fact that growth in urban population entailed a much greater proportionate increase in such social evils as pauperism, intemperance, and crime. The American Social Science Association, formed in 1865, accounted rationally for the frightful increase in human misery and made clear that plans to remove it must take

[1] See, for example, Anon., "The duties of the Rich in Christian Society," *Catholic World*, XV (April 1872), 37–41.

[2] Henry J. Browne, *The Catholic Church and the Knights of Labor* (Washington, D.C., 1949), pp. 12–33, passim.

into consideration its organic character — that is, attack the problem in whole and in part, with appropriate remedies for specific
defects, each of which was related to others as both cause and effect.[3]
Though impressed by the findings of social science, Catholic leaders
were more immediately affected by other phases of the urban crusade. The temperance forces, in their efforts to revive the earlier
battle against the drink evil, formed in 1865 the National Temperance Society and Publication House which relied for success largely
upon churches, Catholic no less than Protestant.[4] Catholics felt the
stimulus of competition from the American Christian Commission,
also organized in 1865, which through city missions planned to
counteract the growing strength of Catholicism and to rescue the
abandoned classes, especially vagrant children, inebriates, discharged convicts, and fallen women.[5] On the other hand, the
Church found an ally in the new state boards of charity which for
the most part urged their jurisdictions to subsidize "the private
foundations, of whatever sect . . . rather than to establish new public
institutions." [6]

In this changing climate of opinion, Catholic zeal in behalf of the
"dangerous classes" appreciably mounted. Noting that Catholics
comprised nearly half the people of New York City and a much
larger part of its destitution, which was increasing ten times faster
than the rapidly growing population, the *Catholic World* insisted
that the time had come "when the physical wants of these unfortunate classes should awaken in us serious consideration." [7] The
evil was primarily physical since the "packing system of the tenement
houses" plagued the metropolis with the highest death rate in the
world and led to a devitalization of the human organism from which
stemmed intemperance and frightful debauchery. The journal
doubted "if throughout Europe, and certainly in no other part of

[3] William Strong, "The Study of Social Science," *Journal of Social Science*,
No. 4, 1871, pp. 1–7.
[4] A. I. Abell, *Urban Impact on American Protestantism*, p. 47.
[5] Ibid., pp. 11–15.
[6] George William Curtis, "Speech before New York Constitutional Convention, 1867–1868," quoted in the Catholic Publication Society Company, *Grants
of Land and Gifts of Money to Catholic and Non-Catholic Institutions* (New
York, 1879), p. 19.
[7] "The Charities of New York," VIII (November 1868), 282.

America, in the same amount of space, so much vice, immorality, pauperism, disease and fearful depravity could be found, as some of the worst of these locations present daily for our consideration." [8] In all the large cities mortality among the poor in the postwar era was as high, the *Pilot* of Boston recognized, as it had been a half century before. The wretched homes of the people — "a disgrace to our country and the boasted philanthropy of the age" — were mainly responsible for physical and moral deterioration in urban communities.[9]

Strange as it may seem, most Catholics did not think that poverty entered into the situation as a major factor. The Society of St. Vincent de Paul summarized prevailing opinion when in 1865 its distinguished president, Professor Henry J. Anderson, assured the brethren in Paris that "our poor, for the greater part, are only so temporarily. Where there is health, temperance and industry, there cannot be poverty in this country. . . . Intemperance," he emphasized, "is the great evil we have to overcome; it is the source of the misery for at least three fourths of the families we are called upon to visit and relieve." On the chief victims of intemperance, namely, the children of broken homes, the society was obliged, he stated, to expend its principal energies.[10]

The bishops assembled in the Second Plenary Council of Baltimore shortly after the war expressed similar views, attributing "the most frightful scandals" to "excess in drinking" and urging increased attention to the needs of youth. "It is a melancholy fact and a very humiliating avowal for us to make," they said, "that a very large proportion of the idle and vicious youth of our principal cities are the children of Catholic parents." In some of the dioceses — "would that we could say in all!" — a beginning had been made toward remedying matters through protectories and industrial schools.[11] In

---

[8] "The Sanitary and Moral Condition of New York City," VII (July 1868), 554.

[9] "The Homes of the Poor," May 10, 1873; "Topics of the Hour," *Catholic Review*, November 2, 1872.

[10] *Report of the Superior Court of New York, 1864–1865* (New York, 1866), pp. 7–8.

[11] Peter G. Mode, *Source Book and Bibliographical Guide for American Church History* (Menasha, Wis., 1921), 473–74; *Pilot*, July 12, 1873.

the years that followed the Catholic press alerted the faithful to the calamity that awaited the Church from the loss of vagrant children. Their number in New York City alone would suffice, lamented the editor of the *Catholic World*, "to people a respectable Southern or Western diocese." [12] Unable to retain "what it gets," wailed the *Catholic Universe* of Philadelphia, the Catholic Church in America, "a section from the bleeding side of Ireland," lost two hundred thousand children yearly.[13] For these children, deprived of both asylum and reformatory inasmuch as they were mostly neither orphans nor criminals, the Church as yet possessed few, if any, institutions comparable to the Children's Aid Society, the Howard Mission, and other agencies operating under Protestant auspices. Although Protestants were "working hard to effect a reform" of the destitute class, the *Catholic World* discovered, their institutions however honestly conducted were "powerful engines of proselytism." "If we do not take care of our own poor," the Paulist organ concluded, outsiders "will not only provide for their physical wants, but will soon acquire charge of their souls." [14]

In Catholic striving to meet the enveloping challenge, the lower New York Church of St. James scored the most brilliant record on the parochial level. Becoming its pastor in 1865, the able and resourceful Felix H. Farrelly soon revealed the opportunities for social service open to a congregation in a neighborhood chiefly distinguished for tenement-house rot. Central in its operations was a parochial school, spaciously housed and staffed by twenty-two teachers drawn from both sexes. At a yearly cost of twelve thousand dollars the school educated fourteen hundred pupils tuition-free. Though it met well the needs of the children from the better tenements, this school left untouched the vagrant and neglected children, largely half-orphans. For these the parish employed Sisters of Charity to conduct an industrial school which provided free lunch and suitable clothing to about two hundred children. To the end that its instruction be thoroughly effective, the congregation in 1867 erected St. James' House, whose extensive work in a twenty-one-

[12] "The Sanitary and Moral Condition of New York City," VII ,(August 1868), 713.

[13] Quoted in J. F. Rowe, "Phases of Religion in the United States," *Christian Quarterly*, I (April 1869), 179–80.

[14] "The Charities of ·New York," loc. cit., 282.

room building rivaled that of Protestants at the Five Points House of Industry and at the Howard Mission.[15]

The care of children did not exhaust the efforts of this famed congregation, which only less thoroughly provided for the physical and moral needs of all its members. On poor relief the parish spent five thousand dollars yearly through a conference of the St. Vincent de Paul Society, forty of whose several hundred members were "constantly on duty visiting the sick, counseling the erring, helping the needy and performing other works of charity." Nine hundred men, organized in two temperance societies, not only rid themselves of intemperance, but by weekly meetings, lectures, and other popular attractions sought "to win others to follow their example." [16] With its social work planned to cover the whole field of human suffering, St. James' anticipated by two decades the great "institutional" churches of the Protestant bodies. Only a few Catholic congregations commanded sufficient zeal and resources to become "working" churches in the full sense. One of these was St. Stephen's Church in New York, which in 1868 established St. Stephen's Home for Children. Except for the parochial school of which the pastor, the celebrated Edward McGlynn, did not approve, St. Stephen's provided agencies to meet most human needs.[17] McGlynn's willingness to serve for only eight hundred dollars a year and to spend his considerable private fortune on charity partly accounted for St. Stephen's success. A social center for its neighborhood, the church was visited daily by ten thousand people.[18]

McGlynn's and Farrelly's work suggested the possibility of similar efforts on a broad extraparochial basis. A group of New York women proposed that Catholics the country over establish and maintain a Central Mission House, pointing out that "as the poverty of the Old World finds its first refuge in our city, so the charity of the New World should be concentrated there to meet it." [19] Although their

[15] "The Sanitary and Moral Condition of New York City," loc. cit., VII (July 1868), 561–63; "The Charities of New York," loc. cit., 283.

[16] "A Word to the Independent," ibid., XIII (May 1871), 254.

[17] L. B. Binsse, "The Catholic Charities of New York," *Catholic World*, XLIII (August 1886), 685; Edward Irenaeus Stevenson, "Representative Roman Catholic Clergy," *Independent*, December 30, 1886.

[18] *Pilot*, January 13, 1900.

[19] "The Sanitary and Moral Condition of New York City," loc. cit., (August 1868), 714.

grandiose plan failed of fruition, they realized part of their dream in the Association for Befriending Children and Young Girls. Formed in 1870, the group operated in the neighborhood of St. Bernard's parish, which was located in the west-central section of the city. Here was found opportunity for the exercise of the most unflinching zeal. The first twenty-five girls ushered from the streets into an industrial school presented a pitiful spectacle of degradation and poverty, several being drunkards and prostitutes and all needing food, clothing, and training. These requirements were amply supplied to an ever increasing number by a day school for the virtuous and by a home, the House of the Holy Family, for the fallen. After 1876 the association extended temporary outdoor relief to young women who for lack of employment might yield to temptation. It also served as an employment agency for respectable women as well as for its own reformed inmates. Aiming to train women thoroughly in some branch of industry, the institution redeemed fully three fourths of its charges, nearly eighteen thousand by 1895. The management, long in the hands of a matron, was entrusted in 1886 to the Sisterhood of the Divine Compassion formed expressly for the purpose by Monsignor Thomas S. Preston, the association's spiritual director. In 1890 the institution moved its reformatory work to Good Counsel Farm near White Plains in Westchester County.[20]

Though the Association for Befriending Children and Young Girls stressed reformation, it also valued and demonstrated the effectiveness of protective measures.[21] Pre-eminent in preventive charity were the Sisters of Charity and the Sisters of Mercy, who were able after 1865 to expand their prewar protective work to a conspicuous degree notwithstanding the pressure of other duties including parochial school teaching.[22] Several other sisterhoods now

[20] "The Association for Befriending Children," *Catholic World*, XI (May 1870), 250–53; Thomas F. Ring, "Catholic Child Saving Agencies in the United States," *St. Vincent de Paul Quarterly*, I (August 1896), 267–77; "The Sisters of the Divine Compassion," *American Ecclesiastical Review*, XVIII (May 1898), 484–501.

[21] John J. Delaney, "What Catholic Agencies Are Doing for the Reformation of Juvenile Delinquents," *Charities Review*, VI (July–August 1897), 443–44.

[22] Mary E. Herron, op. cit., pp. 118–19, 136, 139–40, 175, 185–86, 189; *Sadlier's Catholic Directory, 1865*, pp. 82, 160, 196, 206, 209; ibid., 1869, pp. 64, 238, 259; ibid., 1871, pp. 85, 121, 261; ibid., 1872, pp. 86, 97, 111, 155; ibid., 1874, p. 98; ibid., 1875, p. 116; ibid., 1877, p. 332; ibid, 1880, pp. 58, 153–54, 306, 400.

entered the field with an occasional "home of industry." [23] A typical example was the House of Industry opened in 1873 by the Sisters of St. Joseph in Rochester, New York, "to educate young girls, destitute of parents, friends and employment, in some useful trade for which they seem qualified." [24] Even the Sisters of the Good Shepherd, whose magdalen asylums rapidly multiplied, stressed prevention increasingly, sometimes through industrial schools but more generally in "preservation" classes which housed and trained "truant" girls until the end of their eighteenth year.[25] By the same token, institutions for the innocent and helpless often attempted to reform delinquents. This was notably true of the foundling agencies, the best known of which was the New York Foundling Hospital opened in 1869 by Mary Irene Fitzgibbons, a Sister of Charity. In order properly to rear the children, Sister Irene found it necessary to reform and shelter their mothers, an endeavor in which she was extraordinarily successful.[26]

However, most Catholic doers of good preferred education to rescue, none more so than the Society of St. Vincent de Paul, which pioneered in the movement soon to be known as the "new charity." Besides helping many charities with advice, labor, and money, it supported a few industrial schools and established several boarding homes for young working boys, one of which, the New York lodging house, attained world-wide renown. Shortly before the society opened this home, John C. Drumgoole was ordained to the priesthood in his fifty-third year. Long active in the New York Society, he was thoroughly familiar with the abandoned classes of the city. Appointed city missionary by Archbishop McCloskey, "this humblest and most benevolent of New York's priests" took over the lodging house in 1872, renaming it the Mission of the Immaculate Virgin

[23] Ibid., *1867*, pp. 98, 187; ibid., *1872*, p. 87; ibid., *1874*, pp. 92, 139, 303; ibid., *1878*, p. 216; ibid., *1880*, pp. 142, 214; Elinor Tong Dehey, op. cit., pp. 311, 444, 547.

[24] *Catholic Review*, November 11, 1874; Blake McKelvey, *Rochester: The Flower City, 1855–1890* (Cambridge, 1949), pp. 146, 278, 370.

[25] *Sadlier's Catholic Directory, 1865*, p. 113; ibid., *1867*, pp. 79, 136, 165, 185; ibid., *1873*, 323; ibid., *1880*, p. 306; Dehey, op. cit., p. 283.

[26] Mrs. J. V. Bouvier, "New York Foundling Hospital," *St. Vincent de Paul Quarterly*, I (May 1896), 163–69; Ring, op. cit., pp. 265–66; S.C., "Sister Irene, Founder of the New York Foundling Hospital," *Charities Review*, IX (September 1899), 297–301; Lane, op. cit., pp. 129–31; O'Grady, *Catholic Charities in the United States*, pp. 132–39.

for the Protection of Homeless and Destitute Children.[27] Not a reformatory, the mission aimed to instruct and train thoroughly as many youngsters as possible, mostly boys between the ages of four and twenty-one. Under Drumgoole's "admirable management" the work "made rapid strides," reported the Presbyterian *New York Observer* in 1893, "from a modest beginning to a noble self-supporting institution, caring for and instructing one thousand seven hundred boys and girls." [28]

From bazaars and concerts and after 1875 from a St. Joseph's Union of some sixty thousand members,[29] more than a million dollars was raised for a spacious boys' home at Lafayette Place in the city and for a large farm school at Mount Loretto on Staten Island. Here the boy passed from the nursery through seven classes to apprentice rank. After serving his apprenticeship he completed his industrial education in the Trades Hall where as a "trades boy" he enjoyed many social and educational advantages. His trade mastered, the youth was promoted to the Free Trades Hall where he worked for regular wages or if unusually skilled secured a "professorship." The many boys securing jobs in New York City boarded at the Lafayette Place home until they reached their majority. Those of superior mind could have a college education if they wished it. The relatively few girls accepted by the mission received training in the literary and useful arts at St. Elizabeth Home, Mount Loretto. Well before his death in 1888 Father Drumgoole had made of the Mission of the Immaculate Virgin one of the finest protective institutions in the modern world.[30]

In much greater degree than at the Drumgoole institution, the Boston Home for Destitute Catholic Children, opened in 1864,

[27] James E. Dougherty, "John Christopher Drumgoole, Founder of the Mission of the Immaculate Virgin for Homeless and Destitute Children," *Charities Review*, VIII (August 1898), 323–27.

[28] Quoted in R. H. Clarke, "Catholic Protectories and Reformatories," *American Quarterly Review*, XX (July 1895), 615.

[29] Thomas Church, "Father Drumgoole's Work — The Origin and Growth of the St. Joseph's Union," *Donahoe's Magazine*, II (November 1879), 427–33.

[30] "Rome in New York," in Committee on Catholic Interests of the Catholic Club of the City of New York, compiler, *Catholic Charities and the Constitutional Convention of 1894 of the State of New York* (New York, 1894), pp. 3–5.

extended fostering care to both boys and girls. Maintained at great expense by Catholics throughout New England, the agency provided children temporary refuge and the rudiments of education while awaiting their placement in Catholic homes.[31] Nearly all the protectories and larger industrial schools, however, were for boys, few, if any, training the two sexes after the example of Ives's great institution in New York. But they resembled the New York Protectory in the emphasis placed on reforming incorrigibles. This generalization is less applicable, perhaps, to the later than to the earlier establishments such as St. John's Protectory in Buffalo and the Chicago Reform and Industrial School, both dating from 1864,[32] and St. Mary's Industrial School, opened near Baltimore in 1866 and widely known from the prominence in the youth training movement of its distinguished founder, Archbishop Martin J. Spalding, and from the success of its religious and trade instruction in reforming its charges, nearly four thousand by 1895.[33] Much the same could be said of the Chicago reformatory which in 1882 expanded into St. Mary's Training School, a combined farm and trade school, at Feehanville, Illinois.[34] The boys here were "on the alert, responding quickly and cheerfully to the call for their services. Though nothing stronger than a low picket fence surrounds the premises," it was proudly reported, "no thought of leaving enters their minds. . . ." [35]

Although most states liberally subsidized private institutions training wayward youth, the Catholic reformatories proved an almost insufferable drain on the Church's limited financial resources and managerial personnel.[36] Opportunely the need for these schools diminished as Catholics after 1870 won steadily their battle for religious liberty in public institutions. After the example of the cities of New York, Philadelphia, and Boston, Ohio and Massachusetts, in 1874 and 1875 respectively, acknowledged the right of Catholic clergymen to free and equal access to all public agencies of an

[31] Lane, op. cit., pp. 124–26; *Pilot*, November 5, 1870; ibid., April 19, 1873; ibid., May 3, 1873; ibid., September 29, 1883.

[32] *Sadlier's Catholic Directory, 1865*, p. 168; ibid., *1866*, p. 184.

[33] John Lancaster Spalding, *The Life of the Most Reverend M. J. Spalding, Archbishop of Baltimore* (Baltimore, 1873), pp. 288–94, 374; Ring, op. cit., p. 270.

[34] "Save the Boys," *Donahoe's Magazine*, VIII (December 1882), 540–43.

[35] *Report, 1895*, quoted in Ring, op. cit., pp. 273–74.

[36] *Catholic Review*, March 17, 1877.

eleemosynary and penal character.[37] Since most legislatures refused to act, the right was secured over the years through administrative rulings. The fact that Protestant denominations did not establish reformatories also helped check the Catholic trend in that direction. By 1885 scarcely a dozen of the large predominantly reformatory institutions existed — a poor showing compared to the 37 homes for the aged, 154 hospitals, 272 orphan asylums, and 46 industrial schools and related agencies for needy youth.[38] But "where needed" — in the larger cities — they constituted the "most important" aspect of Catholic charity, being, as Richard H. Clarke so well observed, "the most direct efforts to solve the paramount problem of the child...."[39]

Charities for both youth and adults derived no little help before 1880 from Catholic societies or associations, even from the ones primarily concerned with personal or social reform. Charity was of course the main business of the thousands of Catholic benevolent societies, nearly all of which were organized along nationalistic lines.[40] Thus the societies represented in the Central Verein spent yearly about seventy-five thousand dollars on sickness benefits while the more numerous Irish societies paid sick or disabled members from four to six dollars a week.[41] In a meeting at Dayton, Ohio, in 1869, several of these latter societies federated into the Irish Catholic Benevolent Union under the leadership of Judge Dennis Dyer of that city who served for a time as its president. Growing rapidly during the next decade, the union was soon recognized as a powerful factor in the country's benevolent enterprise.[42] Although indifferent to the implications of the word "Irish" in its title, the organization insisted on Catholicity as a basis of membership, adopting in

[37] *Pilot*, June 21, 1873; August 9, 1873; October 11, 1873; January 10, 1874; April 4, 1874; November 7, 1874; December 12, 1874; September 18, 1875.

[38] *Sadlier's Catholic Directory, 1885*, pp. 345, passim.

[39] Op. cit., pp. 610, 612.

[40] For the beginnings of union among French and Polish Catholic benevolent societies, see *Pilot*, March 21, 1874, and New York *Freeman's Journal and Catholic Register*, December 26, 1874.

[41] Steckel, op. cit., pp. 260–61; *Pilot*, March 6, 1875.

[42] Joan Marie Donohoe. S.N.D., *The Irish Catholic Benevolent Union* (Washington, D.C., 1953), views the organization as largely a training school for political leadership.

1871 a statement drawn up by the Reverend John J. Keane of Washington, D.C., that affiliated societies shall not "admit knowingly into their body any other than practical Catholics, nor any member of secret or sworn societies condemned by the Church." [43]

The fear [44] that politics might disturb the union duly materialized. Curiously enough, rabid opponents of the public school system, not office-seekers, fanned the flames of discord. At its convention of 1873 in St. Louis, the Reverend D. S. Phelan, editor of the *Western Watchman* of that city, introduced a resolution that "the present system of public schools . . . is a curse to our country, and a floodgate of atheism and sensuality, and of civil, social and national corruption." [45] These infuriating words were repudiated by the convention, which expressed its disapproval of purely secular schools in milder language and elected A. M. Keily, mayor of Richmond, Virginia, the leader of the moderate elements, as the union's president for the ensuing year.[46] The rebuffed extremists were somewhat mollified by the obviously good works of the union, which some years spent considerably over a hundred thousand dollars on charity, some of it on protectories and reformatories.[47] In 1874

[43] "Sketch and History of the Irish Catholic Benevolent Union of the United States and Canada," Twenty Fourth Annual Convention, *Proceedings*, 1892, pp. 3–8.

[44] "Irish Catholic Benevolent Union," *Pilot*, July 26, 1872.

[45] Quoted in the *Pilot*, October 25, 1873.

[46] The amended resolution read, "That the system of State education now established in most States by its failure to provide proper religious instruction for the young, and its enlightening the head to the entire neglect of heart-culture, meets with our unqualified reprobation; that it unjustly taxes a large class of our people, who cannot without danger to the faith and morality of their offspring, avail themselves of its advantages." Ibid. Even this statement was too extreme for Mayor Keily, who believed that "the public school system which generally prevails in the United States, in which sound and exclusively secular education is imparted, without assailing or defending any religious tenets, is, under the conditions generally prevailing in the United States, a wise and beneficent system." He added, however, that "whenever the zeal or piety or opportunity of the Church succeeds in erecting by the side of the public school a Catholic school of training, let us avail ourselves of it, and thank God for the privilege." Letter to editor of the *Pilot*, January 31, 1874. Somewhat heatedly Keily explained that his views did not conflict with Article 48 of the Syllabus of Errors, as charged by the *Pilot* and other commentators. The *Pilot* was satisfied with his explanation. "The Syllabus and Mayor Keily's position on the Public School Question," March 7, 1874.

[47] *Pilot*, October 31, 1874; ibid., October 30, 1875.

the union pledged itself to help bishops establish or maintain protectories in which "destitute children of members of this Union
may be taught some means of earning a subsistence, and eventually
becoming an honor to their faith and country." For the benefit of
old and young alike, the union urged "each local society to form or
organize reading rooms or literary societies among its members." [48]

Of more interest, however, was life insurance, which from the outset was suggested as a desirable means "of increasing the utility of
the Union." [49] Though it hesitated to embark upon so hazardous
an enterprise, its discussions of the subject presumably hastened
the formation of such mutual life insurance associations as the
Catholic Knights of America, the Catholic Mutual Benefit Association, the Catholic Benevolent Legion, and others of a local character. Determined to be on this issue no less Catholic than the Masonic
orders, the union finally set up a widows' and orphans' fund in
1877,[50] an example followed by the Central Verein four years
later.[51] The two groups were also interested in the care and distribution of immigrants arriving from Europe. In 1873 the Irish organization established a board of immigration whose designated agents,
co-operating with the union's local committees, were to meet immigrants at the major ports of entry and to assist them in reaching
their destination.[52] The board's chairman was the Reverend T.
Ambrose Butler, Catholic prairie poet, who reported the following
year that in some places, notably Philadelphia, Baltimore, and St.
Louis, immigrants had been given material relief and secured employment.[53]

Aid for German Catholic immigrants was first proposed in Germany
when in 1866 at the Catholic Congress of Treves Peter Paul
Cahensly urged the formation of a St. Raphael's Society for the
Protection of European Emigrants.[54] Aware of Cahensly's plan,

[48] New York *Freeman's Journal*, November 21, 1874; *Catholic Review*, August 26, 1876.

[49] "Sketch and History of the Irish Catholic Benevolent Union . . . ," loc. cit.

[50] Ibid.

[51] Joseph Matt, op. cit., pp. 15–20.

[52] *Pilot*, October 25, 1873; Irish Catholic Benevolent Union, *Proceedings*,
1875, p. 30, appendix.

[53] "Committee on Immigration," ibid., 19–20.

[54] Colman J. Barry, O.S.B., *The Catholic Church and German Americans*
(Milwaukee, 1953), pp. 3–43.

the Central Verein in its convention of 1867 appointed a committee, headed by A. B. Schwenninger, pastor of the Church of the Assumption in New York City, to draw up a program. His committee, reporting the following year, recommended that the Verein provide spiritual and material help at the ports of entry and erect an immigrant house in New York City. The Verein refused to accept these proposals, alleging that so heavy a burden was quite beyond the capacity of a mutual benefit society. It did not disclaim all responsibility, however, naming five New York residents to a Central Committee on Immigrant Affairs and appointing two unsalaried representatives to befriend immigrants arriving at New York and Baltimore. Contributions for a time enabled these men to begin operations.[55] Schwenninger, as chairman of the Central Committee, circularized the bishops of Germany on the preparations being made in America to safeguard the newcomers, and the New York agent of the committee, Joseph Kölble, visiting Europe at his own expense, encouraged Cahensly to persevere in his eventually successful campaign to put emigrant care on an international basis.[56] But in the absence of assured financial backing from the Central Verein the work soon languished: the repeated pleas of Father Schwenninger for a hospice in New York on the model of the Lutheran Pilgrims' Home fell on deaf ears.[57] Only when German immigration swelled to unprecedented volume in the early 1880s did German Catholics take the problem seriously in hand. They were encouraged by Cahensly, who in 1883 established a branch of the St. Raphael Society in New York. In co-operation with the society, German-American Catholics raised by 1889 a hundred thousand dollars with which to build and equip Leo House, "a departure in organized Catholic charity." [58]

55 Brophy, *The Social Thought of the German Roman Catholic Central Verein*, pp. 36–37, 87–89.

56 Thomas F. Meehan, "Emigrant Aid Societies," *Catholic Encyclopedia*, V, 403; Joseph Schaefer and Charles C. Herbermann, "The Society of St. Raphael and the Leo House," United States Historical Society, *Historical Records and Studies*, I (January 1899), 110–17.

57 Helen M. Sweeney, "Handling the Immigrant," *Catholic World*, LXIII (July 1896), 503; Abell, op. cit., p. 41.

58 Schaefer and Herbermann, op. cit., 110–29; I. M. O'Reilly, "The Leo House for Immigrants, A Departure in Organized Catholic Charity," *Records of the American Catholic Historical Society*, XVI (1905), 445–52.

For the same reasons, as will be seen, Irish Catholics took similar action in the mid-1880s. Meanwhile the social movement continued its course. As the benevolently minded exhausted their slender resources on charitable institutions, they determined to strike at intemperance, which necessitated most of the heavy outlays. Besides bringing pauperism and misery, the widespread and excessive drinking, from the unseemly conduct it entailed and paraded before the public eye, compromised the Church's claim to be an unfailing source of public and private virtue. Determined to end these evils and scandals, a small but aggressive minority after 1865 revived along more constructive lines the prewar crusade of the beloved Father Mathew. Though all agreed that the zealous friar had well performed his pioneering tasks, many were convinced that his work exhibited a fatal defect: it had failed to persuade Catholics in sizable numbers that religious duty even more than humanitarian concern must impel men to fight intemperance. Thus in the opinion of most laymen the Reverend Patrick Byrne of Jersey City was a full-bloom fanatic when he made temperance a part of religion in the parochial total abstinence societies he began organizing in 1860. Nor did many of his fellow priests — "brethren far above" him "in learning, zeal and piety" — see the need of special aids to sobriety; for them the ordinary means of grace sufficed.[59]

Yet the new idea caught on, for the religiously motivated societies actually safeguarded their own members, who by example persuaded others to mend their evil ways, neighborhood after neighborhood showing marked improvement in manners and living standards. In all urban communities societies proliferated after the war, the result partly of the numerous missions conducted by the Jesuits, Paulists, and other religious orders. Beginning with Connecticut in 1870, many of the rapidly multiplying societies grouped themselves into metropolitan, diocesan, and state unions. In a speech before the New Jersey union in November 1871 the Bishop of Newark, James Roosevelt Bayley, long an active foe of the liquor interests, strongly endorsed the temperance movement in its new

[59] Patrick Byrne, "Utility of Our Societies," in James W. O'Brien, editor, *Lectures and Addresses of the Very Rev. Thomas N. Burke, O.P.* . . . (New York, 1872), p. 68; James W. O'Brien, "The Catholic Total Abstinence Union of America," in W. H. Daniels, *The Temperance Movement and Its Great Reformers* (New York, 1878), pp. 207–11.

phase. Regretfully he expected little from legislation "though it might do much good if wisely directed and effectively carried out." Politicians, he recalled, had thwarted the attempts of Catholic and Protestant clergy to secure restrictive measures in Newark. The failure strengthened his conviction "that any great permanent reform in this matter can only come from religious influences." [60] In the six months following this, his first "temperance speech," more societies were formed than "in all the years since Father Mathew's death." [61] Bayley also approved the New Jersey union's invitation to temperance groups throughout the country for a meeting in Baltimore to survey the possibilities of a national organization. Here was formed in February 1872 the Catholic Total Abstinence Union of America.[62]

In its first resolutions and statements the new body shaped its program in accordance largely with the Bayley viewpoint. "Our motto is 'moral suasion,'" read its address to the Catholics of America. "With prohibitory laws, restrictive license systems, or special legislation against drunkenness, we have nothing whatever to do. . . ." [63] Although chiefly interested in promoting total abstinence, the union, believing that temperance and benevolence should "go hand in hand," endorsed the "attractive" mutual relief features which with scarcely an exception Catholic societies had "blended" with their temperance work. But the temperance societies intended

[60] "Intemperance — How to Check Its Ravages," O'Brien, editor, op. cit., 45–48.

[61] James W. O'Brien, "The Catholic Total Abstinence Union of America," in National Temperance Society and Publication House, *The Centennial Temperance Volume. A Memorial of the International Temperance Conference, Philadelphia, June, 1876* (New York, 1881), p. 726.

[62] For a detailed discussion of the C.T.A.U. of A., see Bland, *Hibernian Crusade*, pp. 43ff.; and James J. Green, "The Organization of the Catholic Total Abstinence Union of America, 1866–1884," *Records of the American Catholic Historical Society of Philadelphia*, LXI (June 1950), 71–97.

[63] Joseph C. Gibbs, *History of the Catholic Total Abstinence Union of America* (Philadelphia, 1907), p. 20. But the union was not opposed in principle to prohibitory legislation, recognizing in Resolution 7 "the great good that would result from the suppression of public drinking places, and from such legislation as would restrain the manufacture of intoxicating liquor within bounds consistent with public morality and will gladly hail such legislation whenever the public authorities may grant it." "Baltimore Resolutions," in O'Brien, editor, op. cit., p. 52. In the meantime, the union informed the Prohibition party, it would steer clear of political movements "looking only to the supply" and "rely upon the power of religion to destroy the demand by conquering the appetite." Ibid.

to supplement, not antagonize, the efforts of the recently founded Irish Catholic Benevolent Union. The temperance union also favored counterattractions to the saloon in the way of lectureships, reading rooms, and temperance halls which local societies as well as metropolitan unions were urged to provide.[64] The union's belief that religion must motivate temperance work was underscored by the ruling that the presidency of the new organization should be entrusted only to clergymen. The first two presidents, James McDevitt and Patrick Byrne, had been among the first to stress the religious factor.

In the years immediately following its organization the union distributed over a million tracts and edited a journal, *The Catholic Total Abstinence Union of America*. This literary activity partly accounted for the movement's rapid growth as did also the agitational campaign of several great leaders, among them a second Irish friar, the Dominican Thomas N. Burke, more eloquent if less great than Father Mathew, and the Reverend John Ireland, whose bold and sagacious promotion of the cause stamped him as "the Father Mathew of the West." The extent of the movement was easily exaggerated. Thus James W. O'Brien's estimate that by the centennial year two hundred thousand members were enrolled in Catholic temperance societies seems wide of the mark notwithstanding the momentum of the American temperance crusade in this period.[65] O'Brien was nearer the truth in his belief that the strong temperance sentiment weaned perhaps a million Catholics away from saloons.[66] Invariably Protestant observers of the Catholic crusade paid tribute to its salutary influence, none more so than John Wanamaker, who reported to the National Temperance Society in 1873 that in a Philadelphia neighborhood where he supported a mission the Catholic temperance societies had destroyed the patronage of the tavern and forced the rum seller to give up "his trade as a bad business." [67]

[64] Ibid.

[65] Abell, op. cit., pp. 47–50.

[66] "The Catholic Total Abstinence Union of America," *The Centennial Temperance Volume . . .* , pp. 732–33.

[67] Quoted in the *Pilot*, November 8, 1873; see also J. B. Harrison, *Certain Dangerous Tendencies in American Life and Other Papers* (Boston, 1880), pp. 190–91.

However impressive their agitation against intemperance, the societies devoted some of their time and most of their resources to charity. Though a growing number of persons questioned the adage, "Temperance and benevolence go hand in hand," the union of the two remained unshaken in this period when charity was the chief social concern of the Church.[68] Nearly all temperance societies contributed from time to time charitable objects, though few to the extent of the Metropolitan Union of New York, which in a single year, 1875, raised over eighteen thousand dollars.[69] Some members suggested that the societies discontinue this practice in order to increase the funds available for distribution as sickness and death benefits.[70] But most critics preferred that the benefits be curtailed or eliminated altogether and the money thus saved used for temperance halls. Every Catholic society should establish places of recreation for young men, urged the Philadelphia *Catholic Herald.* "The Halls, in part," it wrote in October 1873, "become in time the successful rival of the tavern." [71] The *Pilot* editorialized a year later to the same effect. "What a blessing it would be to the whole country," it surmised, "if these 400 temperance societies had each a pleasant reading room, open every night in the year, with perhaps a coffee-bar in place of the liquor-bar. . . ." Should the temperance society "set up as a rival" to the "drinking saloon," the national temperance union, "instead of having 60,000 members, would have 600,000 in a short time." [72] The *New York Herald* pronounced the *Pilot* editorial the "most seasonable and sensible article that has yet appeared on the temperance question. . . ." [73]

Thus prodded by a portion of the Catholic press as well as by the officers of the national union, numerous societies provided the desired substitutes. If in New York State the number by 1873 was "very small," there were "a few, especially in the larger cities." In Ohio some of the societies, it was further reported, "have large and elegant halls, where public and private meetings are held," while

[68] *Pilot,* May 23, 1874.

[69] "The Catholic Total Abstinence Union of America," *Constitution and Proceedings, 1875,* p. 24.

[70] *Pilot,* March 20, 1875.

[71] Quoted in the *Pilot,* October 4, 1873.

[72] "A Serious Word with Our Temperance Societies," October 24, 1874.

[73] Quoted in the *Pilot,* October 31, 1874.

in Philadelphia the societies were "procuring permanent halls, where books, periodicals, newspapers, and games of various kinds are furnished. . . ." [74] A reading room in Fisherville, New Hampshire, appealed to the whole Catholic population and reduced the number of barrooms from seventeen to three.[75] Money saved from reducing the number of expensive St. Patrick's Day parades, against which the temperance forces launched a slashing attack,[76] provided funds for many of the saloon substitutes. In the end Philadelphia scored the best record, twenty-five of its sixty temperance societies erecting halls which appreciably influenced the subsequent course of the American temperance movement.[77]

The substitutional phase of the Catholic temperance movement was strongly reinforced by the young men's societies. Numbering perhaps a thousand by 1875, these associations, the newer as well as the older ones formed before the war, were primarily literary and debating organizations.[78] An increasing number, however, taking their cue from the Newark Catholic Institute and the Young Men's Christian Association, erected or rented buildings in which to carry forward a vigorous work for the educational, physical, and recreational benefit of male youth, some of whom lacked education and all needing safeguards to faith and morals. Among the first to enlarge their work were the Xavier Union of New York in 1871, the Carroll Institute of Washington, D.C., in 1872, and St. Stephen's Institute of Buffalo in 1875.[79]

None of the young men's halls was better equipped or more favorably known than the institute of the young men's literary association at the Brooklyn Church of the Assumption. In 1875 this congregation and its pastor, William Keegan, provided at a cost of thirty-five thousand dollars a spacious three-story brick building which housed a bowling alley and a dance hall as well as a library

[74] C.T.A.U. of A., *Constitution and Proceedings*, 1873, pp. 45–48.
[75] *Pilot*, October 18, 1873.
[76] Ibid., November 7, 1874; ibid., February 20, 1875.
[77] Raymond Calkins, *Substitutes for the Saloon* (Boston, 1901), p. 377.
[78] "Catholic National Unity" (ed.), *McGee's Illustrated Weekly*, II (June 16, 1877), 50.
[79] "Catholic Young Men's Associations," *Catholic World*, XVIII (November 1873), 273–74; Cleveland Papers (Library of Congress), February 12, 1897.

and reading room.[80] An Episcopalian journal commended Father Keegan's work with the observation that "the supervision of amusements is a right and privilege which belongs to the church and not to the devil," [81] while a Catholic layman wrote that the Brooklyn priest had done more for temperance than all the total abstinence societies of the city.[82] Inasmuch as many societies planned to broaden the scope of their work, they sensed the value of national federation. The *Catholic World* suggested that they unite under the constitution of the Sodality of the Blessed Virgin Mary, a youth organization three centuries old, of which the Xavier Alumni Sodality of New York with its Xavier Union was a member.[83] But the men themselves preferred the leadership of the Newark Catholic Institute under whose auspices forty-two societies in February 1875 formed the Catholic Young Men's National Union. Destined to a long life of slow, steady growth, the new body, the better to emphasize its religious motivation, restricted its early presidency to clergymen.[84]

The second president, John J. Keane, by now Bishop of Richmond, did much to clarify the purposes and to enhance the importance of the union. In his view the young men's society was potentially the most useful of all lay organizations, for in addition to meeting needs peculiar to youth it was in a position to recruit and train active workers for the Church's various benevolent and social reform groups.[85] In the end the union did promote objects of broad scope, notably the Catholic reading circle and summer school movements.[86] For the immediate present, however, it attended to the interests of its own constituency.[87] It maintained a lecture bureau

---

[80] "The Assumption Literary Society," *Catholic Review*, June 20, 1874; ibid., July 25, 1874.

[81] *Working Church*, II (August 1874), 117.

[82] Daniel Flanagan, "A Question for Irish Societies," *Pilot*, March 6, 1875.

[83] "Catholic Young Men's Associations," op. cit., pp. 269–76.

[84] *Pilot*, March 6, 1875; ibid., September 30, 1899; Michael J. Slattery, "Fraternal Societies of the Laity," *Catholic Builders of the Nation*, II, 319–20.

[85] "Our Catholic Young Men," *Catholic Review*, September 6, 1879; "Catholic Young Men's National Union," ibid., November 8, 1879.

[86] James Addison White, *The Founding of Cliff Haven. Early Years of the Summer School of America* (New York, 1950), pp. 5–6, 17–18, 59–60.

[87] Some societies, particularly those affiliated with the Young Men's Institute, founded in California in 1883, provided sickness and death benefits. "The Young Men's Institute," *Catholic Encyclopedia*, XIV, 736.

and after 1878 helped numerous affiliates to establish night schools for the benefit mainly of those who had not received an elementary education through regular channels. Some societies, however, provided vocational training. The school managed by the Catholic Young Men's Association of Boston imparted both general and vocational instruction to over two thousand students annually.[88]

Implicit in the origin and growth of all Catholic associations was the desire to steer Catholics away from secret societies. The sickness and death benefits offered by most societies were expected to counteract in some degree the attractions of the Masonic groups. When the "great beneficial feature" extends "from one end of the country to the other," affirmed the founders of the Catholic Total Abstinence Union, "Catholics will not seek it in objectionable orders, where many soon forget the teachings of religion as well as the practice of temperance."[89] As the struggling labor movement erupted into fury and violence during the economic depression following 1873, some Catholics hoped that charitable associations might also substitute for trade unions. Thus in 1874 Bayley, now Archbishop of Baltimore, endorsed the Irish Catholic Benevolent Union on the ground that it exerted "a proper influence. . . . guarding from what is worse than secret societies — that is, the miserable associations called labor organizations. Their idea is communistic," he insisted, "and no Catholic with any idea of the spirit of his religion will encourage them."[90] Others expressed similar sentiments though as a rule[91] indirectly in the course of pleas for a greater charity.[92]

[88] Slattery, op. cit.

[89] "Joint Address of the State Catholic Total Abstinence Unions," in James W. O'Brien, editor, op. cit., p. 51.

[90] *Pilot*, October 31, 1874.

[91] But the Louisville *Catholic Advocate*, October 29, 1874, commended Bayley's "words of wisdom to the careful perusal and serious consideration of members of Catholic societies, and especially to those who are identified with organizations which, in a spirit of recklessness that chafes under wholesome religious restraint, are disposed to array themselves in opposition to the moral precepts of the Church."

[92] See Rt. Rev. Thomas A. Becker, "Secret Societies in the United States," *American Catholic Quarterly Review*, III (April 1878), 193–219, which is cautiously favorable to trade unions; and John Gilmary Shea, "The Rapid Increase of the Dangerous Classes in the United States," ibid., IV (April 1879), 255, 263, 265, 266, and Rt. Rev. Francis S. Chatard, "Catholic Societies," ibid., 215–17, 219–21, which are implicitly opposed.

In fact, a genuine trade unionism won little, if any, recognition in Catholic circles until the mid-1880s. Even the *Pilot*, always something of a working-class journal, warned trade unions as late as 1875 to seek no more than the "market value" of the wage earner's labor.[93] This advice suggests no doubt that *laissez-faire* notions had penetrated the Catholic body. But it can scarcely account for the Catholic distrust of trade unionism during the depression years of the 1870s. The Church's leadership feared that workingmen's associations scheming in secret were responsible, at least in large part, for the bloodshed and destruction that marked the conflict between capital and labor in that turbulent decade. In the mining regions of eastern Pennsylvania the notorious "Molly Maguires," an inner ring of Irish Catholic labor leaders in the Ancient Order of Hibernians, perpetrated murder after murder.[94] Although many Catholics recognized that these outrages and particularly the railway riots of 1877 were provoked by employer greed for dividends at the expense of wages, they insisted, nevertheless, that violent strikes were not only morally debasing but also powerless to restore work and wages. Moreover, if persisted in, labor "insurrections" would undermine the constitutional structure and open the way for a Communist revolution. More wisely, workers should strive through united political action to secure needed legislation: comprehensive public-work projects to provide employment, progressive income taxes, and checks on corporate power.[95] "Charity is good enough in its way for those who are not competent physically to help themselves," observed *McGee's Illustrated Weekly*; "but what the mass of able-bodied desire is employment at reasonable wages." The government should disregard the law of supply and demand, and "help the poorer classes in time of need." [96]

[93] March 15, 1873; April 12, 1873; May 10, 1873; May 31, 1873; May 29, 1875; June 19, 1875.

[94] Walter Coleman, *Labor Disturbances in Pennsylvania, 1850–1880* (Washington, D.C., 1936).

[95] "Lawless Violence," *McGee's Illustrated Magazine*, II (August 11, 1877), 178; "Labor and Capital," ibid. (August 18, 1877), 194; "New York's Danger," ibid. (September 15, 1877), 258; *Catholic Advocate*, July 5, 1877; July 26, 1877; August 2, 1877; August 9, 1877; *Catholic Columbian*, July 28, 1877; August 4, 1877; October 28, 1877; "The Workingman's Remedy," *Pilot*, June 15, 1878; "Wages and the Cost of Living," ibid., August 17, 1878.

[96] "Who Will Help the Poor?" *McGee's Illustrated Weekly*, I (December 23, 1876), 66; "In answer to a Calumny," ibid., IV (July 13, 1878), 114.

While some Catholics could see no ultimate solution short of state socialism (public ownership of major utilities), they currently urged only that employers pay higher wages and alongside government bestow philanthropic benefits on the laboring masses. Besides providing ample wages to cover living costs, education of children, and compensation "for accidents, sickness or enforced idleness," employers, wrote Bishop James O'Connor of Omaha, should establish "reading rooms, libraries, gymnasiums, building associations, and insurance companies" for the workers' benefit.[97] Under the impact of economic depression, not many Catholics continued to believe that urban charity could allay social discontent. On this point most Catholic thinkers were at one with the jurist, T. Wharton Collens of New Orleans, who was widely known as Catholic Communist, labor reformer, and co-founder of the Christian Labor Union.[98] At the crest of postwar interest in charity Collens penned for the *Catholic World* a most revealing analysis of the labor question [99] in which he declared flatly that no system of public or private alms could put a stop to labor agitation or arrest the progress of revolutionary socialism. Only as Catholics found and applied "the just principle of economic distribution" could they remove the "deep and widespread disagreements . . . between the laboring man and his employers." [100] Trade unionism and labor legislation, while in no sense contrary to religion, were ineffectual remedies since they were powerless to realize that perfect charity which had been announced by the early Christians, universalized in theory by More's *Utopia*, and applied with partial success by various religious groups, notably the Jesuits in their Paraguay missions. Christians wishing to solve the modern labor problem should, he believed, "separate from the world," and in families vowed to poverty and obedience form closely knit communities wherein to strive for perfection and to produce surplus wealth for the poor — not for themselves but for

[97] "Socialism," *American Catholic Quarterly Review*, VIII (April 1883), 240; see also George D. Wolff, "Socialistic Communism in the United States," ibid., III (July 1878), 522–62; Anon., "Some Barriers Between Labor and Capital," *Catholic World*, XXVIII (November 1878), 230–42; Anon., "Some of Our Present Weapons Against Socialism in America," ibid., XXXI (September 1880), 721–35.

[98] Abell, op. cit., pp. 21–23.

[99] "View of the Labor Movement," X (March 1870), 784–89.

[100] Ibid., 784–89.

the benefit of "any and all men." [101] Thus in colonization Collens discerned a remedy for all urban ills as well as an alternative to labor organization.

This view, progressively divested of its utopian imagery, won favor in all Catholic circles by the late 1870s when labor grew dangerously belligerent and outlays for urban social service exhausted the people's resources. A few thinkers defended the feasibility of Western colonization under the leadership of religious orders.[102] From members of the St. Vincent de Paul Society — and from others too — came the truly realistic plea for partial colonization — that is, for the housing and training of orphans on Western land where they could mature amid surroundings favorable to the farmer's life.[103] In actual practice, however, colonization advanced in accordance with the prewar suggestions of the Buffalo colonizing convention whose program was kept alive and to some extent carried out by western Catholics, notably bishops.[104] Most successful was John Ireland, who on becoming Coadjutor Bishop of St. Paul in 1875 founded within four years five saloonless colonies on land purchased from railroads.[105] But his plan was little more than a real estate arrangement enabling Catholics having the means to buy and equip land to settle together. It lacked benevolent features, as Ireland himself was the first to emphasize, whereby the really poor could be helped to become self-supporting farmers.

For correction of this deficiency Bishop Ireland at first relied upon the Irish Catholic Benevolent Union, which in 1875 appointed a Colonization Board with Father Butler as chairman. After securing information from bishops and priests as to the location of desirable lands Butler recommended that the union through local

---

[101] Ibid., 792–95.

[102] Anon., "Who Shall Take Care of Our Poor?" *Catholic World*, VIII (March 1869), 734–40.

[103] *Catholic Review*, July 22, 1876; "Open Catholic Agricultural Homes in the West," ibid., January 4, 1879; *Sadlier's Catholic Directory*, 1880, p. 400.

[104] *Pilot*, May 2, 1874; December 8, 1898.

[105] James P. Shannon, *Catholic Colonization on the Western Frontier* (New Haven, 1957); "Colonization and Future Emigration," *Catholic World*, XXV (August 1877), 685–88; "Catholic Colonization as Actually Established," ibid., XXIX (April 1879), 120–26; "Roman Catholic Colonization," *Christian Union*, March 26, 1879; Raymond Philip Witte, S.M., *Twenty-Five Years of Crusading. A History of the National Catholic Rural Life Conference* (Des Moines, 1948), pp. 25–27.

boards raise funds for colonization on the joint-stock principle.[106] "By no other means," Ireland declared in a letter to Butler, "can the poor among our people — those most in need of homes — be colonized." Until now Catholic colonization, "the great question for our race in America," Ireland believed, had failed for lack of organized support. In the Irish Catholic Benevolent Union, with its four hundred societies, he discerned a great instrumentality for definite accomplishment. He urged speedy action. "Whatever is done," he said, "must be done quickly before the frontier lands are exhausted." [107]

The union organized colonization boards in Philadelphia, St. Louis, and St. Paul, each of which founded a colony. The Philadelphia colony in Virginia did not thrive; the others, one each in Nebraska and Minnesota, prospered from the beginning. As soon as the union evidenced its inability to mobilize the full Catholic strength, a further attempt was made by a specially created organization, the Irish Catholic Colonization Association of America, with Bishop John Lancaster Spalding of Peoria as president and William J. Onahan, a Chicago businessman, as secretary.[108] In behalf of the association Spalding published *The Religious Mission of the Irish Race and Catholic Colonization* (New York, 1880), in which he vividly portrayed the well-nigh hopeless condition and future of urban Catholics. He believed that comparatively few Catholics had abandoned their faith: the Church's heavy losses were to be sought chiefly "in the almost incredible infant mortality among our people, in the high death rate among the immigrants themselves and in the fact that large numbers of them have not married at all." In his opinion only colonization could cope with such evils as drunkenness and revolutionary strife. "The perfectly sober" among crowded tenement dwellers "would die," he alleged, "from mere loathing of life." Although Catholics had been singularly free of communistic infidelity, they could not long escape its influence. Even if the

---

[106] I.C.B.U., *Proceedings of Convention, 1875*, p. 20; ibid., *1876*, pp. 11–12
[107] Ibid., 13–16.
[108] Sr. Mary Evangela Henthorne, *The Career of the Right Reverend John Lancaster Spalding, Bishop of Peoria, as President of the Irish Catholic Colonization Association of the United States, 1879–1892* (Urbana, 1932), 35–59; for Spalding's Catholic humanism, see Thomas T. McAvoy, C.S.C., "Bishop John Lancaster Spalding and the Catholic Minority (1877–1908)," *Review of Politics*, XII (January 1950), 3–19.

labor movement went no further than strikes and trade unions, "this will be enough to undermine" their moral character "and wean them from the Church." [109]

Though strongly put, these arguments carried little weight with the rank and file of Catholic people. Only with difficulty and after Ireland and Spalding literally "stumped the country" was the new association able to raise the hundred thousand dollars deemed essential to the prosecution of its work. With this fund the association successfully colonized during the early 1880s ten thousand acres in Minnesota and twenty-five thousand acres in Nebraska.[110] It proceeded no further partly because so few urban dwellers were genuinely interested in becoming farmers but mainly because with the great increase in immigration the problem of befriending the newcomers at the ports and helping with their distribution assumed greater urgency.[111] At its annual meeting in 1883 the association thoroughly discussed immigration, and through Bishop Stephen V. Ryan of Buffalo requested the Archbishop of New York to establish a mission at Castle Garden. Assured of financial support by neighboring prelates, Cardinal McCloskey took the requisite action, selecting for missionary the Reverend John J. Riordan, who in January 1884 opened the Mission of Our Lady of the Rosary, to which was soon added a lodging house for destitute girls. Fully equipped and well managed, the mission during its first ten years befriended fifty thousand immigrant girls and helped two hundred thousand people to reach their destinations safely. In order to facilitate the orderly distribution of new arrivals Riordan in cooperation with the Irish Catholic Colonization Association set up numerous bureaus in inland cities.[112] In 1886 the St. Vincent de Paul societies assumed responsibility for the support and extension of the bureau network.[113]

Attention to the problem of immigrant distribution did not sig-

---

[109] Pp. 118, 121, 205.

[110] Henthorne, op. cit., 61–89; *Pilot*, April 3, 1880.

[111] "Secretary's First Annual Report," *Catholic Review*, May 29, 1880; Stephen Byrne, O.P., "Irish Settlers in the West," *Pilot*, February 3, 1883.

[112] John J. Riordan, "The Priest at Castle Garden," *Catholic World*, XLIII (July 1896), 505–7; "A Shelter and a Home," *Catholic Review*, October 24, 1896.

[113] *Report of the Superior Council of New York to the Council General at Paris, 1886* (New York, 1887), pp. 16–17.

nify that the country's Catholic leadership no longer valued agriculture as a superior way of life. The realization dawned, however, that destitue Irish immigrants could become successful farmers only after they first acquired skill and competency in some remunerative trade or industrial occupation. Pointing out that German Catholics for the most part labored at the better-paying urban jobs before taking up land on the frontier, the *Pilot* urged Catholic societies and the parochial schools to stress industrial education in order to make possible a like course for Irish Catholics.[114] For the immediate present this influential journal was sure that relief from the exactions of oppressive corporations must be sought not in colonization but in the "dangerous and expensive" resort to the "general strike."[115]

Few clergymen shared the *Pilot's* increasing sympathy with militant trade unionism.[116] On the contrary, numerous priests and a few bishops openly antagonized in the early 1880s the growing influential Knights of Labor notwithstanding the largely successful efforts of its Grand Master Workman, Catholic Terence V. Powderly, to conform the order's ritual and use of secrecy to Catholic moral requirements. In the interest of ecclesiastical uniformity and of freedom of association for the Catholic laity, the bishops in their Third Plenary Council of Baltimore in 1884 ruled that pastors and other ecclesiastics, without the "previous explicit authorization" of a specially designated committee, must not condemn societies, including labor unions charged with abusing the device of secrecy or with perpetrating injustices upon employers. From this and other statements in the council's Pastoral Letter the implication is clear that the hierarchy did not object to Catholics joining secularly led labor unions provided their end and means were "consistent with truth, justice and conscience." It is equally clear that the council relied for social reform mainly on Catholic societies, all of which it warmly endorsed, including "the various forms of Catholic beneficial so-

---

[114] "Arguments and Suggestions Addressed to the Irish Catholic Benevolent Union," January 20, 1877; "Contemporary Views," *McGee's Illustrated Weekly*, II (September 29, 1877), 291.

[115] "The Coming Lock-out in Fall River," June 28, 1879.

[116] "Rings and Strikes," *Pilot*, January 20, 1877; "Strikes and Their Results," ibid., February 28, 1880; "The Power of Discharge Must Be Taken from Employers," ibid., July 3, 1880.

cieties and kindred associations of Catholic workingmen." As late as 1884 the Church saw no need, apparently, to modify existing economic arrangements. In his sermonic address on "the church in her councils with special reference to her moral, social mission," the Archbishop of Philadelphia, Patrick J. Ryan, stated that "Christian kindness to the poor and the working men and women, and the inculcation of patience in poverty, after the example of Our Lord," were "the best securities against the communism and anarchy that seem to threaten society."

Not alone this distinguished archbishop but the Third Plenary Council as a collective body seemed oblivious to the bearing of civil legislation on the course of moral and social reform. On one issue, that of Sabbath observance, imperiled by the spirit of greed and dissipation, the bishops favored a more rigid enforcement of Sunday-closing laws. But they mainly relied on moral suasion not only to keep Catholics out of saloons and beer gardens on the Lord's Day but, more important, to induce the "faithful," engaged in the sale of liquors, "to abandon as soon as they can the dangerous traffic, and to embrace a more becoming way of making a living." Although the bishops urged Catholics "for the love of God and of country" to keep holy the Lord's Day, they did not clearly realize that many Americans were coming to view not only temperance but all social reforms as manifestations of patriotic Americanism. Not fully grasping this phase of the situation, the bishops at the Third Plenary Council failed to portray the Catholic crusade for urban welfare as added proof that the Catholic Church and American institutions were perfectly compatible — a claim they stressed and defended on abstract theological grounds.

CHAPTER III

Catholic Reactions to Industrial Conflict

During the 1880s Catholic social interest shifted from urban charity and rural colonization to the labor movement. In this decade the frontier disappeared and agriculture, notwithstanding its vast expansion, failed to keep pace with the growth of manufacturing in the nation's economy. With accelerated speed grew also the traditional concomitants of industrial advance, conspicuous among them being urbanism, pauperism, intemperance, and crime, and the wage-earning population which continued to be drawn in large part from Catholic lands — relatively less now from Ireland and Germany and increasingly from Italy, Hungary, and the Slavic peoples of central and southeastern Europe. Inevitably the economic transition engendered bitterness between employers and employees. Their profits imperiled in the new highly competitive national markets, businessmen sought, first, to reduce costs by mechanizing their plants and cutting wages, and, secondly, to maintain or raise prices through pools and more permanent forms of monopolistic combination. Determined to arrest profits at the expense of wages, workers engaged in strikes and boycotts, many of which entailed violence, bloodshed, and the destruction of property. The workers' cause was spearheaded by the Knights of Labor and by the craft unions associated after 1886 in the American Federation of Labor. Relying upon legislation as well as collective bargaining to secure labor's emancipation, these organizations numbered perhaps a million members at the height of the Great Upheaval of Labor, 1884–87.

Mainly wage earners, Catholics tended to take labor's side as industrial conflict became chronic and widespread. But they did not believe that labor partisanship necessarily conflicted with the public interest and the common good. On the contrary, they voiced the opinion that the peace and welfare of society could be maintained only if the working people secured a substantial improvement in living conditions. Implicit in the attitudes of all Catholic thinkers was the conviction that the blurring of spiritual insights accentuated economic conflict — that preoccupation with materialistic objectives generated greed and social discontent. Industrial peace stemmed from the disposition of employers and employees to deal fairly and justly with each other, and this willingness in turn sprang from the subsoil of a vital religion. Pending the attainment of saner ideals, and as one means perhaps to the desired result, workers were justified, not a few Catholic thinkers insisted, in battling for higher wages. "The definition of a strike remains," wrote E. W. Gilliam, a Washington, D.C., attorney, "a method forced upon workingmen to keep them from starvation wages." [1] Averring that employers, by putting the atheistic "supply and demand" philosophy into practice, infuriated workers into lawlessness and violence, the *Catholic Review* of New York believed that unions would discipline workingmen and enable them to secure justice with minimum resort to strikes and boycotts. [2]

Few, if any, Catholic newspapers or periodicals denied that workingmen rightfully struggled to better their condition. None, however, rivaled the Boston *Pilot* in its uncompromising advocacy of labor's cause. With the brilliant John Boyle O'Reilly as its editor during the 1880s, the *Pilot* devoted more attention, perhaps, to the working-class agitation than did any other journal not published under labor auspices. Especially important were the weekly comments of "Phineas," the paper's anonymous labor correspondent during the culminating phase of the Great Upheaval. "Phineas" exultantly approved the profusion of strikes and boycotts which accompanied the mushroom growth of the Knights of Labor and the trade unions during the sixteen months after February 1885. [3]

[1] "Some Aspects of Private Fortunes," *American Catholic Quarterly Review*, XII (October 1887), 649.
[2] "The Lawlessness of Capital," July 12, 1885; "Labor Organizing," March 6, 1886; "Organized Labor Necessary for Peace and Justice," May 9, 1886; "A Crisis for Capital," May 23, 1886; "Mistakes of Workingmen," June 13, 1886; "Mistakes of Employers," June 20, 1886.
[3] "What the Workmen Demand," April 3, 1886; "Strike and Boycott," May 8, 1886; "Powderly's Recommendations," September 24, 1887.

This militant uprising marked the first great stride in the emancipation of labor from thralldom to capital. "The consolidation of huge
blocks of capital has rendered possible," he wrote, "the subjection
of millions of workmen. And it is by counter-organization," he
claimed, "that the latter can regain the lost ground." [4] The workers
must keep up the agitation until all their rights were recognized:
"Phineas" was displeased when, in order to appease "public opinion," officialdom in the Knights of Labor took steps to halt the
struggle.[5]

For "Phineas" believed that public opinion as molded by capitalists, journalists, clergymen, educationalists, and other professional
leaders was hostile to workingmen and unwilling to champion their
demands, however reasonable and just.[6] Workers, he repeatedly
emphasized, must rely upon their own concerted efforts. Through
constant study, planning, and agitation the relatively few workers
belonging to labor organizations must win the support of the twelve
million wage earners in America along with their twenty-four million dependents.[7] Not until the wage-earning class as a whole had
rallied behind organized labor could workingmen forgo the use of
the costly strike and boycott and secure the enactment and enforcement of needed social legislation. But "Phineas" did not envisage
a major role for the state in industrial relations. Rather he looked
forward to the day when capital and labor, each equally well organized, would jointly determine the volume of production, the
hours of labor, the rate of wages, and through other forms of collective action seek to mitigate the severity of industrial depression.[8]
He could see no reason "why the workman and employer should
not meet on equal terms." [9] Only in the event that capital went
"on strike" would workingmen take over and "conduct the business

[4] "The Workman's One Way to Protect Himself," August 14, 1886.
[5] "Mr. Powderly's Advice to Workingmen," April 3, 1886; "Is Labor Losing
Ground?" June 26, 1886; "The Coming Labor Convention," September 4, 1886;
"Close up the Ranks," December 18, 1886.
[6] "The Masters' Weapon," July 24, 1886; "The Irrepressible Conflict," June
19, 1886.
[7] "The Great Convention of the Knights of Labor." October 23, 1886.
[8] "The Workman's One Way to Protect Himself," August 14, 1886; "Professor Sumner Attacks Labor Unions and Is Answered," September 18, 1886.
[9] "What the Labor Unions Are Good For," July 19, 1886.

of the country with intelligence, with enterprise and with success." [10]

"Phineas" did not, however, expect socialism to conquer the country. On the contrary, he defended the thesis that the contemporary drive toward labor organization had already thwarted socialist objectives. From the vantage point of 1886, he surmised that in the summer of the previous year the unorganized masses, oppressed by capital and ignored by legislatures, were strongly drawn toward anarchistic socialism.[11] But they were saved at "the edge of the precipice." A fraction of the downtrodden "rallied at last," he explained, "made a stand, and began to organize." With no aid from the "better classes," with, in fact, only maledictions from pulpit, press, and study, workingmen by their own concerted effort had put an end to wage cuts and other indignities. "The success of the labor organizations," he further explained, "gave courage and confidence to the hitherto hopeless masses; thousands of them flocked to the labor organizations," and the other millions closed up quickly behind and around "until organized labor formed but a mere corporal's guard in a vast army of toilers." [12]

This turn of events posed, "Phineas" reflected, a question of momentous importance: should the armies of toil be controlled by the labor organizations or led by the extreme socialistic element? In contrast to the socialists who make no concessions to capital, pronounce the American system a hideous failure, and "hesitate at nothing, not even at violence and bloodshed," the labor organizations, he said, "sanction no methods more violent than the strike and boycott and these only in exceptional cases. It is only when arbitration has failed," he asserted, "that the strike or boycott is adopted." [13] He forgot to point out that unions in a strong position sometimes would not agree to arbitration. In his view workers did not demand any "right to rule capital," only the right to bargain and to "a voice in the regulation of wages, and in fixing the conditions under which they shall labor." [14] Organized labor was interested in "immediate results," not in utopian solutions of the social question.

[10] "What the Workmen Demand," April 3, 1886.
[11] "The Masters' Weapon," July 24, 1886.
[12] "Workmen Winning," May 15, 1886.
[13] Ibid.
[14] "Are They at War? A Needless Fight That Wastes the Country," December 25, 1886.

For this reason "Phineas" hoped the public, including the employer part, would uphold the unions and encourage workers to join them "that they may be placed beyond the reach of selfish demagogues and crackbrained agitators." [15]

Divested of its belligerently pro-labor overtones, the "Phineas" view was certain to find defenders. One such was the Vicar-General of the Archdiocese of Chicago, Patrick J. Conway, who encouraged labor organizations because they practiced secrecy for business, not evil, purposes, did not teach the destruction of property, and believed "in settling their troubles by arbitration." [16] Highly significant was the endorsement of organized labor by great colonization and temperance leaders, notably William J. Onahan and Bishops Spalding and Ireland. Though he no doubt regretted the passing of the independent craftsman, Onahan was sure by the mid-1880s that the aggregation of capital was "the logical and perhaps inevitable result of our modern social system — in which wealth and 'greed of gain' is held to be the chief end of life." Inasmuch as the great corporations and exacting monopolies "little regard the rights of the day laborer," his desire "to combine and unite with other toilers for purposes of mutual protection" could not "be seriously questioned." Employees by the "tens of thousands" had no redress or alternative unless to "strike" when confronted, as they sometimes were, with arbitrary wage cuts ranging from ten to twenty per cent. For the removal of this and other injustices, he suggested that the two parties have recourse to the peaceful processes of arbitration. Workers would recognize and respect the rights of capital only if capitalists recognized and performed their duties to labor, the chief of which was "frank and honest arbitration." Should employers meet operatives "on this half-way neutral ground, an adjustment may be confidently looked for in most cases," he predicted, and the "arts of the demagogue and the threats of the socialists" would no longer "be effective with the laboring classes." Disputes not arbitrable by "mutual agreement" could be appealed to legislative boards of arbitration which should "be provided for by law in every state." [17]

[15] Ibid.; "Workmen Winning," loc. cit.
[16] "Knights of Labor," *Donahoe's Magazine*, XV (May 1886), 433–34.
[17] "Capital and Labor: Philosophy of 'Strikes,'" *Donahoe's Magazine*, XV (March 1886), 232–34.

Like "Phineas" in the *Pilot*, Onahan did not seriously think that labor unions were steppingstones to socialism. He expected the unions to repel the aggressions of capital without seeking to bring about fundamental changes in the existing order. For Onahan attributed the miseries of the poor less to economic oppression than to moral deficiency. "The labor question," he stated at the climax of the Great Upheaval," is not so much a question of labor as it is of liquor, laziness, and loafing." [18] With this diagnosis Bishop Spalding substantially agreed. Repeatedly the Bishop of Peoria pointed out that, with property in the United States widely diffused, the socialist propaganda lacked a factual base. Notwithstanding, workingmen had "legitimate claims," he conceded, which could best be met by trade unions. "They exist, and the ends for which they exist, in spite of incidental abuses connected with their working, are praiseworthy," he wrote in 1886, "and there is no power that can put them down." Spalding looked to the labor movement to exalt the ideals of morality and intelligence above those of commercialism. "If the trade-unions shall succeed in forcing politicians to recognize that financial interests are not the only or principal human interest, they will have conferred a benefit upon the nation," he believed.[19]

As his special contribution to the discussion of labor attitudes, Bishop Ireland [20] insisted that immigrant workingmen, no less than native ones, were hostile to socialism. He was incensed at stories in public print portraying foreign-born workers in Chicago as gory

[18] Quoted in "Evils of the Saloon," *Catholic Review*, January 1, 1887. For varying opinions concering the bearing of character defects on labor unrest, see John Talbot Smith, "Kitchens and Wages," *Catholic World*, XLIV (March 1887), 799–86; same author, "Liquor and Labor," ibid., XLVII (July 1888), 539–44; M. F. Foley, "Drink and Drink-Sellers the Nation's Bane," ibid., XLVIII (December 1888), 311–18; "Labor and Temperance," *Catholic News*, September 12, 1888; "Bishop Ireland on Socialism," *Northwestern Chronicle*, May 13, 1886; "The Friends of Labor," ibid., September 23, 1886; "Gravity and Meaning of the Social Question," ibid., May 25, 1888; "The Catholic Church and Socialism," ibid., June 20, 1890; "The Church and Poverty," ibid., August 7, 1891; "The C.T.A. Convention," ibid., July 17, 1892; "Poverty," ibid., January 6, 1893; "The Church's Social Duty," ibid., May 19, 1893; "C.T.A.U. Convention," *Voice*, August 13, 1891; "Temperance, Bulletin of the General Secretary," *Catholic Herald*, February 23, 1895.

[19] "Are We in Danger of Revolution?" *Forum*, I (July 1886), 405–15.

[20] James H. Moynihan, *The Life of Archbishop John Ireland* (New York, 1953), esp. pp. 20–32, 211–33.

insurrectionists who caused the Haymarket Square Riot of May 3, 1886. The immigrants were of the best intention, he asserted, but, not understanding the language or customs of the country, were at the mercy of demagogues. "I do not put the labor question on the same footing as socialism. There is a wide difference," he wrote, "but socialistic leaders take advantage of the opportunity to draw the labor question into the present difficulty." [21]

For the most part, Catholic reformers believed that the labor movement must and in fact would steer clear of socialist ends and means. Also implicit, if not openly expressed, in every Catholic defense of unionism was the assumption that it would help mobilize public opinion behind needed social legislation. The *Pilot*, it is true, favored legislation only if its "immediate benefits" increased attachments of workers to labor organizations on whose militant activities their emancipation primarily depended. In this spirit, "Phineas" urged laws to protect, if not to insure, workmen against industrial accidents.[22] But other reformers expected protective labor laws to take the place of "foolish and expensive" strikes and boycotts. These weapons, when employed against great corporations, "were totally incompetent," insisted the Reverend John Talbot Smith, "to achieve a radical and permanent success." [23]

Smith complained that in their preoccupation with the strike weapon workmen had paid too little attention "to the defective statute, or to the preparation and passage of good laws." One cause of low wages, he pointed out, was "the employment of children where adults should be employed." Rather than exhaust their energies futilely attempting to change the "law of supply and demand" through strikes and boycotts, the unions should combine with wealthy philanthropists and other reformers not of the wage-earning class to end by law the child labor abuse, wipe out rotten tenements, curtail the liquor traffic, increase the number of public parks, extend factory inspection, and chain the coal and food monopolies — all measures bearing directly on the workers' standard of living.[24]

[21] "Bishop Ireland on Socialism," loc. cit.; "Know-nothingism vs. Anarchy," ibid., May 20, 1886.

[22] "The Knights of Labor. Some of the Work They Have to Do," June 12, 1886.

[23] "Workmen Should Not Only Act but Think," *Catholic World*, XLVII (September 1888), 842.

[24] Ibid., pp. 842–43.

If workers were slow to move in the right direction, the general public, as another critic, Edward Priestley, noted, was also at fault: it had refused to exercise its inherent power to regulate wages, hours, and other vital working conditions. Through fear of paternalism employers and employees had been left free to associate and to fight out their differences on the industrial battlefield. Brawn being no match for money, the workers had failed to win a decent support. With the growing realization that poverty not only debased the masses but also menaced society, many were coming to Priestley's conclusion: "that we must, more than we have hitherto done, make over to the state a closer oversight of the relations between the classes." [25]

Some Catholics subscribed to a theory of state intervention which proclaimed its power to remove the causes of industrial conflict. They were followers of the agrarian radical, Henry George, whose brilliantly written *Progress and Poverty* (New York, 1880) aroused interest in social reform not only in the United States but in all English-speaking lands, especially in Ireland.[26] Labor's real exploiter under the existing system, George taught, was not the employer or capitalist (merely the custodian of "stored-up labor") but the landowner whose rents, increasing without effort on his part as civilization advanced, tended to impoverish all producers, employers, and employees alike. Should the state confiscate to public uses, as he proposed, the "unearned increment" (leaving the "possession" of land and improvements in private hands), industry would be unburdened and conflicts between employers and employees eliminated or greatly lessened.[27]

Grateful to George for his journalistic efforts in behalf of the Irish Land League, many Catholics believed his principles, properly applied, would relieve urban poverty, and accordingly supported his independent candidacy for mayor of New York in 1886. The heated campaign attracted national attention. Not only workingmen but also many middle-class people — professional men, clerks, merchants,

[25] The Wage Earner and His Recreation," ibid., (July 1888), 513.

[26] Charles Albro Barker, *Henry George* (New York, 1955), esp. pp. 265–304, 341–416.

[27] See Peter Alexander Speek, *The Single Tax and the Labor Movement*, Bulletin of the University of Wisconsin, No. 878, Economics and Political Science Series, Vol. 8, No. 3, pp. 247–426, for a detailed analysis.

and clergymen — supported George because they wished to rebuke corrupt politics and irresponsible wealth. The most widely known of George's backers was the zealous pastor of St. Stephen's parish, Dr. Edward McGlynn, powerful orator and impassioned crusader for social justice. Although George lost the election, he piled up a heavy vote and won something of a moral victory. Many rejoiced at his courageous attempt to effect great social changes through peaceful and constitutional means. In contrast to the revolutionary anarchists, George's agitation, some thought, tended to check social disorder. "Instead of the large vote cast by the labor party being a menace to society," wrote the *American Catholic News* (New York), "it actually demonstrated the safety of society from dynamite bombs of the Nihilists and the riots of the socialists." [28]

Not many Catholics accepted the whole of George's economic theory. To James A. McMaster, veteran editor of the New York *Freeman's Journal*, Henry George was an "unbalanced Turgot," [29] an economic individualist in the traditions of Rousseau and the Manchester School, a reformer who ignored or minimized the need for protective labor legislation, for trade unionism, and for the "establishment of confidence between the employer and the employed. . . ." [30] To most of his Catholic critics, however, George was no individualist, not even a false one, but an unbridled socialist intent on wiping out private property. In this vein wrote the newly elevated Archbishop of New York, Michael A. Corrigan, who in a pastoral letter shortly after the election warned the faithful "to be zealously on guard against certain unsound principles and theories which assail the rights of property." [31] Admitting inequities in the existing system, Corrigan seemed indifferent to current reform: he counseled the rich to treat the poor charitably and the latter in turn to await patiently "the rewards of eternal happiness." As if anxious to incur the archbishop's wrath, Father McGlynn heaped scorn upon the pastoral letter. The slaves of poverty and oppressed toil would not, he surmised, derive much comfort from

[28] November 17, 1886.
[29] "Rome and the Knights of Labor," March 19, 1887.
[30] "Mgr. Freppel on the Labor Question," ibid., November 20, 1886.
[31] Frederick J. Zwierlein, *Letters of Archbishop Corrigan to Bishop McQuaid and Allied Documents* (Rochester, 1946), 7–11.

Corrigan's condescending reminder that Christ bade them hope for reward in the next world. "This is not the doctrine to preach to honest laborers of this century," McGlynn retorted. So long as "ministers of the gospel and priests of the Church tell the hard working poor to be content with their lot and hope for good times in heaven, so long," he warned, "will skepticism increase and 'Bob' Ingersoll have many believers." He did not hesitate to say that in charities, which "relieve, not eradicate" poverty, he retained only "a languid interest": the "true and only adequate remedy for social evils lay in the abolition of private ownership of land" through the confiscation of economic rent.[32]

Socially minded critics denied, however, that land, though of the greatest public importance, required socialization or more extended regulation than other kinds of property. The community right in land "would be no greater," asserted Judge F. McGloin, "no different from what it would be where strict popular necessity demanded interference with proprietary interests in things of any other character."[33] So long as the civil authority acknowledged "theoretically and practically the right of private property in land or as a result of men's labor and exertion," explained the Jersey City canonist, Monsignor J. de Concilio, it could regulate the exercise of the right "by just and equitable laws, in view of the common good of the social body. . . ."[34] More specifically, the Reverend Edward McSweeny contended that as a rule the rich owned the land while the poor depended upon their labor for support. Although each was ultimately useless without the other, land was more independent of labor than labor of land. Self-interest, therefore, sometimes failed to make the rich consider the needs of the poor. If after being reminded of Christ's law of charity they continued to neglect the poor and needy, society was at liberty to employ force, because "in justice as well as charity," he said, "what-

[32] "Dr. McGlynn's Pessimistic Philosophy," *Nation*, December 3, 1886. See McGlynn's two statements of his attitudes, "Justice Wanted More Than Charity," *Independent*, December 11, 1890, and "Large Fortunes and Low Wages," *Donahoe's Magazine*, XXXIV (July 1895), 749–53.

[33] "Individual Property in Land: Its Justice," *Freeman's Journal*, March 19, 1887.

[34] "The Right of Individual Ownership — Does It Spring from the Natural or the Human Law?" *American Catholic Quarterly Review*, XIII (April 1888), 297.

ever remains after the legitimate wants of the rich are supplied belongs to the poor." [35] More specifically still, the Jesuit M. Ronayne stated that the burden of relieving the hardships of labor "rests directly on the State." He meant not alone the time-honored relief of indigence by state alms but "that distress which lies on ablebodied men and women who are willing to work and can find no one to hire them or those who have work but receive for it, we may say, starvation wages." Laws effectively controlling corporate monopolies, eliminating child labor, wiping out rotten tenements, and curtailing the liquor traffic would help workers directly or indirectly to secure living wages. [36]

The moderate state interventionists sought a *via media* through the land controversy. But their views were temporarily lost on the extremist camps. Enough of a theologian, as he claimed, to know that the Church had "never condemned" common property in land "as contrary to Catholic faith," McGlynn was heedless of Corrigan's demand that he abandon the Georgist agitation. Thereupon the archbishop first suspended and then removed the rebel cleric from the St. Stephen pastorate. Uncompromising, selfrighteous on occasion, and always defiant, McGlynn helped to organize and headed the Anti-Poverty Society from which he gained a livelihood and a social gospel pulpit. When he refused to go to Rome under censure to explain his opinions and conduct, he was excommunicated. Both men were stubborn and doctrinaire; each was unduly sensitive to inroads on his canonical rights. [37]

The public was interested chiefly, however, in the social implications of the controversy. The attempt to silence McGlynn encountered frenzied resistance from his parishioners and from Catholics everywhere who sincerely believed in the single-tax theories. These defenders in New York City led parades and protest meetings and raised funds for the support of McGlynn and the "crusade" — all in total disregard of Archbishop Corrigan and his wishes.

---

[35] "Lacordaire on Property," *Catholic World*, XLV (June 1887), 345–46.

[36] "Land and Labor," *American Catholic Quarterly Review*, XII (April 1887), 250.

[37] See Stephen Bell, *Rebel, Priest and Prophet. A Biography of Dr. Edward McGlynn* (New York, 1937), for an extended discussion of the controversy from McGlynn's side; and Frederick J. Zwierlein, *The Life and Letters of Bishop McQuaid*, III, 1–83, for the Corrigan viewpoint.

McGlynn's following was mainly recruited from citizens who believed that the archbishop had unjustifiably curtailed liberty of discussion in a controversy that was primarily political and economic and only incidentally religious in nature. All the priest's defenders, whatever their religious or economic views, appealed to liberty and Americanism.[38] In a letter addressed publicly and privately to Pope Leo XIII, a distinguished Brooklyn priest, Sylvester Malone, stated that "as understood by the American people," the charges against Dr. McGlynn "raise the question of the right of the citizen to express his views fully and openly on all questions that are non-essential. Nothing can alter this view of the case," he emphasized as he asked His Holiness, "is it wise to give our fellow-citizens cause, even for suspicion, that Catholics are enemies of this principle of civil liberty, held so sacred by all Americans?" Inasmuch as McGlynn, widely known and highly respected, was the advocate of America's dependent citizens, his condemnation would likely alienate millions of the poor, and should be avoided, Malone suggested, "unless the Holy Church . . . teaches that the state must hold that it is not true in morals that she can take into her own hands the dominion of the land for the benefit of all, the poor as well as the rich." [39]

Malone spoke, no doubt, for many clergymen, especially the younger ones, who had succumbed, in Bishop McQuaid's words, to the "pernicious influence" of McGlynn and "his pernicious notions." [40] From the outset, laymen, especially workingmen, demonstrated attachment to McGlynn. At the overflow meeting of January 17, 1887, held in Cooper Institute to protest the rector's deposition, Corrigan was denounced for "interposing his influence and authority against the efforts of the toiling masses to gain a peaceful redress for their grievances. . . ." [41] But mainly the meeting elaborated on the theme that ecclesiastical authority could not rightfully

38 This is brought out in James Jeremiah Green, "The Impact of Henry George's Theories on American Catholics," a doctoral dissertation, 1956, University of Notre Dame.

39 Sylvester L. Malone, editor, *Memorial of the Golden Jubilee of the Rev. Sylvester Malone* (Brooklyn, 1895), 61–62.

40 Letter to Corrigan, December 11, 1886, Archdiocesan Archives of New York (photostatic copy, University of Notre Dame Archives), Box C–16.

41 Bell, op. cit., p. 51.

"prescribe for American Catholics, lay or cleric, what economic opinions they shall express or what line of political action they shall pursue or abstain from. . . ." The meeting declared that "the Catholic priest does not and ought not to cease to be an American citizen, and should enjoy, unquestioned by ecclesiastical authority, the full rights of his citizenship, so long as he does not seek to intrude his opinions or politics into his priestly office." Finally, these Catholic workingmen protested "against Dr. McGlynn's summons to Rome to account for his political opinions and action as an attempt to establish the dangerous precedent that an American citizen can be questioned in a foreign country for his course in American politics." [42]

McGlynn's treatment, in the view of non-Catholics, was a shining example of ecclesiastical tyranny. The Unitarian *Christian Register* of Boston wrote that in trying to be both a priest and a free man McGlynn had made an experiment about as successful as it would be "for a fish to attempt to walk on dry land." [43] When Corrigan's friends noticed this aspect of the controversy, they contended that for Catholics Rome was not a "foreign power" and that, since McGlynn "was sustaining men who preached false and dishonest doctrines" — that is, "socialistic theories that have been conceived to be inimical to lawfully constituted authority" — his civil rights had not been violated by ecclesiastical authority.[44] Without denying the force of this argument, socially liberal members of the American hierarchy sided with Corrigan's critics. Many of his colleagues, notably the newly designated cardinal, Archbishop James Gibbons of Baltimore, viewed the unfolding controversy with deep misgivings. They feared that McGlynn's condemnation would not only alienate many of his sympathizers but would also help to turn the entire labor movement against the Church. To many workingmen, McGlynn's treatment seemed to climax or intensify current ecclesias-

[42] "Vindication. Know-nothingism Strangled by Catholic Laymen," *Catholic Herald,* January 29, 1887.

[43] "New York Notes," January 27, 1887; Adolf Hepner, "A German Free-thinker," in *Ultramontanism Is Unlawful in the United States. A plea for Home-Rule, an Account of the McGlynn Case* (Philadelphia, 1887), urged the federal courts to enjoin McGlynn from going to Rome.

[44] "Henry George's Sophistry," and "Minor Education," *American Catholic News,* January 12, 1887.

tical attitudes unfriendly to labor. In July 1886 Rome reaffirmed its earlier condemnation of the Knights of Labor in the ecclesiastical province of Quebec. Inasmuch as only a few American bishops wished to have the Knights in this country condemned, they were apprehensive lest the Quebec ban be extended into their jurisdictions. They failed, however, to present a solid front in behalf of the Knights. When in late October 1886 the archbishops met as a committee to consider the question, two of their number voted to disapprove the order. Lacking unanimity, the committee was obliged in accordance with the ruling of the recent Third Plenary Council of Baltimore to refer the issue to Rome for settlement.

Convinced that condemnation of the order would "expose the Catholic Church to many dangerous losses," [45] Gibbons resolved to bring pressure on the Holy See to lift the ban. To this end, he made good use of his visit to Rome early in 1887 to receive the red hat. Besides discussing the subject with various ecclesiastical officials, the new cardinal prepared with the aid of Bishops Ireland and Keane and presented to the Holy Office a lengthy memorial which would show, he wrote Archbishop Elder, "the injustice, danger and folly of denouncing the Knights." If, as he intimated to the Cincinnati prelate, the suspension of McGlynn, the laborer's friend, had disturbed the Church's peace, "what a tumult would be raised if we condemned the laborers themselves." [46] Not writing with a view to publication, Gibbons was under no temptation to court public opinion and felt all the freer therefore to address the curial officials with the utmost frankness and candor.[47] By doing so, he undoubtedly laid bare the true state of the American Catholic mind on the labor question.

At the outset of his plea Gibbons insisted that in neither its constitution nor its mode of operations did the order violate the rulings of the Church respecting societies and associations. The Knights did not exact of its members either an oath or a promise of blind obedience. The resort to secrecy for the purpose of guarding its

[45] Henry J. Browne, *The Catholic Church and the Knights of Labor*, p. 192.
[46] Ibid., p. 238.
[47] The Memorial was published, March 3, 1887, by the New York *Herald*, its Roman correspondent having procured a copy probably through bribery of a minor curial official. John Tracy Ellis, *The Life of James Cardinal Gibbons, Archbishop of Baltimore* (Milwaukee, 1952), I, 511.

business against enemies and strangers did not preclude Catholic members from revealing everything "to competent ecclesiastical authority, even outside of confession." Moreover, the order was friendly to religion and anxious to keep its policies in line with Catholic moral requirements. Powderly, its "president," other prominent officers, and two thirds of the members were loyal adherents of the Church. The memorial, written in French, played up the Catholic complexion of the organization; the English translation, made to influence public as well as Catholic ecclesiastical opinion, minimized this aspect of the document's contents.[48] Gibbons was also at pains to show that the Knights were not subversive of government and political authority. He pointed out that "the heads of our civil government" did not eye the Knights with disfavor but rather "treat with the greatest respect the cause which they represent." The President and the Congress were planning ameliorative measures in labor's behalf and the political parties vied with each other "in championing the evident rights of the poor workmen who seek not to resist the laws, but only to obtain just legislation by constitutional and legitimate means."

In the face of undeniably grave social evils, "which call for strong resistance and legal remedy," the Knights of Labor seemed an effective instrument with which to combat oppression and injustice. The malady stemmed mainly from private and corporate monopolies which "to their own profit" corrupted legislatures, imperiled liberty, and through greed of gain pitilessly ground "not only the men but particularly the women and children in various employments. . . ." All lovers of humanity and justice were coming to realize that "it is not only the right of the laboring classes to protect themselves, but the duty of the whole people to aid them in finding a remedy against the dangers with which both civilization and the social order are menaced by avarice, oppression and corruption." The remedy lay obviously in association or the organization of all interested persons, "the most efficacious means . . . almost the only means to invite public attention, to give force to most

---

[48] Allen Sinclair Will, *Life of Cardinal Gibbons* (New York, 1922), I, 337–52, and Zwierlein, *The Life and Letters of Bishop McQuaid*, II, 445–55, reprint the original English translation, which is an abridged and inexact text. Browne, op. cit., pp. 365–78, gives a complete and accurate translation.

legitimate resistance, to add weight to the most just demands." In obedience to the Church and their consciences, Catholics shunned the Masonic brotherhood, joining instead workingmen's associations for mutual protection and help, and the legitimate assertion of their rights. Not surprisingly, they were grieved and astonished to find themselves, for no satisfactory reason, threatened with condemnation and thereby "deprived of their only means of defense."

As to objections to the socially inclusive Knights, Gibbons stoutly denied that exclusively Catholic trade unions were feasible or necessary in America; "in a mixed people like ours, the separation of religions in social affairs is not possible." Intermingling with Protestants in trade unions did not, however, imperil the faith of the Catholic workers of America, "who are not like the workingmen of so many European countries — misguided and perverted children, looking on their Mother the Church as a hostile stepmother — but they are intelligent, well instructed and devoted children ready," he declaimed, "to give their blood, as they continually give their means for her support and protection." The cardinal was no less sure that Catholics knew "how to disregard with good sense and firmness" the machinations in the Knights of Labor of the "destructive element" comprising atheists, Communists, and anarchists. The union between the Church and her children reduced to a minimum the danger from violent and aggressive characters in the labor movement. The "only grave danger," he warned, "would come from an alienation" of the faithful, "which nothing would more certainly occasion than imprudent condemnations."

While the Knights sometimes resorted to violence and bloodshed, they did not monopolize these deplorable evils against which "the laws" and "chief authorities" of the organization exerted a decidedly restraining influence. The Baltimore prelate reminded the Holy Office that in the struggle of the masses against the "mail-clad" power of "hard and obstinate monopoly," it was "vain to expect that every error and every act of violence can be avoided. . . ." The labor movement being irrepressible, Christian prudence counseled ecclesiastical authority, he suggested, "to try to hold the hearts of the multitude by the bonds of love . . . to acknowledge frankly the truth and justice in their cause, in order to deter them from what would be false and criminal, and thus to turn into a legitimate, peaceable and beneficent contest what could easily become for the masses of our people a volcanic abyss, like that which society fears and the Church deplores in Europe."

On this phase of the subject, Gibbons discoursed with special earnestness, pointing out that the question at issue involved not only the rights of the working classes but also "the fundamental interests of the Church and of human society for the future." The Church must continue to hold the affections of the masses lest they be impelled by the "prince of darkness" toward "the ruinous paths of license and anarchy." Now that the people ruled, especially in America, "social amelioration" was the "inevitable programme of the future," opposition to which would alienate popular support and esteem, a main source of the Church's influence. "To lose the heart of the people," he warned, "would be a misfortune for which the friendship of the few rich and powerful would be no compensation." Somewhat inclined to overestimate labor's real strength, the cardinal feared that condemnation of the Knights might antagonize the political power of the country and thereby tear down the whole edifice of Catholic patriotism. Recalling the erstwhile Know-Nothing persecution, Gibbons observed that the accusation of being "un-American," that is to say, "alien to our national spirit, is the most powerful weapon the enemies of the Church know how to employ against her." In months past, angry threats had been made against the Church on this score.

Inasmuch as Catholic workingmen considered condemnation to be "both false and unjust," they would not accept it. "They love the Church, and they wish to save their souls, but they also must earn their living, and labor is now so organized," as he explained, "that without belonging to the organization there is little chance to earn one's living." Should the Knights be put under the ban, Catholics by the thousands would leave the Church and swell the ranks of the secret societies. The revenues of the Church, including Peter's pence, "would suffer immensely. . . ." If the condemnation of a single priest had so deplorably disturbed the Church's peace, "what will not be the consequences to be feared," he asked, "from a condemnation which would fall directly upon the people themselves in the exercise of what they consider their legitimate rights?"

Even if condemnation "were just and prudent," it was wholly

unnecessary. For the Knights of Labor, only one among several forms of labor organizations, was "so little permanent" in its form that "it cannot last very many years." While, indeed, social agitation would continue so long as there are social evils to be remedied, forms of organization and procedure "are necessarily provisional and transient." For the Church to strike at one of these forms would be to commence an exhausting war against changing and uncertain phantasms — "without system and without end." Moreover, the American people did not fear that the social movement would get out of hand, standing ready to deal with "any excesses or dangers that may occasionally arise." For this reason, if for no other, the Church "should not offer to America an ecclesiastical protection for which she does not ask, and of which she believes she has no need."

The cardinal's warning advice, so strongly put, did not go unheeded. Immediately the Holy See lifted the penalties which had been imposed on recalcitrant Knights in Quebec, and after more than a year's delay ruled that the order could be tolerated provided "words which seem to savor of socialism and communism" were removed from the preamble of its constitution. This condition, something in the nature of a face-saving reservation, was never complied with by the Knights of Labor whose officers, including Powderly, were unwilling to antagonize socialist and anti-Catholic groups in the order. Although Archbishop Corrigan, Bishop McQuaid, and other Catholic conservatives saw duplicity and sinister purpose in the order's failure to act, the Catholic liberals with Gibbons at their head were not greatly perturbed, especially in view of the Knights' rapid loss of influence and membership in the late 1880s and the early 1890s.[49]

Henry George's agitation similarly lost most of its mid-1880s impetus. Owing, however, to McGlynn's and Corrigan's uncompromising attitudes, the single-tax theory continued to be of major Catholic concern. As a means of undermining McGlynn, Corrigan pushed plans in Rome to have Henry George's *Progress and Poverty* put on the Church's Index of Prohibited Books. Not a few members of the hierarchy doubted the justice or wisdom of the New York prelate's project. In a letter to the Holy Office Gibbons pointed out

[49] Zwierlein, *Life and Letters of Bishop McQuaid*, I, 458–61; Browne, op. cit., pp. 259–69, 307–12, 322–38, 344–46.

that "the relation of the State to the ownership of land" is "a very complicated question, governed by differing circumstances of time and place and never fit to be resolved by a peremptory sentence." While "the theories of Henry George differ," as he emphasized, "from those ordinarily called Communism or Socialism," they did involve a profound change in social relations, not likely to be undertaken "in a country like the United States, which is not one for doctrinaires and visionaries." If left alone, the agitation would "in all certainty die of itself"; if condemned, it would spread "immensely," he predicted. "Prudence should suggest," he concluded, "that we should not incur the risk of giving to these theories a vital importance and an artificial force by the intervention of the Church tribunals." [50]

In the spring of 1888 Gibbons addressed a second letter to the Holy Office, in the hope of thwarting the renewed efforts of Archbishop Corrigan to achieve his purpose. At the cardinal's prodding, more than a score of bishops urged Rome not to place the treatise on the Index. Although not a single one of these bishops believed that the single-tax proposal in its entirety was either just or practicable, they opposed condemnation largely on the ground that it would expose Catholics to the charge that their Church was hostile to civil liberty. The issue was compromised: early in 1889 the Holy Office decided that Henry George's doctrines were "deserving of condemnation," but refrained from promulgating the decree.[51]

Aside from its prudential deference to American public opinion, this decision reflected the lingering belief in papal circles that solutions of social questions were to be found only in the religious and moral realm in which the rich exercised benevolence and patronage and the poor cultivated the virtues of industry, Christ, and contentment with their lot. In the more Catholic parts of continental Europe this was the viewpoint of various study and agitational groups under the influence of the sociologist Le Play and often referred to as the Angers School from their favorite assemblage or convention site. As against these Catholic conservatives who relied on charity and alms, the so-called Catholic reformers — the Liège

[50] James Cardinal Gibbons to Cardinal Simeoni, February 26, 1887. Richmond Diocesan Archives, quoted in Green, op. cit., pp. 193–95.
[51] Ellis, op. cit., I, 574–85.

School — demanded social justice, to be ushered in through social legislation establishing a minimum wage for every industry, providing insurance against industrial hazards, limiting the working hours of women and children, and prohibiting work on Sunday. Gradually Pope Leo XIII veered in the direction of the Liège School. He told a delegation of French workingmen on October 17, 1887, that should morality, justice, man's dignity, or the domestic life of workingmen be menaced or jeopardized "the State by a right measure of intervention will be working for the common wealth, for it is its duty to protect and watch over the true interests of its subjects." [52]

In the years immediately following, Leo was constantly importuned to elaborate an authoritative statement of principles underlying social thought and action. Beset with controversy involving labor and land issues, American bishops called upon the Holy See for theoretical guidance. Their wishes were voiced by Archbishop Elder, who in opposing the condemnation of *Progress and Poverty* also wrote, "It is desirable to have a clear statement of Catholic doctrine" concerning the rights and duties of land, capital, and labor, the "exposition" to deal only incidentally with "George's particular notion" and "without reference to his name or his book."[53] In the hope of putting an end to rifts among American as well as European Catholics, the Pope carefully formulated a social justice program, giving to the world in May 1891 the *Rerum novarum*, a masterly encyclical on the condition of labor.[54] In Leo's view social justice must mediate between the two clashing systems of the day: on the one side economic liberalism with its scornful rejection of moral and political intervention in industry, and on the other socialism, which magnified the place of the State and the community in industrial life. That his plan for radical though non-Socialist reform would only with difficulty gain a hearing, Leo was well aware. The *laissez-faire* policy, as he realized, was deeply intrenched in the thought and practice of politicians and statesmen, and socialism

[52] Quoted in Edward McSweeny, "State Socialism," *Catholic World*, XLVI (February 1888), 690; Priestley, op. cit., 518; *Catholic Review*, November 19, 1887; ibid., December 24, 1887.

[53] Browne, op. cit., pp. 319–21.

[54] Aaron I. Abell, "The Reception of Leo XIII's Labor Encyclical in America, 1891–1919," *Review of Politics*, VII (October 1945), 464–67.

as a political movement resting on a highly developed economic theory was mobilizing millions of adherents for a social overturn. The wealthy, he knew, would not willingly subordinate their realm of industry and trade to the Christian social law, however just and reasonable. The poor, indoctrinated by two generations of Socialist teaching that all humanly created wealth rightly belonged to them, would likely reject his plan, which assigned them only a part, though a greatly enlarged part, of total earnings.

Obstacles did not, however, deter the Pope from his determination to formulate the truly Christian remedy for the "misery and wretchedness" of the world's poor. At the outset of his short treatise, Leo insisted that two fundamental principles must be accepted, the one economic and the other religious. Over against "the main tenet of Socialism, the community of goods," he placed "the inviolability of private property" as a guiding social principle. The maintenance and extension of private property in "land or movable goods" accorded with natural law by stimulating the individual to self-improvement, by supplying the basic needs of human personality, and by safeguarding the integrity of family life. That some, even much, common property might be desirable and legitimate in modern society, he did not deny; he merely insisted that every man has by nature the right to hold property as his own in "stable and permanent possession."

Nor would any "practical solution" of the social question be found, said Leo in passing to his second fundamental principle, "without the assistance of Religion and the Church." Apart from reconciling mankind to the pains, hardships, and inevitable inequalities of life, the Christian religion obliged conflicting groups to adjust their differences in accordance with the precepts of justice and charity. Since "capital cannot do without labor, nor labor without capital," the two should co-operate, and nothing is more powerful than religion in bringing them together "by reminding each . . . of its duties to the other, and especially of the duties of justice." Thus religion enjoined employees to carry out all equitable agreements freely made and employers to respect the human and Christian dignity of their workpeople, and to pay them just and adequate wages. The Church also enjoined persons whose possessions more than sufficed for their support at a becoming level to give of their surplus to those in need. "It is a duty," he explained, "not of justice (except in extreme cases), but of Christian charity — a duty which is not enforced by human law."

Private property resting on justice and charity, therefore, was the firm foundation on which men and women 'by appropriate means should erect the enduring structure of labor's welfare. The Church itself, with benevolent agencies "efficacious in the relief of poverty," was one means. The others were the state and workmen's associations. In serene defiance of the current "police" theory, the Pope made promotion of human welfare the chief business of government, stating that when "the general interest of any particular class suffers, or is threatened with, evils which can in no other way be met, the public authority must step in to meet them." Since the working people contributed more than any other group to the prosperity and material well-being of the commonwealth, justice required the commonwealth in turn to remove or lessen the burdens inflicted upon them by modern industry. Thus the public administration should eliminate Sunday labor, shorten the workday, prohibit or regulate the labor of women and children in factories, and use the taxing power to favor the multiplication of property owners.

Leo was particularly interested in administrative agencies, presumably under state authority, to guarantee workers a "living" wage. He granted that, as a rule, workmen and employer should freely agree as to wages, but "there is a dictate of nature," he solemnly affirmed, "more imperious and more ancient than any bargain between man and man, that the remuneration must be enough to support the wage-earner in reasonable and frugal comfort." If out of weakness he accepted less, he was "the victim of force and injustice." On the modest goal of "comfort" — a standard midway between the extremes of luxury and subsistence — Catholics in America and elsewhere were to focus effort in social reform. The wage system in this sense they accepted, knowing full well that it would vastly improve living conditions and realize, to some degree, the fond ideal of widely diffused private property.

Private as well as public effort must be resorted to in order to solve "this most difficult question." Through workmen's associations employees could better their condition in body, mind, and property. The two kinds of associations present in Europe Leo emphatically endorsed — the association consisting of workmen alone (the independent trade union) and the type including workmen and employers together (the guild or *syndicat mixte*). Also with an eye to Socialist-Christian schism in the European trade union movement, he urged Catholic associations, to the organization, management, and benefits of which he devoted considerable space. But by unmistakable implication he approved labor unions of the British and American type which, while conforming in their ends and means to Christian principles, eschewed formal religious leadership.

Taken as a whole, the encyclical marked the emergence of three new trends, interpreters pointed out: first, the decision of the Church in a democratic age to seek popular in place of princely support; second, a Christian desire for industrial peace — "a kind of truce of God," in Father Zahm's telling phrase; [55] and third, the victory of progressive Catholics the world over who wished "to unite justice with charity" in order to usher in "a new organization of society based upon some conception of equality." [56] The Pope had "gone into the details of labor questions," editorialized the *Catholic Citizen* of Chelsea, Massachusetts, "as if he were a Powderly or a Gompers charged with the interests of organized labor." [57] This journal's prediction that the encyclical "will strengthen laboring people everywhere in their demand for justice" was verified in the sense that union labor made use of the document "in hundreds of labor organizations" and "before innumerable labor audiences." Reformers outside the ranks of organized labor acknowledged its constructive power. Among economists, Carroll D. Wright, distinguished labor statistician, considered Leo's encyclical "the foundation for the proper study of social science in this country," and "I know," he was to report, "that it has had an immense influence in steadying the public mind." The friends of "social Christianity" among Protestants, by 1891 a fairly large group, admitted

[55] J. A. Zahm, "Leo XIII and the Social Question," *North American Review*, CLXI (August 1895), 203–4.

[56] John Graham Brooks, "The Papal Encyclical upon the Labor Question," *American Economic Association, Publications*, IX (1894), 546. See also "The Pope and the Poor," *Nation*, January 7, 1892; and M. Anatole Leroy-Beaulieu, "State Intervention in Social Economy," *Popular Science Monthly*, XLI (August 1892), 463–68.

[57] "The Encyclical: A Comment That Will Be Interesting," June 20, 1891.

that Leo's program sanctioned effective methods of industrial reform. "The authority of the encyclical lies in its unqualified assertion of the doctrine of private property," wrote the *Andover Review*;
"its wisdom lies in its concessions respecting the present economic
and social function of the state." By urging the state to help relieve
social distress, the Pope "has ranged himself unmistakably on the
side of the new Political Economy." [58]

Not essentially different was the main body of Catholic comment.
The "deep import" of the encyclical, wrote Bishop Spalding, lay in
its "pronouncement that the mission of the Church is not only to
save souls, but also to save society." But he did not believe that
social salvation could be gained through state intervention. Since
poverty, no less than vice and crime, stemmed chiefly from ignorance and moral weakness, the betterment of labor, in the future
as in the past, presupposed a gradual evolution in which education,
individual and social, rather than legislation was to be principally
stressed. "We are convinced," he stated, "that the great aim should
be not to provide for all men, but to train and educate all men to
take care of themselves." While taking sharp issue with the socialist
claim that the "present economical system" was "organized injustice," he readily admitted that it often produced "an incalculable
amount of physical and moral evil." We may not, however, he
warned, "trample on rights to secure greater distributive justice,
or approve of schemes which if they promise a greater abundance
of material things to the poor, would lead to a general enfeeble-
ment and lowering of human life." [59]

In the opinion of at least one Catholic editor, J. Talbot Smith
of the *Catholic Review*, the Peoria bishop failed to stress sufficiently
the plight of workers who in major occupations "were worse paid
than at any time since the war, and inadequately paid if we consider
the work they do and the profits of their employers." The "des-
picable" condition of American labor derived less from "the poverty
that prevails" than from "the systematic injustice" practiced upon
the laborer, by employers, landlords, and government. Not by reference to general principles in the Spalding manner was the labor

[58] See Abell, "The Reception of Leo XIII's Labor Encyclical in America,
1891-1919," loc. cit., 476.
[59] "Socialism and Labor," *Catholic World*, LIII (September 1891), 791-807.

question to be understood and solved; existing facts must be studied and disseminated through continuous agitation.[60] Less concerned than Spalding and Smith with specific working conditions was Bishop John J. Keane, rector of the newly founded Catholic University of America, whose commentaries on the Leonine document were as judicious as they were luminous and masterly.[61] More than other Catholic interpreters, Keane viewed *Rerum novarum* in terms of social justice and its attainment. He noted that "the majority of workers for `social reform have been convinced that all volunteer efforts would fall short unless aided by legislative reform, wisely framed and gradually applied." [62] Inasmuch as experience demonstrated that "the wealthy cannot be trusted to see to" the amelioration of the poor, the task "must be accomplished by organized endeavor on the part of the laboring classes, and where this falls short, by legislative enactments prompted by humanity and justice." [63] Owing to Leo's moderation on the issue of state intervention as evidenced by his zeal in upholding private and public rights in due proportion, Keane thought that the labor encyclical would go "far towards securing unity of view and action" among American Catholics.[64]

This was a fond expectation because, if unified, Catholics had it "in their power," as the *Catholic Record* of Indianapolis asserted, "to do an infinite amount of good in improving the condition of the poor." [65] Temporarily, however, the continuing single-tax controversy encouraged confusion and discord.[66] From his failure to understand the true nature of private property, the Pope had floundered in the remedies he proposed from near anarchy to "extreme socialism," contended Thomas B. Preston, ardent Catholic Georgist. In his opinion Leo was no true individualist, favoring, as he did, compulsory Sunday rest, an eight-hour day, trade unionism, and

---

[60] "Bishop Spalding and the Labor Question," *Catholic Review*, October 11, 1891.

[61] "The Encyclical 'Rerum Novarum,'" *American Catholic Quarterly Review*, XVI (July 1895), 595–611; "The Catholic Church and Economics," *Quarterly Journal of Economics*, VI (October 1891), 25–46.

[62] Ibid., 44.

[63] "The Encyclical 'Rerum Novarum,'" loc. cit., 604–5.

[64] "The Catholic Church and Economics," loc. cit.

[65] July 9, 1891, quoted in Green, op. cit., pp. 241–42.

[66] Green, op. cit., Chapter VII.

regulation by Church societies, "all of which savor of the very socialism which he is combating." [67] Henry George, who believed with Preston that Leo had condemned his scheme, speeded to His Holiness an "Open Letter," in which he painstakingly explained that single taxers would transform only rent (a social creation or value) into common property. Since they would leave the possession of land and the fruits of capital and labor applied to land in individual hands, single taxers upheld private property and opposed socialism as truly as the Pope himself did.

Unimpressed by this rather labored distinction, Archbishop Corrigan forced public disclaimers from the numerous priests in his jurisdiction who found "good and perfect thoughts" in George's reply to the Pope.[68] No less bluntly single taxers, Catholic and non-Catholic alike, rejected the archbishop's interpretation of the Pope's words as infallibly defending the present system of landownership. Archbishop Corrigan "grossly misrepresents the laymen of his church," claimed a Missouri Catholic.[69] Another lay theologian was sure that every Catholic who understands the single tax "knows that it is in strict harmony with Catholic doctrine" and that "private property in land is opposed to every established rule of the Catholic Church." [70] But Edward Osgood Brown, well-known Catholic lawyer of Chicago, was on firmer ground when he recalled that "no well-instructed Catholic supposes the Encyclical to be such an utterance of the Holy See as is held by Catholic doctrine to be infallible." He regarded the encyclical as no more than "a sermon from the highest pulpit in Christendom." [71]

As the controversy progressed, Catholics more and more agreed with Cardinal Gibbons and his friends that, while a doctrinal point was involved, it was not conclusive and that the fate of the single tax must rest with the whole people judging its expediency and justice as freely as any other proposed public policy. To forbid Catholics to participate in the discussion and decision, as Archbishop Corrigan wished, would be to acknowledge "the truth of the accusation of our enemies," wrote the *Catholic Standard* of Philadelphia,

[67] "Pope Leo on Labor," *Arena*, IV (September 1891), 461–63.
[68] *Standard*, November 11, 1891.
[69] Ibid., November 25, 1891.
[70] Ibid., December 16, 1891.
[71] Ibid., August 12, 1891; ibid., November 18, 1891.

"that Catholics are not and cannot be truly loyal to the civil authorities of their country." [72] Sharing these sentiments and believing that progressive Catholics deserved encouragement, Monsignor Francis Satolli, the Pope's representative, lifted in late 1892 the sentence of excommunication against Father McGlynn on the ground that "there is nothing" in his opinions "contrary to the faith and teachings of the Church." Though the Church had not been converted to McGlynn's views, they "are now free doctrine," as the Reverend Richard L. Burtzell rightly observed. The decision that a man has a right to be a Catholic priest and at the same time an American citizen was a solution, editorialized an "institutional church" journal, "over which all good men will rejoice." [73]

While McGlynn's restoration marked a great advance in Catholic Americanization, it was something of an anticlimax in the Henry George movement. Even before Satolli's decision, most Catholic social thinkers were acutely aware that, viewed practically, the single-tax theory had little or no bearing on the resurgent industrial conflict that was to characterize the 1890s. If in his great encyclical Leo XIII had not in so many words placed the wage contract within the scope of public authority,[74] many American Catholics assumed that by implication the document approved state oversight of industrial relations. With few exceptions, Catholic publicists urged reformers and statesmen to include legally enforced arbitration in their plans for allaying social discontent and industrial strife during the depression of 1893–97 and the phenomenal business consolidation which ensued with the return of prosperity. In the discussions regarding the Homestead strike of 1892 and every major industrial disturbance in the decade thereafter, Catholic reformers almost uniformly endorsed compulsory arbitration, however widely they differed on other solutions.

In the vanguard of reform was the wealthy convert John Brisben Walker, whose social criticism was not confined to the shortcomings of the Catholic clergy. When the Carnegie interests at Homestead employed armed Pinkertons against the Amalgamated Association

---

[72] Ibid., December 23, 1891.

[73] *Church Work* (St. Paul, Minn.), IV (January 1892), 2.

[74] "Pope Leo on the Condition of Labor," *Independent*, XLIII (June 18, 1891), 909–13; "The Pope and the Poor," *Nation*, LIV (January 7, 1892), 7–8.

of Iron and Steel Workers, this "Catholic Mugwump" [75] branded the action an assault on the people's liberties. "For if one man may hire 300 poor devils ready to shoot down their brothers in misery," he editorialized in his magazine, the *Cosmopolitan*, "there is no reason why he may not hire 10,000." [76] The inequality which encouraged arbitrary displays of industrial power Walker would lessen through high income taxes; public ownership of railways, telegraphs, and telephones; heavy taxation of land and other properties held for speculative purposes; and a currency system, self-regulated by means of postal savings banks. "Finally, let it be a recognized principle," he wrote, "that when men employ many laborers their business ceases to be a purely private affair, but concerns the State, and that disputes between proprietor and workmen must be submitted, not to the brute force of many Pinkerton mercenaries, but to arbitration." [77]

Catholic journals echoed Walker's demand for arbitration, pointing out that great corporations must be operated to "public as well as private advantage." No writer more convincingly called attention to the "overlooked third interest in the contentions between labor and capital," namely, that of "the public and the public interests," than the veteran Catholic journalist, George Dering Wolff, whose remarks on Homestead were destined to be his last commentary on the labor question. "Neither employers nor employees," he categorically asserted, "have any rights over or against the public welfare." He readily admitted, to be sure, that in ordinary disputes, where neither party was sufficiently powerful to disturb the public peace or injure other interests, the state wisely held aloof. The situation changed radically when immense corporations and labor associations asserted unqualified rights. Then pride and self-will usurped the place of prudence and mutual consideration; neither side would yield, "and the interests of others, both public and private, necessarily suffer, even if violence and bloodshed do not ensue; and it

---

[75] The epithet is from the *Catholic Review*, March 29, 1891, which took exception to Walker's recent address at the Catholic University of America in which he had alleged priests favored the rich and shunned social reform. See "The Church and Poverty," *Lend a Hand*, III (November 1891), 338–43, for a sympathetic reference.

[76] "The 'Homestead' Object Lesson," XIII (September 1892), 572.

[77] Ibid., pp. 574–75; cf. "Echoes from Homestead," *Pilot*, September 3, 1892.

is seldom that they do not." Wolff was sure that when powerful corporations and "less powerful yet still very powerful associations of workingmen" came into conflict, there was "no other way, consistent with the public welfare, to settle the contention . . . than that of enforced arbitration." [78]

Within limitations set by the public welfare, Catholic advocates expected compulsory arbitration to secure higher wages and better working conditions for the laboring population. In support of their proposal, they appealed to the Irish Land Act of 1881 and to Pope Leo XIII's labor encyclical of a decade later, each of which, the one in practice and the other in theory, had reconciled public and private interests. The New York *Freeman's Journal* believed that industrial courts of arbitration, composed equally of representatives from the state, capital, labor, and religion, would give life to one of Leo's celebrated formulas: "Whenever the general interest of any particular class suffers, or is threatened with evils which can in no other way be met, the public authority must step in to meet them." From the proposed courts, this influential newspaper envisioned decisions so just and reasonable that employees would abandon the strike, and even their unions, while employers, forced into compliance by public opinion, would in the course of time accept profit-sharing arrangements. [79]

In a less lyric mood, the Indianapolis *Catholic Record* observed that neither profit sharing nor compulsory arbitration would function properly in the absence of strong unions equipped to present the labor viewpoint. [80] Other journals voiced the same opinion, none more emphatically than the *Colorado Catholic* whose Populist-inspired editor, Father Thomas H. Malone, was thoroughly committed to the economic and political organization of farmers and workers. In his view, a compulsory arbitration law was but the first step in the united drive of the two groups to "create legislative

[78] "An Overlooked Third Interest in the Contentions between Labor and Capital," *Catholic Standard* (Philadelphia), July 30, 1892.

[79] "Leo XIII and Labor Adjustment," August 13, 1892; "The Labor Battle," ibid., July 16, 1892; "The Remedies for Labor Troubles — Arbitration and Profit-and-Loss Sharing," ibid., July 30, 1892; "Industrial Arbitration," ibid., August 6, 1892.

[80] Ibid., July 28, 1892; ibid., August 4, 1892; ibid., August 11, 1892.

safeguards to protect the laboring man from the greed and heartless aggressiveness of capital." [81] By the same token, the conservative New York *Catholic Review* sought in compulsory arbitration a check on lawless labor. This journal feared that troops sent to quell strikes would desert to the side of the idle and unemployed and reproduce on American streets the frightful scenes of the French Revolution. Even if militiamen remained loyal, employers inevitably incurred immense damage from industrial conflict. "Better run the risk of having their profits cut down by judicious arbitration," the editor advised, "than to provoke the hostility of a maddened crowd of excited workmen." [82]

While seemingly convincing, the New York journal's argument failed to anticipate changing realities: employers need not arbitrate in view of the growing willingness of the federal judiciary to outlaw strikes and boycotts against railroads and other quasi-public corporations. Mainly on the ground that the public welfare required uninterrupted service, several federal judges, conspicuous among whom was William Howard Taft, limited in 1893 the exercise of the strike right in decisions which were reaffirmed on a national scale during and after the violent and destructive Pullman strike the following year. Barring a few exceptions, representative Catholics believed President Cleveland's sending troops to Chicago was necessary to restore law and order.[83] Some of them, however, thought that the federal authority would have re-established peace more wisely and justly had it forced the parties to arbitrate the contest rather than obliging labor in effect to yield it.[84] Over and above their conflicting estimates of the Pullman struggle, reforming Catholics insisted that curtailing the strike right, without replacing it by arbitration or something equally advantageous to labor, was socially dangerous: the poor would conclude that they no longer

[81] "Compulsory Arbitration," August 27, 1892.
[82] "The Carnegie Collision: An Object Lesson," July 17, 1892.
[83] "The Western Riots," *Catholic Mirror* (Baltimore), July 14, 1894; James R. Randall, "Washington Letter," *Catholic Columbian* (Columbus), July 21, 1894; "Modes of Enforcing the Law," *New World* (Chicago), July 14, 1894.
[84] "A Way Out of the Difficulty," *New World*, July 14, 1894; "The Railroad War," *Pilot*, July, 14, 1894; "A New Kind of Heresy," ibid., September 1, 1894; "The Haughty Railroad Managers," *Northwestern Chronicle*, July 20, 1894.

enjoyed equally with the rich the law's protection and must, therefore, seek relief through revolutionary action.[85] The *Pilot* could visualize no solution short of government control or ownership of the railway network. "It is an undemocratic and paternal cure," it admitted, "but the disease is desperate, and calls for desperate remedies. ..." [86]

Sharing the *Pilot's* willingness to face reality, other journals also regretfully conceded that the Jeffersonian principle of as little government as possible needed modification. Sure that government ownership would be "the entering wedge of socialism." [87] the *Catholic Record* did not think this objection was valid against compulsory arbitration. The supposition that the decisions "would be in favor of labor and always adverse to employers" was as erroneous as it was widespread. "The judgment of the court," the editor, Alexander Chomel, believed, "would be founded on the merits of the case as in other tribunals." [88] Paternal government was needed to protect workers "not only against capital, but also against demagogues and false leaders." [89]

At least one Catholic journal, the *Catholic Columbian*, published in Ohio's capital city, expected as a sequel to the Pullman strike "the enactment of a compulsory arbitration act by Congress." [90] Although no law resulted, President Cleveland under existing statutes appointed a strike commission to investigate the causes of the recent conflict with a view to future legislation. The commission's report suggested that Congress establish for the railroads a permanent national strike commission with authority to investigate disputes, recommend settlements, and enforce them with the aid of

[85] "Is Wealth to Trample on Freedom and Stamp Out Life?" *Catholic Advocate* (Louisville), July 14, 1892; "Is Law Tyranny?" ibid., October 13, 1892; "The Masses and the Classes," *Catholic Herald* (New York), April 1, 1893; "The Conflict of Labor and Law," ibid., April 8, 1893; "The Law and Labor," *Pilot*, April 8, 1893; "The Arrest of Debs," *New World*, July 14, 1894; *Catholic Review*, January 6, 1894; ibid., February 17, 1894; *Review* (St. Louis), September 1, 1894.

[86] "The Railroad War," July 14, 1892; cf. "The Pullman Boycott," *Catholic Advocate*, July 12, 1894; "The Big Strike," ibid., July 19, 1894; "Anent the 'Walking Delegate,'" *Catholic Telegraph*, October 27, 1892.

[87] "Our Labor Troubles," July 12, 1894.

[88] "Compulsory Arbitration," August 9, 1894.

[89] "Our Labor Troubles," July 12, 1894; "The Hope of Labor Is in a Paternal Government," July 12, 1894.

[90] "Two Good Results," July 21, 1894.

the federal courts.[91] In his editorial approving these and other suggestions, including one on employer recognition of the railway unions, Dr. Michael Walsh, editor of the New York *Catholic Herald*, urged that compliance be exacted through a license system. Requiring all corporations to take out licenses, the government should grant them "only on condition that all disputes with employees be submitted to arbitration. A refusal to submit," he insisted, "should entail a forfeiture of the license." This plan, the "only legitimate way" government could interfere with contracts between wage earners and their employers, would, he believed, make rich and poor "really equal in the eyes of the law." [92]

Walsh was unique among Catholic editors of the 1890s for the thought and space he devoted to the religious and social aspects of the economic crisis, styling his journal a labor paper along *Rerum novarum* lines.[93] He tried to demonstrate, among other things, that adjustment of disputes, in accordance with Leonine principles, served to check, not strengthen, as many employers assumed, the Socialist menace.[94] Not all Catholics, to be sure, interpreted *Rerum novarum* in a radically progressive sense. Thus William J. Onahan found in the Leonine teachings a great and comforting "bulwark" of the *status quo*. "An evil spirit seems to have taken possession of the masses — a rage against capital and authority," wrote this Chicago philanthropist and public servant to his friend, Monsignor Denis O'Connell, in the wake of the Pullman strike. "It is the Catholic Church chiefly," he continued, "that will be the bulwark of society and even of government in trials like the present and Pope Leo has made the attitude of the Church invulnerable at all points." [95]

[91] United States Strike Commission, "Conclusions and Recommendations," Report on the Chicago Strike of June–July, 1894 (Washington, 1895), XLVI–LIV.

[92] "Cleveland's Strike Commission," November 24, 1894; cf. "The Strike Commission's Report," *Church Progress*, November 17, 1894.

[93] "The Strike Commission and the Press," November 24, 1894.

[94] See "Beware of False Teachers," July 30, 1892; "The Labor Question," November 4, 1893; "The Pope and Trades Unions," September 29, 1894; "Agitate! Agitate!" October 13, 1894; "Cardinal Gibbons on Strikes," October 13, 1894; "A Lesson from the Strike," February 9, 1895; "No Place for Socialists," April 18, 1897.

[95] July 17, 1894, Denis O'Connell Correspondence (Microfilm Copy), Box 10, University of Notre Dame Archives.

More pronouncedly, Onahan's friend, Archbishop Ireland, wanted to quell social agitation associated during the depression of the mid-1890s with the strikes of militant labor and the political demands of workers and farmers in the Populist and related movements. With Catholics "numerous in strikes and riots," as he reminded Cardinal Gibbons in a letter justifying his open denunciation of the Pullman strike, it was all the more necessary to keep the Church "before the American people as the great prop of social order and law. . . ." Ireland distinguished less sharply than formerly between socialism and the labor movement. "Socialistic ideas have gone into our people and into many of our priests," he now believed. "We have been siding with labor in its grievances: the unthinking ones transgress the golden mean, and rush into war against property." [96] The Archbishop of St. Paul could not contain his alarm when in 1896 the armies of discontent gathered around Bryan, seeking the presidency on a nominally Democratic but essentially Populist platform. Bryan's election, Ireland announced, would bring "destruction of social order," "lawlessness and anarchy," and rule by the "International." [97] He was outraged by the Democratic promise to free labor from "government by injunction." The courts "are to be shorn of their power," he lamented, "and shorn of it in favor of mobs, bent on rioting and the destruction of property." [98]

Apart from partisan politics, Ireland's social attitudes strongly appealed to a small but enlarging group of Catholics able and willing to rely for the improvement of their social status on thrift, sobriety, and the other economic virtues. But rank-and-file Catholics, along with most of their lay and clerical leadership, refused to follow the archbishop [99] and deeply resented the attempts of business interests

[96] Archives of the Archdiocese of Baltimore, 93–J–4, Ireland to Gibbons, July 21, 1894.

[97] Moynihan, op. cit., p. 261.

[98] "John Ireland," *Colorado Catholic*, October 17, 1896.

[99] Reputedly, only two Catholic newspapers, *Der Wanderer* (St. Paul) and the *Catholic Herald* (New York), supported Ireland on Bryan's defeat, "The Church and the Wage-Earner," *Catholic Herald*, October 24, 1896. Father Thomas H. Malone exaggerated in saying the "Catholic Church and the Catholic Clergy as a whole are working night and day for the election of Bryan and the silver cause," "Bryan and Martin Luther," *Colorado Catholic*, October 24, 1896.

to represent his position as that of the whole Church.[100] They contended, on the contrary, that property and income regulations were now more necessary than ever before. By the new business consolidations, which gained mastery over the American economy around the turn of the century, workingmen as consumers, along with the rest of the population, were often forced to pay extortionate prices, and as producers to forgo justifiable wage adjustments.[101] Although in meeting this situation a few Catholics, among them the priests Thomas J. Hagerty and Thomas McGrady, affiliated with organized socialism,[102] the Catholic body desired only a more vigorous trade union movement and the legislative program as it had come from the intertwining hands of Knights of Labor, single taxers, and Populists.[103]

No person at the turn of the century represented with more force and distinction the continuing Catholic interest in the labor question than the Most Reverend George Montgomery, Bishop of Monterey-Los Angeles, California. In an open letter to American workingmen the Bishop urged them to set the labor cause on a religious pedestal. Inasmuch as capital possessed an "undue purchasing power" in courts and legislatures, labor's only hope of securing justice lay in the emergence of honest and conscientious representatives and public servants. So long "as gold can buy votes and legislation, the laboring man will be the victim of capital," he warned, "and gold will have that power wherever religious principles do not form and control men's consciences." [104] As the routine of government became more responsible, Montgomery looked

[100] "Socialism and Catholic Education," New York *Sun*, January 2, 1898; *Northwestern Chronicle*, January 7, 1898; "Hanna and Socialism," *Challenge* (*Wilshire's Magazine*), December 26, 1900, p. 6; Pittsburgh *Observer*, May 1, 1902.

[101] "State Interference with Strikes," *Catholic Herald*, September 4, 1897; "Pagan Views of Labor," New York *Freeman's Journal*, September 22, 1900; "The Labor-Robbing Trusts," ibid., November 24, 1900.

[102] Alfred W. Cook, "The Bugbear of Socialism," *Midland Review* (Louisville), December 7, 1899; Mary Bryne Carroll, "The Tempest Confronting Humanity," ibid., February 22, 1900; G. Rybrook, Ord. Praem., "The McGrady Scandal," *Review*, November 21, 1901; "What a Priest Says," *Wilshire's Magazine*, II (March 13, 1901), 10; "Father McGrady Resigns," ibid., No. 54 (January 1903), 34–37.

[103] Pittsburgh *Observer*, July 17, 1902; ibid., October 9, 1902.

[104] "Labor and Religion," *Catholic Herald*, August 28, 1897.

for a solution of the labor question in terms of compulsory arbitration, income taxes, municipal socialism, and nationalization of railways and telegraphs.[105]

In urging these measures, Bishop Montgomery suggested the continuing vitality of the attitudes and policies long extolled by large and influential segments of the Catholic body. Major strikes and strike threats in coal, steel, and urban utilities evoked renewed calls in the Catholic journals for a compulsory arbitration system. Perhaps the clearest, most succinct, and most cogently reasoned defense of the scheme at the turn of the century came from the pen of Populist-inspired John A. Ryan, a young priest studying for the doctorate at the Catholic University of America. As it had done in New Zealand, so also in America compulsory arbitration would put an end, Ryan thought, to "industrial anarchy," raise wages, eliminate sweatshops, encourage labor organization, and establish wage minimums — all requirements of industrial justice.[106] The right of free contract was a lesser right which "ceases," he insisted, "when it comes in conflict with the right to a living wage." If courts of arbitration ought in most cases to rule in favor of labor, they should also prohibit worker excesses. "If an employer is in danger of being forced out of business by the unjust demands of his men, the state is bound to protect his natural right to fair profits," he affirmed, "and to compel the men to work under reasonable conditions, or else seek other employment." [107]

Although fervently committed to the compulsory principle, Ryan viewed it as only a secondary phase of the broad effort to secure living wages for all workers. The responsibility here rested primarily on employers, as he demonstrated in his treatise, *A Living Wage: Its Ethical and Economic Aspects*, published in 1906 and destined to become the "Uncle Tom's Cabin" of the minimum wage law movement. In Ryan's judgment neither custom nor bargaining nor equivalence between work and pay, but the essential needs of the human personality must determine the minimum just wage. From a

[105] "Bishop Montgomery . . . Advocates Municipal Socialism," *Wilshire's Magazine*, II (February 6, 1901), 3.

[106] "A Country without Strikes," *Catholic World*, LXXII (November 1900), 145–57.

[107] On this point, see John Bates Clark, "Do We Want Compulsory Arbitration?" *Independent*, November 13, 1902.

careful study of available statistics, Ryan concluded that the average family of that day — husband, wife, and four or five children — could not live decently on less than six hundred dollars a year and that at least sixty per cent of adult male wage earners received less than this sum. In view, however, of the country's ample productive resources, a living wage for all was morally imperative and ultimately attainable. While employers were morally bound to pay living wages, the enforcement of the duty must come through trade union action, the payment of sufficiently high prices by consumers, and minimum wage boards under public authority.

CHAPTER IV

Battling for Social Liberalism, 1884–1901

By its increasingly sympathetic attitude toward the labor movement of the late nineteenth century, Catholic leadership laid the foundations for cordial relations between the Catholic Church and the working people of America. Moreover, the Church's reaction to the industrial crisis favorably impressed other Americans, men and women of discerning mind who were not affiliated with either the Catholic Church or the wage-earning population. These generous folk were quick to realize that the Church, besides being an uncompromising foe of violence, anarchy, and socialism, sanctioned worker demands only in so far as they advanced the general welfare. No Protestant publicist more ably vindicated the social effectiveness of the Catholic Church than the Reverend Lyman Abbott. As editor of the widely read undenominational weekly journal, the *Christian Union* (the *Outlook* after 1893) and successor of Henry Ward Beecher in the pulpit of Plymouth Church, Brooklyn, this "Protestant of Protestants" branded as "fatal folly" the campaign of sectarian zealots to undermine the authority of the Catholic priesthood over urban immigrants,[1] and joyfully proclaimed the virtues of reforming Catholics as he recorded their deeds in his own community and throughout the country.

If numerous Protestants, notably persons under the influence of liberal theology, shared Abbott's views, the rank and file looked upon Catholics as a group apart and consequently ignored or minimized their potential contribution to the reform cause. "At the moment," complained the *Catholic Review* (New York) in May 1886, "when various important civic and social reforms are promised, and a crisis in the labor and temperance questions threaten the

[1] "Dangers Ahead," *Century Magazine*, XXXI (November 1885), 51.

country," Catholics are not invited to help, even though "the national movement which gains their entire support will march to victory as surely as that the sun will rise tomorrow." Their "rigid faith" will not allow Catholics "to stand on the same platform with us," the editor represented Protestants as saying. "Let them go and we shall get along without them." [2] To some Protestants the words "Catholic" and "reform" were contradictory terms, the juxtaposition of which provoked hilarity and mirth. Thus the report that in the summer of 1888 Catholics had joined with other denominations of Chicago to suppress the saloon evil and Sunday desecration aroused the risibilities of the Philadelphia *Protestant Standard*. The "faithful" would find things to do in plenteous abundance. A good start would be to wash "the whiskey stench out of St. Patrick's Cathedral in New York, and from a good many other Mass-houses that have been built up with beer, whiskey and lotteries." Properly indignant that Catholics after mass on Sundays sought amusement and recreation, the paper did not doubt that the godly might with more reason "ask a prostitute to preach virtue than to look to the Church of Rome to stop Sabbath desecration." [3]

Catholics on their part could be equally insulting. Many of their newspapers heaped contempt and ridicule on Protestant social service as an ill-conceived and thoroughly mischievous enterprise. In 1888 the New York *Catholic News*, edited by the historian John Gilmary Shea, pronounced the recently formed Charity Organization Society "a sort of infidel Trust Combination. . . ." Its principles, he insisted, "are bad, essentially bad, and Catholic societies should have nothing whatever to do with the concern, which," he warned, "is a ravenous monster that eats up charity itself and causes the deserving poor to be sent to prison as criminals." [4] The Reverend Patrick F. McSweeney was amazed, as were other priests no doubt, at the "petty, prejudiced and narrow-minded way" Catholic journalists often belittled non-Catholic efforts to improve society. "Liberalism is, no doubt, a bad thing," he mused, "but so is un-Christian Illiberalism and calumny, were it even directed against Satan him-

[2] "Points of Agreement," May 2, 1886.

[3] "A Comical Idea," June 21, 1888, in "Collection of Newspaper Clippings Relating to the Situation of the Roman Catholic Church in America," New York Public Library, Vol. 2, pp. 293–94.

[4] "An Evil Institution," May 6, 1888.

self." [5] Shea retorted that the belligerent overtones of the Catholic press were necessary weapons against unscrupulous enemies of the Church, conspicuous among whom were ex-priests and "escaped nuns." [6]

If all Catholics wished to guard against the "no-popery" virus, many scented danger to the faith of immigrants in their rapid Americanization and therefore opposed all forms of religious co-operation which presumably accelerated the process. Under the influence of this conviction, some leaders of the Catholic foreign-born urged immigrants during the 1880s and 1890s to cling tenaciously to their Old World habits and customs. They apparently did not realize that social isolationism as they conceived it was sure to provoke a Know-Nothing revival. The new form of nativist wrath centered in the American Protective Association. Beginning in 1887 in the Middle West, the APA had by the time it ran its course in the middle 1890s inflicted political defeat and business failure on many hapless Catholics in all parts of the country. Meanwhile, the agitation of disgruntled Catholics, here and abroad, came to a climax in the Lucerne Memorial presented to the Holy See in 1891 by the German merchant, Peter Paul Cahensly, lifelong benefactor of immigrants, and by his associates in the St. Raphael's Society for the Protection of Catholic Emigrants.[7] The memorial claimed that over ten million Catholic immigrants had lost their faith in America and requested the Pope to appoint bishops for the aggrieved nationalities in order that religion might be safeguarded through the perpetuation of foreign customs and speech. In a subsequent memorial Cahensly hiked the losses to sixteen million souls!

His suggestions enraged American public opinion, especially the idea that the United States was not truly a nation, only a juxtaposition of jarring colonies from abroad. Cahensly was villified as a defamer of the American hierarchy and as the central figure in nefarious plots to advance German imperial interests at the expense

---

[5] "The Church and the Classes," *Catholic World*, XLVII (July 1888), 478–79. P. A. Tracy, "Condition of Catholics in the United States," *Donahoe's Magazine*, XVIII (July 1887), 61–62.

[6] "The Catholic Press," *Catholic News*, June 2, 1888.

[7] Colman J. Barry, O.S.B., *The Catholic Church and German Americans* (Milwaukee, 1953), an exhaustive study portraying Cahensly as a genuine benefactor of immigrants without ulterior political or ecclesiastical motives.

of the United States. But Cahensly was not the man to bathe his philanthropy in perfidy and intrigue. He was blameworthy only in the sense that he planned to isolate immigrants from American influences, including trade unions and other secular associations whose inclusion of "atheists, infidels and Protestants" endangered, as he believed, the faith of Catholic members. He urged the Church in America to encourage with all her strength the formation of additional mutual aid, benevolent and protective associations, "having different ones for different nationalities, if need be, in which Catholics will have the same advantages, the same temporal benefits as those offered by the secret societies and societies based on religious indifferentism." [8] Cahensly's program, which recalled the erstwhile opposition to the Knights of Labor, posed a threat to the Church's labor policy as expounded by Cardinal Gibbons and his fellow seekers of industrial justice. Moreover, it played into the hands of the APA, which used its influence in the trade unions to exclude and expel Catholic wage earners in fulfillment of the oath to counsel only with Protestants on wage disputes and to enter into no "agreement with a Roman Catholic to strike or create a disturbance. . . ." [9]

With the influence of Catholics in the general labor movement thus imperiled by religio-social extremism without and within the Church, middle-of-the-road Catholics bestirred themselves to promote understanding and good will among all religious groups. Even before Cahenslyism and APAism took formal and final shape, discerning Catholics had pointed out that on many moral and social questions Catholics and non-Catholics "almost precisely" agreed and could "work together on a common platform without sacrificing one tittle of their religious belief. . . ." [10] Of most concern to Protestants were measures to combat the lawless liquor traffic and its interference with Sabbath observance. Inasmuch as so many Catholics were personally implicated in these scandals, the bishops in 1884 at their Third Plenary Council of Baltimore had, as has been seen, condemned the continental Sunday and admonished Catholics "engaged in the sale of liquors to abandon . . . the dangerous traffic and to

---

[8] "Cahensly's Second Report," *Catholic Review*, July 25, 1891.
[9] "Topics of the Hour," *Catholic Review*, November 26, 1892.
[10] "Points of Agreement," loc. cit.

embrace a more becoming way of making a living." To the surprise and satisfaction of non-Catholics generally, the Church in immediately following years not only continued to employ moral suasion against drinkers and sellers of intoxicants, but also lent support to legislative restrictions on saloon activity — expensive license, no sale to drunkards and minors, and Sunday closing. While neither the Church officially nor Catholic temperance leaders personally considered prohibition on a national or state-wide basis to be wise public policy, they refused to condemn it. Thus in 1891 at the convention of the Catholic Total Abstinence Union of America the delegates agreed with Bishop Keane: "There are honest men who believe the only cure is by striking at the root and enforcing Prohibition. Many think Prohibition will yet be the only remedy, and we have no right," he stated, "to slap them in the face." [11]

To promote temperance and other reforms many Catholics were inspired by the example of the English cardinal, Henry Edward Manning, whose success as a social reformer stemmed largely from his willingness to work with men of every religious persuasion. One of Manning's devoted American disciples, the Reverend Edward McSweeny, insisted in 1887 that while "the publicist is training the voters to correct some of the social wrongs by the ballot," all men, "the Jew and the Samaritan, the Catholic and the infidel," should unite to extend and perfect the ever needful practice of private and public charity. This endeavor, apart from bringing benefits to the Catholic poor, would remove from all Catholics the reproach of incivism, multiply conversions, and infuse into charitable associations something of the spirit of the St. Vincent de Paul Societies. "We ought to be very grateful," he thought, "for the Christian spirit that prevails" in the various societies for the diffusion of beneficence, the suppression of vice, the prevention of cruelty, and the promotion of temperance. He also thought that Pope Leo XIII included this type of citizen co-operation in his advice to Catholics, in the encyclical *Immortale Dei* (*Christian Constitution of States*) of November 1885, to "take part in public affairs" with a "fixed determination to infuse into all the views of the state, as most wholesome sap and blood, the wisdom and virtue of the Catholic religion." [12]

[11] "C.T.A.U. Convention . . .," *Voice*, August 13, 1891; see Joseph V. Tracy, "Prohibition and Catholics," *Catholic World*, LI (August 1890), 669–74.
[12] "Social Problems," *Catholic World*, XLIV (February 1887), 586–88.

Actually, American Catholics, especially those identified with the urban welfare and labor movements, were ready in full measure to perform "the duties of individual citizens" to which the Pope alluded at the close of his encyclical. Above all they realized that only as religious animosities were softened could the Catholic Church contribute fruitfully to the public welfare. They possessed in Cardinal Gibbons a leader who personally embodied public and private virtue, a man whose every thought and deed aimed to manifest the inner harmony of Catholicism with liberty and lofty patriotism, an ecclesiastic who could press Catholic claims without becoming uncharitable or needlessly offensive. In his two most widely read books, *The Faith of Our Fathers* and *Our Christian Heritage*, popular expositions of Catholic and Christian doctrines respectively, he was conciliatory in tone. The latter book, a Protestant admirer wrote, "did not contain six pages which would not be endorsed by any Protestant divine from the right reverend bench in the House of Lords to the pastors of the Reformed Church in France." [13] After noting that much of the Christian heritage found "able and zealous advocates in Protestant writers," Gibbons stated that "far from despising or rejecting their support, I would gladly hold out to them the right hand of fellowship, so long as they unite with us in striking the common foe. It is pleasant," he observed, "to be able to stand sometimes on the same platform with our old antagonists." [14]

In this spirit Gibbons, his associates, and his followers worked to ease the controversy and friction on socially divisive issues. Of these the most troublesome was the public school question, the legitimacy of which had been challenged by Catholic authority in America on the fundamental ground that, while the state should support or subsidize education, it had no right to impart or control it. Sensing by the late 1880s that this more than any other Catholic attitude generated community resentment against the Church and its people, Catholics re-examined their position, to find that in Catholic thought education was the proper function of all groups qualified to teach — the state no less than the family and the Church. At Stillwater and Faribault, Minnesota, Archbishop Ireland hoped

[13] J. E. C. Bodley, *The Catholic Democracy of America* (Baltimore, 1890), p. 72.
[14] *Our Christian Heritage* (Baltimore, 1889), p. 1.

to transform parochial into public schools, the essential features of
the arrangement being that the boards of education lease the Catholic school buildings for a nominal sum, pay the salaries of the Catholic teachers, and authorize formal religious instruction after regular
school hours. "Religion a side-show!" exclaimed parochial school
enthusiasts who along with equally partisan public school champions
heaped abuse and insult on the archbishop. When the furor failed
to subside quickly, Leo XIII sent an ablegate, Archbishop Francis
Satolli, to America, to clarify the Church's stand on popular education and other issues involving social morality and clerical discipline.

Lasting five years, Satolli's mission, as his sojourn was called, resolved numerous disputes and prepared the way for the establishment of an Apostolic Delegation, its first head being Satolli himself.
Inasmuch as a papal representative in America curtailed somewhat
the discretionary power of bishops, many of them, with Spalding
of Peoria as their mouthpiece, did not look favorably upon the new
arrangement. On the other hand, it provided, as many, especially
priests, were quick to realize, a measure of "home rule" for the
Church in the sense that now most ecclesiastical decisions would
be made in America itself and slow, costly appeals to Rome would
be limited to matters of the gravest moment. On the school question
Satolli finally approved Archbishop Ireland's experiments and the
public school philosophy underlying them, making clear, however,
that pastors and people must continue to erect parochial schools
as decreed by the Third Plenary Council. Well-disposed Protestants
joined with reforming Catholics to play up the social significance
of Satolli's ruling: it would encourage co-operation for common
American ends. Listing Satolli's mission "among the most important events in American history since the close of the civil war,"
Lyman Abbott's *Christian Union* believed the decision meant that
in the future the Catholic Church "is to work for spiritual ends
through methods not inconsistent with American life and institutions." [15] An "Onlooker," apparently a Catholic, emphasized in
an article in the New York *Independent* that Satolli's ruling would
give Catholic clergymen of American spirit more liberty of action to
co-operate in philanthropic work with their non-Catholic brethren. Recalling Archbishop Corrigan's attempt to suppress the McGlynnites,

[15] "The Roman Catholic Issue," January 21, 1893.

he observed that there had been "less freedom of discussion among Catholics here than among their brethren in the British Isles. Questions free in the schools of theology," he stated, "are frequently forbidden of discussion here." [16] Bishop Keane was sure that Satolli's mission "will give the country clearly to understand that we recognize and admit civil rights and are ready to co-operate fairly in education as in all else that concerns the public welfare." [17]

From time to time, as opportunity offered, reforming Catholics — increasingly referred to as liberals — insisted that the Church must keep in step with human progress. Since progress involved adjustment and change, Catholic social philosophers, especially Ireland and Keane, explained that there were two elements in the Church's constitution — the one essential and divine, the other human and accidental. The first must never change; the second must change in order to keep the Church abreast of the age. "Progress," asserted Ireland, "is the law of God's creation." God has implanted the desire for improvement in the hearts of men. The vast material and scientific progress of the nineteenth century was an essentially divine event — a providential step in the onward march of humanity. The new age had intensified, however, some of the old evils such as pride, thoughtlessness, and indifference to the laws of justice. The problem facing the Church was that of balancing material and intellectual progress with a corresponding development of moral and spiritual progress. Only as the champions of morality and justice moved in concert could the herculean task be accomplished.[18]

In this practical or social sense the reforming Catholics did not object to the qualifying term "liberal," with which they were tagged by friend and foe. Theirs was a true liberalism, they boasted, as against a false liberalism which denied the primacy of divine authority in human affairs. A penetrating student of religious trends, Merwin-Marie Snell, Keane's secretary until he apostatized — he soon returned to the Church — pointed out that American Catholic liberalism was social and ethical in origin and purpose, and was not to be confused with the theological movement bearing the same

16 "The Catholic Outlook," April 34, 1893.
17 John J. Keane to Archbishop Ireland (in Rome), April 9, 1892, Denis O'Connell Correspondence, microfilm copy, University of Notre Dame Archives.
18 See A. I. Abell, "Origins of Catholic Social Reform in the United States: Ideological Aspects," *Review of Politics*, XI (July 1949), 304–6.

name in the Protestant world.[19] Only Bishop Spalding and Monsignor Denis O'Connell among the great Catholic liberals exhibited rationalizing tendencies. A member of an old colonial family of unbroken Catholic traditions, Spalding was "by far the most scholarly and cultured man in the hierarchy; but his clear, cold intellectuality is unrelieved," Snell thought, "by any of the practical energy, the warm enthusiasm or the fervid ideality which characterizes in different degrees Archbishop Ireland and Bishop Keane." The cool, levelheaded, sagacious, and observing O'Connell was "one of the most active and liberal of thinkers," always asking questions on the issues of the day, "especially those connected with scientific and scriptural problems — evolution and the destructive criticism." But the other leaders were "Protestantizing" liberals in the sense that they shared the moral outlook of conservative orthodox Protestantism, "which is really of all religious schools," Snell believed, "the least congenial with true traditional Catholicism." Like all his party, "Bishop Keane," Snell reported, "is very much in touch with Evangelical Protestantism. His principal point of contact with it is on the spiritual side, while Archbishop Ireland's Protestant sympathies are altogether in the field of ethics, and Cardinal Gibbons combines to a certain extent the two." [20]

Brief, blunt, and written for the information of puzzled Protestants, Snell's comments illumined some aspects of the American Catholic social movement. The full scope of the movement as well as its basic motivations were displayed by the two Catholic Congresses, the first one at Baltimore in 1889 during the celebration of the hierarchy's centennial and the second at Chicago in 1893 as part of the Columbian Exposition.[21] In years past some Catholics,

[19] "The Ethical Kinship between Protestant Radicalism and Catholic Conservatism," *Christian Register* (Unitarian), July 27, 1893. See also press quotations in Arthur Preuss, editor, *Review*, especially IV (February 10, 1898), 3, and V (December 8, 1893), 1–2.

[20] "Pen-Pictures of the American Hierarchy," *Independent*, April 27, 1893.

[21] William H. Hughes, publisher, *Souvenir Volume Illustrated. Three Great Events in the History of the Catholic Church in the United States* (Detroit, 1889), pp. 1–84; J. S. Hyland and Co., compilers, *Progress of the Catholic Church in America and the Great Columbian Catholic Congress of 1893*, (4th ed.; Chicago, 1897), II; Patrick J. Ryan, "The Columbian Catholic Congress," in J. W. Hansen, editor, *The World's Congress of Religions* (Chicago, 1894), pp. 984–1024; The William J. Onahan Papers, University of Notre Dame Archives.

notably Father Hecker, had urged their co-religionists to assemble at regular intervals to discuss religious and social problems on the model of the great Belgian and German Catholic Congresses whose proceedings attracted world-wide attention.[22] Apart from the labor and expense of convening a truly representative congress, the fear of augmenting anti-Catholic feeling caused Catholics of influence and discernment to hold back. They knew that, as viewed by Protestants, the Old World congresses were convened merely to secure the restoration of the Pope's temporal power. "It would be a difficult task," thought John Gilmary Shea, "to undertake the work of dispelling the idea" than an American congress "was not convened for the same purpose and designed to inveigle the United States Government into a stand on a question which would lead us into undesirable international complications." [23]

Apprehension on this point lessened as in the late 1880s industrial, social, and racial tensions took on menacing proportions. "If the Catholic Church in the United States is a great and growing moral power . . . why should not we American Catholics meet together annually," asked the Reverend Bernard O'Reilly, Cardinal Gibbons' confidante, "in order to perfect every institution pertaining to education, to charity, to solving the great social problems of labor and capital, and even to impel mightily forward, on the lines of Christian philosophy, all the intellectual forces of the modern world?" [24] The *Church News*, published in Washington, D.C., believed that a congress would magnify the two forces holding the Know-Nothing spirit in check, namely, the conservatism of the majority of Americans regardless of creed, and the numerical strength and the intellectual acquirements of Catholics.[25] In noting these and other reasons for holding a congress, Shea ridiculed them as "silly reasons, every one of them." He assumed that the existing Catholic societies sufficed "for the interchange of Catholic thought and experience." [26] Other Catholics, countering that the societies served special, often racial, interests, wished for a general organization. "I look to the day," declared the distinguished president of the

22 "Shall We Have a Catholic Congress?" *Catholic World*, VIII (November 1868), 224–28.
23 "A Congress of Catholic Americans," *Catholic News*, May 26, 1889.
24 Quoted in ibid.
25 "The Catholic Congress," September 8, 1889.
26 "The American Catholic Congress," *Catholic News*, November 11, 1888.

Central Verein, Henry J. Spaunhorst of St. Louis, "when we shall have one grand national convention of Catholics all over this country regardless of nationality. In spite of language we are Americans," he stressed, "and must follow the guide of this country, and I never found a good Catholic," he told his Columbus, Ohio, centennial audience, "but who held that view." [27]

As a German-American, Spaunhorst believed that within their limitations Catholic national organizations accomplished much good. This was his attitude toward Katholiken Tag, a German-American congress of Catholic layman under the leadership of the German-American Society of Priests and meeting annually after 1887 (until 1898) alongside conventions of the Central Verein. Americanist extremists feared, however, that these congresses were more interested in preserving German language and customs than in discussing the social questions, the solution of which was admittedly their ultimate objective.[28] The Americanists demanded a nationally inclusive congress. "Why confine the convention to Germans?" asked the *Catholic American* of New York. "Why not make it a Catholic congress in every respect?" [29] To no avail Bishop Gilmour of Cleveland and others urged the Germans to transform their organization into a genuine American Catholic lay congress.[30] The *Catholic Review* of New York thought an American congress necessary to rid Catholics of "old and worn-out methods." We have communities, argued the editor, which are "usually dominated by methods — not by ideas, for all our ideas are American — but by methods which were born in Bavaria, Quebec and Connaught, not on this soil." [31]

While interested Catholics discussed the congress idea, one of their number, Henry F. Brownson of Detroit, the late philosopher's son and apparently the first to suggest that lay Catholics convene at Baltimore during the centennial celebration in November 1889, was successfully engaged in securing episcopal approval. "If the pro-

---

[27] "The Church and the State. What Catholics Have Done for the United States," ibid., September 19, 1888.

[28] Barry, op. cit., 104–27, 169–72, 210–15; "German Roman Catholics," *Christian Union*, October 3, 1891; "Priester Verein," *Northwestern Chronicle*, September 25, 1891; ibid., September 20, 1895.

[29] "Collection of Newspaper Clippings Relating to German Catholics in the United States, 1888," New York Public Library.

[30] Archbishop Ireland to Cardinal Gibbons, July 16, 1889, Baltimore Cathedral Archives, 86–E–9; Barry, op. cit., pp. 113–14.

[31] "The Catholic Congress of the United States," June 9, 1889.

41523

moters," chiefly Brownson, Onahan, and Spaunhorst, "are very prudent," Archbishop Ireland informed Cardinal Gibbons in the early spring, "and work in preparing the programme with yourself or a committee of bishops approved by you, and knowing your mind, I am inclined to think that good would come from the project." [32] Gibbons acted on these suggestions, appointing a committee of bishops, with Ireland as chairman, to advise and, if need be, to control the laymen lest they overstress Catholic grievances or air them in a belligerent or unseemly manner. Against his will, it may be pointed out, Brownson, chairman of the committee on papers, was obliged to submit the essays, written mainly by lawyers and editors, to the advisory committee of bishops. [33] The committee apparently found little to disapprove in the manuscripts which, despite their hurried composition, presented well-digested information on nearly every topic of current social interest.

How to deal wisely with the loss of the temporal power caused, not unexpectedly, the greatest anxiety. Already the hierarchy had informed Leo XIII, to his great chagrin no doubt, that Rome need not expect American Catholics to demonstrate for the restoration of papal sovereignty. [34] At the cardinal's suggestion, the editor of the Baltimore *Mirror* stated in the issue just previous to the opening of the congress that the transfer of the Papal States to the Kingdom of Italy "though achieved by fraud and robbery cannot be regarded as a deprivation affecting the spiritual interests of the Catholic world." But the nations must guarantee the Pope perfect freedom to exercise his spiritual functions in the Eternal City, the proper seat of his power. [35] In his paper on "The Independence of the Holy See," Charles J. Bonaparte, Gibbons' personal selection, expressed similar

[32] Archbishop Ireland to Cardinal Gibbons, April 20, 1889, Baltimore Cathedral Archives, 85–W–13.

[33] John Hyde, editor of *Michigan Catholic*, to William J. Onahan, October 20, 1889, "Catholic Congress, 1889," Onahan Papers, University of Notre Dame Archives; M. Sevina Pahorezki, O.S.F., *The Social and Political Activities of William James Onahan* (Washington, D.C., 1942), pp. 112–14.

[34] Archbishop Ireland to Cardinal Gibbons, October 27, 1888, Baltimore Cathedral Archives, 85–G–9; ibid., November 23, 1888, 85–I–6; January 11, 1889, 85–O–5; July 20, 1889, 86–F–10; July 24, 1889, 86–F–1; August 9, 1889, 86–G–10; George Zurcher, *The Apple of Discord* (Buffalo, 1905), p. 491.

[35] Quoted in "The Centennial of American Catholicism," *Independent*, November 14, 1889; in the same vein, Father James Nilan, "The Temporal Power of the Pope," ibid., November 13, 1890.

views. While properly indignant at the treatment meted out to the papacy, he bespoke only sympathy for the Pope pending agreement by the Christian world on measures to assure his full independence.[36] In its resolutions the congress recorded its "solemn conviction that the absolute freedom of the Holy See is equally indispensable to the peace of the Church and the welfare of mankind," and pledged to Leo XIII "the loyal sympathy and unstinted aid of his spiritual children in vindicating that perfect liberty which he justly claims as his sacred and inalienable right." [37]

To APAists this pronouncement was "ultramontane and un-American," [38] and to the more conservative Catholics it seemed needlessly evasive if not indifferent to Catholic interests.[39] But to moderates in all camps the "position taken was the logical one," in keeping with the primary purpose of the congress to demonstrate that Americanism and Catholicism were sides of the same shield.[40] The *Independent* was not sure "which was put first, the country or the Church." There was in the participants "something of the assertive, as if they knew that their patriotism had been called in question by a noisy clique in Boston and by a foolish 'American' party elsewhere," the journal observed, "and they would not let it be possible for any but a knave to assert that their submission in religious doctrine to Rome could interfere with their patriotism." [41] As if to reinforce this attitude, the congress was as conciliatory on the school question as on that of the Pope's temporal power. It is true that in his paper on education ex-Judge Edmund F. Dunne denied, as he had been doing

[36] "The Independence of the Holy See," in William H. Hughes, op. cit., pp. 30–32.

[37] Ibid., p. 63.

[38] James Harris, "The Baltimore Congress's Catholicism," *American*, XIX (1889), 149.

[39] Bp. F. A. Chatard to William J. Onahan, March 10, 1890, "Catholic Congress, 1889," loc. cit. Editor Hyde pronounced the statement of the Baltimore Congress concerning the Holy See "the feeblest and most minimized sentiment that has ever come from a body calling itself a Catholic Congress." John Hyde to William J. Onahan, November 15, 1889, loc. cit.

[40] "Stepping Forward," Detroit Evening News, November 13, 1889, in "Onahan Clippings, 1893," Onahan Papers, University of Notre Dame Archives.

[41] "Only Knaves Can Doubt It," New York *Independent*, "Onahan Clippings, 1893," loc. cit.

for years, the right of the state to educate and urged it to distribute its school fund among the various denominations.[42] In its resolutions, however, the congress stated that as, "in the state schools, no provision is made for teaching religion, we must continue to support our own schools . . . so that the benefits of a Christian education may be brought within the reach of every Catholic child in these United States." [43] If these resolutions "mean anything at all, editorialized the Detroit *Evening News*, "they mean that the school question is dead." [44]

The Archbishop of Philadelphia, Patrick J. Ryan, saw in the lay congress refutation of the charge that Catholics are "priest-ridden." [45] But the prevailing attitude was the more positive one that laity and clergy, working together irrespective of national origins and cooperating with friendly non-Catholic reformers, could do wonders for both Church and community. To this end the laity resolved "to co-operate with the clergy in discussing and in solving those great economic and social questions which affect the interests and well-being of the Church, the country, and society at large." They also favored Catholics "taking greater part than they have hitherto taken in general philanthropic and reformatory movements." They noted that the obligation "to help the needy and to instruct the ignorant, is not limited to the needy and ignorant of our own communion" — we are concerned "both as Catholics and as Americans, in the reformation of all the criminals and the support of all the poor in the country. By mingling more in such works of natural virtue, as our non-Catholic citizens are engaged in . . . we might exert a Catholic influence outside of our own body," the congress explained, "make ourselves better known, and infuse into these good works something of supernatural charity. . . ." [46] The laymen also noted that participation would enable the clergy to minister spiritually to Catholic inmates of prisons and hospitals.

Turning from private to public philanthropy, the congress be-

---

[42] "The Rights and Duties of the State, the Church, and the Parent in that Regard," William H. Hughes, publisher, loc. cit., pp. 43–46.
[43] Ibid., p. 63.
[44] "Stepping Forward," November 13, 1889, loc. cit.
[45] "Sermon," Hughes, op. cit., p. 10.
[46] "Resolutions," Hughes, op. cit., pp. 62–63.

lieved that on "many Christian issues Catholics could come together with non-Catholics, and shape civil legislation for the public weal." [47] Of special importance in this area were Sunday observance and the liquor traffic to which the congress in its formal papers devoted careful attention. In his paper denouncing Sunday opening of saloons, beer gardens and theaters, the journalist Manly Tello of Cleveland explained that "there is a distinctive American way, and a people has a right to its own individuality." If within Catholic lines "there are two ways to do a thing, and one is exclusively American, for that very reason," he contended, "that way should be universally adopted." [48] In keeping with this theory of neo-puritanism, the congress resolved to "seek alliance with non-Catholics for proper Sunday observance. Without going over to the Judaic Sabbath, we can," the congress affirmed, "bring the masses over to the moderation of the Christian Sunday." To this end, the sale of intoxicating liquors on Sunday in saloons or elsewhere should be prohibited by law. At no time should the sale of liquor to minors and intoxicated persons be permitted. The corrupting influences of saloons on politics and the crime and pauperism resulting from excessive drinking justified further legislative restriction (excluding prohibition apparently) "which we can aid in procuring," the congress emphasized, "by joining our influence with that of the other enemies of intemperance." [49]

These statements drew much favorable comment from sources friendly to reform. "When the Roman Catholic Church," wrote the Albany *Evening Journal*, "declares for temperance, Sunday observance and good government, it would be well for reckless politicians to stop and consider." [50] Another paper, the St. Louis *Globe Democrat*, insisted that all religious elements in the country must recognize the new situation, which called for better application of Christianity to the duties and responsibilities of citizenship. "The Baltimore Congress has spoken for the Catholics in plain and sensible terms, and there is ample cause to believe that its promises will be kept. Let the Protestants," the editor counseled, "see to it

---

[47] Ibid., p. 63.
[48] "Sunday Observance," Hughes, op. cit., pp. 69–70.
[49] Ibid., p. 63.
[50] "Onahan Clippings, 1893," loc. cit.

that they are not outdone in graces and wisdom." [51] "The Protestant element," the Chicago *Herald* believed, "should eagerly accept this offer of opposition to Sunday liquor selling in exchange for a mild modification of the Puritan Sabbath." [52] The Baltimore Congress "evaded nothing, quibbled at nothing, but spoke out in a voice dominant and daring," the Reverend D. C. Potter informed fellow members of the New York Baptist pastors' conference. "The Protestant Church could stand on its platform," he said, "with hardly a phrase changed." [53]

Some Catholics took special satisfaction in the reformatory pronouncements of the congress. Bishop R. Phelan of Pittsburgh and Alleghany was "particularly pleased" with the spirit manifested on the part of all assembled "to co-operate with people of all denominations in the furtherance of what was called philanthropic work and reformatory movements." [54] The famed Brooklyn priest, Sylvester Malone, was delighted in his old age "to find at last the policy of progress and true Catholicity" which he had so long advocated, "in fact was the first to enunciate," had been "so fully and fairly resolved upon at Baltimore." If in the past Catholics had been misunderstood, "it had been our own fault altogether, or nearly so. We have kept aloof and apart too much," he explained, "from the questions which, as American citizens, we should have met frankly and freely." America was "a great nation, and we should make it known to our Protestant fellow-citizens that on subjects affecting the welfare of the State Catholics and Protestants can stand side by side." [55] No doubt by 1890 many priests shared Malone's views, though few stated them so vaingloriously and bluntly.

Some observers, both Catholic and Protestant, were most impressed by the pronouncements of the congress on the economic aspects of the social question. In the view of the congress the Republic was menaced and society imperiled by "the constant conflict between capital and labor." The congress equally condemned nihilism, socialism, and communism on the one hand, and "the heartless

[51] Ibid.
[52] Ibid.
[53] Ibid.
[54] Ibid.
[55] Sylvester L. Malone, editor, *Memorial of the Golden Jubilee of the Reverend Sylvester Malone* (Brooklyn, 1895), pp. 64–65.

greed of capital" on the other. The remedy must be sought "in the mediation of the Church, through her action on the individual conscience, and thereby on society, teaching each its respective duties, as well as rights, and in such civil enactments as have been rendered necessary by these altered conditions." [56] With Cardinal Gibbons the congress affirmed that paramount among the "sacred rights" of the laboring classes was "their privilege to organize or to form themselves into societies for their mutual protection and benefit." [57] If in its resolutions the congress did not specify the "civil enactments" it deemed "necessary," the formal papers offered many thoughtful suggestions. In his essay entitled "Labor and Capital," William Richards, a lawyer of Washington, D.C., savagely attacked the gospel of wealth. More justifiably workers associated in order to "ward off the evils of a ruinous competition of man against man" than the wealthy owners of great corporations pooled "their issues with impunity, taxing a helpless public *ad libitum*" in order to swell their ill-gotten gains. Richards was aware, however, that trade unions and similar organizations benefited only their members, not all the people. They were "simply voluntary associations, partial and limited, not state organizations embracing all parts of human society." More to his liking was the social insurance system of Bismarckian Germany. He was also cheered by various experiments elsewhere in the direction of state socialism, among which was public control of tenant rights to land in Great Britain and Ireland.[58] Here Richards referred to, but did not name, the Irish Land Act of 1881 which exerted, as has been seen, a marked influence on the social thinking of American Catholics.

Besides approving the sentiments in Richards' paper, the advisory committee of bishops suggested to Peter L. Foy of St. Louis that he expand his original topic on "Charities" into a discussion of "philanthropic movements generally." He obliged in a lengthy paper on "The New Social Order," whose subtle and perspicacious insight into social movements was exceeded only by its brilliant diction and profuse literary allusion.[59] To the lack of balance between

[56] Hughes, op. cit., 62–63.

[57] Quoted from James Cardinal Gibbons, "The Dignity, Rights and Responsibilities of Labor," *Cosmopolitan*, VIII (August 1889), 384.

[58] Hughes, op. cit., pp. 71–74.

[59] Ibid., pp. 36–43.

the two Titans — irrepressible democracy and organized industry — he attributed the evils as well as the gains of the new age. Machine industry, he observed, concentrated in cities both boundless wealth and the children of toil. Since thirty thousand persons owned half the nation's property, wealth obviously gained the advantage in power and influence. "Wealth and population increase," he wrote, "but wealth more than population, and distress more than wealth." The centralizing tendency was enhanced, he emphasized, "by the lucrative privileges which wealth never fails to win from the government. If centralization was unquestionably a law of the industrial as well as the political movement," as he admitted, "the accelerated speed of the centripetal tendency in recent times is attributable not to natural, but civil law." Cities as the foci of new ideas and intelligent plans for their embodiment possessed "subtle powers unknown to the rural population which are periodically called into play in the policy of the state for the benefit of private or corporate interests."

Alive to the abuses of wealth, yet Foy pronounced no "anathema on riches," which, in his view, was but another name for capital, "an indispensable factor of production and the well-spring of wages." Capitalists held "the keys of the workingman's paradise — permanent, remunerative, invigorating employment" — even if, at the best of times, "the gates are held ajar and but comparatively few of the workingmen are admitted." [60] He denied that, since the rich were growing richer, the poor were becoming poorer. In truth, their standard of living was steadily improving, but not speedily enough to invalidate their accusation that capitalists take or get more than their due proportion of the fruits of productive effort, and in addition absorb the whole unearned increment, whether coming from land or from other monopolies. The poverty of proletarians stemmed not from personal defects but from social injustice; their "occasional lapses from sobriety and thrift, and the dissipated habits of some, are in no small degree caused by their wretched, sordid environment. . . . To restore a just and fair balance between the two classes," Foy thought, "is the chief problem in political science in this our day and generation."

The aid of the state was required — if not in behalf of skilled workers, whose fairly good wages and strong trade unions enabled

[60] Ibid., pp. 36–38.

them to take care of themselves, then in behalf of the great horde of unskilled and "sweated" labor whose economic position on account of irregular employment and low wages became increasingly precarious. True "objects of charity," these segments of the working class deserved of the state vastly enlarged relief administered in a kindly and liberal spirit. Workers and their families were also entitled to ample protection by way of compensation against the hazards of industry, among which should be numbered not only accidents but also, as in Germany, ill-health and old age. Foy objected, however, to that feature in the German system whereby the state contributed equally with employers and employees to the insurance fund. He would place the direct burden on employers only, allowing the workers to withdraw the amount of their contributions at stated intervals and confining the government's participation to supervision and enforcement.[61]

Besides insurance and state charities, public policy required, Foy failed not to stress, "a more equitable distribution of the joint productions of land, labor and capital." He understood, of course, the difficulty of devising workable plans of economic reorganization. If we are as yet "incompetent to provide for a fair division of the fruits of industry between the different factors of production, we are at least able to provide," he believed, "provisional or empirical relief for the evils of the existing state of affairs. . . ." He suggested an extension of education along physical, technical, and artistic lines for all age groups, and public hygiene, including sanitary tenements and factories. The rich, whose fortunes had been accumulated with the connivance of politicians, should now be forced through taxation to share their surplus with the poor, and in this way submit to a measure of justice. He did not insist that they restore to the state their ill-gotten gains, but that they contribute more liberally "to the victims of their rapacity." [62]

Becoming more specific, Foy suggested that a small tax on personal and corporate incomes in excess of ten thousand dollars would sufficiently compensate for damages "inflicted on individuals and society by the industrial system, and indirectly by the law." Recalling the blow that laid low the slaveholders, he warned monopo-

---

lists, cattle kings, and the lords of the "unearned increment" on the surface or in the bowels of the earth not to resist the rising demand for an income tax — a demand which would become, he rightly predicted, loud and irresistible. By the same token, organized labor must not through power intoxication plunge the country into revolution and anarchy. Provided their demands were reasonable, workers could confidently count on the public to approve them, whether sought directly by the unions "or indirectly through the medium of the state." While he evidently preferred the latter method, he did not think that strikes and lockouts, which often accompanied the trade union medium, were either illegal or immoral, so long as employers refrained from black-listing union workers and these, in turn, did not destroy capital — the wage fund — or terrorize non-union employees.[63]

In discussing the philanthropic aspects of the labor and other movements, Foy repeatedly alluded to the interplay between private and public action. Though the ministrations of the Church "shall continue whether the state act or not," he noted, "yet it is only when the state has done its part, that voluntary charity can hope to be mistress of the work she has to do — a work that will end only with the consummation of all things. . . ." [64] Since public charity seemed more important, private charity was not seriously studied by Foy or the other speakers at the Baltimore Congress, excepting possibly Spaunhorst, who discussed benevolent societies with special reference to the Central Verein.[65] This limitation was overcome at the Columbian Catholic Congress of 1893, which devoted three of its five days to the social question as illumined by *Rerum novarum*, Leo XIII's great labor encyclical. Not alone the principles of Christian justice and charity but also the techniques for their application were canvassed in papers and discussion meetings which covered a wide range of subjects: the labor encyclical; the rights of labor and the duties of capital; pauperism and the remedy; public and private charities — how to make them more effective and beneficial; workingmen's societies and societies for young men; life insurance and pension funds for wage workers;

[63] Ibid.
[64] Ibid., p. 40.
[65] "Societies," Hughes, op. cit., pp. 58–60.

trade combinations and strikes; immigration and colonization; intemperance; the condition and future of the Indian and Negro races in the United States; and finally the work of women in religion and in the world.[66]

If in the World Fair scheme the Columbian Catholic Congress was a part of the World's Congress Auxiliary, this Catholic gathering was actually the first to be planned and may well have inspired the idea of auxiliary action to make the Fair an exposition of moral and intellectual as well as of material progress. The Baltimore Congress had instructed its committee on future congresses to convene an international Catholic congress during the approaching Columbian Exposition. Aware that Catholics drawn from all over the world would display community of interests only in faith and morals, the committee early decided to confine the congress to American issues. Moreover, an international assembly would most likely highlight the Pope's temporal power, which the projectors of the congress, especially the prelates, wished to keep supplementary to social themes. An indeterminate number of Catholics insisted, however, that the school question and papal sovereignty were "the burning Catholic questions of the day." [67] Conspicuous among the champions of this viewpoint were former Judge Dunne, a member of the committee for the coming congress, and Condé B. Pallen, editor of the St. Louis *Church Progress*. At the committee's meeting in December 1891, Dunne with the backing of a majority of its lay members presented the conservative plan for the Chicago meeting. The proposal was rejected on the urgent advice of Archbishop Ireland and other prelates, only Bishop Spalding feebly upholding Dunne's protest against clerical dictation.[68]

In a letter to Pallen, Dunne gave vent to his anger at Archbishop Ireland. The letter in some unexplained way fell into the hands

[66] Ryan, "The Columbian Catholic Congress," loc. cit., pp. 990–91; "The Catholic Congress," *Christian Union*, January 21, 1893; "Topics of the Hour," *Catholic Review*, July 22, 1893; "On to Chicago," *Northwestern Chronicle*, August 25, 1893; Jane Avery, "Chicago to the Front," *Pilot*, February 25, 1893.

[67] "A Word to an Inexperienced Brother," *Church Progress*, January 16, 1892.

[68] William Lewis Kelly (a Minnesota judge) to William J. Onahan, September 26, 1891, Onahan Papers, loc. cit.; William J. Onahan to W. W. O'Brien, Detroit, February 23, 1892, ibid.

of the Reverend C. Kuhlman, who put it into print, sent copies
to all the cardinals, and urged Rome to raise the education and
temporal power questions from the supplementary to the top position on the program of the forthcoming congress.[69] Ireland successfully belittled this commotion as a tempest in a teapot stirred up
by stubborn soreheads in league with St. Louis Cahenslyites.
Nevertheless Pallen kept up a steady editorial fire on the committee's
evident determination "to minimize," as he contended, "the Catholicity of the Congress" by converting it into a "mere social congress" or a "simple labor convention." [70] In comment on the remark
of the *Catholic Review* that the social program of the congress if
followed up would put the Catholic Church "where she ought to
be — in the van of progress and reform," Pallen wrote that the
Church was already in that position, securing progress and reform
by bringing "truth" to the individual and "by supplying him with
the necessary sacramental strength to walk the narrow path of justice and virtue." [71] When at the conclusion of its work this Columbian Catholic Congress reaffirmed in slightly different phraseology
the attitudes of the Baltimore Congress on the school question and
the temporal power, Pallen continued to voice complaint.[72] The
resolution that the Pope must be independent and autonomous in
the exercise of his spiritual functions "said nothing," he felt, "that
anybody could not have said." Even the Italian government by its
law of guarantees promised as much. "The question to resolute
about," he maintained, "is our conviction, as Catholics, of the necessity of the Temporal Power of the Holy Father." [73]

Pallen was also contemptuous of the fervent professions of
patriotism at the congress, in keeping with its central belief "that
the national welfare and the highest material prosperity are com-

[69] "Republics and Leo," Chicago *Tribune*, February 17, 1892; Kehoe-Hammond
Correspondence, Miscellaneous, Box 3, University of Notre Dame Archives;
Pilot, February 27, 1892; "Editorial Notes," *Independent*, March 10, 1892.
[70] "The Two Leading Issues," November 14, 1891; "What Is the Matter?"
ibid., February 6, 1892; "The Catholic Congress," ibid., October 1, 1892; "The
Program of the Catholic Congress," ibid., December 3, 1892.
[71] "The Catholic Church Progressive," ibid., January 9, 1892.
[72] J. S. Hyland and Co., compilers, op. cit., p. 198.
[73] "Independent and Autonomous," *Church Progress*, September 16, 1893.
See "The Drift of the Catholic Congress," *Independent*, September 21, 1893.

patible with the widest propagation of the Catholic Religion and the fullest freedom of its adherents." [74] Toward the end of his address Monsignor Satolli urged the delegates to "Go forward! in one hand bearing the Book of Christian truth and in the other the Constitution of the United States." [75] It would be better, Pallen thought, for Catholics to march forward with the Bible in both hands! [76] Moreover, the "unseemly exaltation and untimely rant" about American institutions were as un-American as they were unnecessary. "You never find them coming from men born on the soil with native generations back of them," he observed. "Such men never imagine the need of protesting their loyalty or their patriotism." [77]

Friends of the congress countered that, however correct undemonstrative patriotism might seem to old-line Americans like Pallen and Spalding, it played into the hands of the Cahenslyites. That these purveyors of "foreignism" created difficulties for the congress is unmistakable. "I had no idea the national feeling among some of the German clergy was so intense," Spaunhorst informed William J. Onahan after a trip through Wisconsin and Minnesota in the wake of the Lucerne Memorial.[78] In order the better to secure a representative and harmonious congress, Spaunhorst suggested that competent speakers be allotted time on the program to present the viewpoints and contributions of the various national groups.[79] Onahan, as the active organizer of the congress, accepted and carried out this recommendation.[80] Also in the interests of harmony the German-American Society of Priests reluctantly yielded to pressure from Spaunhorst and other German-American social liberals and called

[74] William J. Onahan, "Columbian Catholic Congress at Chicago," *Catholic World*, LVII (August 1893), 607–8.

[75] J. S. Hyland and Co., compilers, op. cit., p. 46.

[76] "Don't Smother Patriotism," *Northwestern Chronicle*, September 22, 1893.

[77] "Buncombe," *Church Progress*, September 16, 1893.

[78] H. J. Spaunhorst to William J. Onahan, June 2, 1891, Onahan Papers, loc. cit.

[79] Ibid., October 1, 1891.

[80] J. W. Rozan to William J. Onahan, August 14, 1893, ibid.; Rozan to Onahan, August 17, 1893, ibid.; August Kaiser, "Immigration and Colonization," J. S. Hyland and Co., compilers, op. cit., pp. 138–40; Michael Callaghan, "Immigration and Colonization," ibid., pp. 140–44; Joseph L. Andreis, "Italian Immigration and Colonization," ibid., pp. 176–79.

off its Catholic Day (Katholiken Tag) for 1893.[81] While many German-American Catholics warmly approved the resolutions of the Chicago Congress, the Central Verein at its annual convention in late 1893 refused to endorse them. The epithet "Freemasonry Resolutions," hurled by one opponent during the heated debate, seemingly epitomized the convention's sentiment.[82]

Involved on the liberal side of the ecclesiastical controversy, the congress project repeatedly neared the brink of failure. That it was finally brought to a successful and fruitful conclusion was owing largely to the efforts of one man, its organizer, William J. Onahan, whose untiring patience, fairness, and negotiating skill inspired the greatest confidence.[83] In a real sense the mouthpiece of the bishops, he frowned upon revolts against clerical supervision. Otherwise, he encouraged liberty of discussion, which secured for the congress highly competent speakers with fresh and often divergent opinions on the many topics of a wide and varied program. He did not object when the Chicago lawyer, Edward Osgood Brown, a champion of Father McGlynn, insisted on presenting the single-tax aspects of the labor question.[84] He permitted, in fact encouraged, Mary Theresa Elder, the Cincinnati archbishop's saucy niece, to present her infuriating essay which in estimating Catholic losses at twenty millions out-Cahensly-ed Cahensly! She attributed this alleged loss, along with the paucity of great Catholic leaders in American history, to the Church's failure to missionize the rural regions.[85] This theory — based as she claimed on a decade's study — was to become sober doctrine in the next century, especially after World War I; at the time it was viewed in the light of a sensational diversion.

[81] H. J. Spaunhorst to William J. Onahan, March 15, 1893, Onahan Papers, loc. cit.

[82] Anonymous letter of a German-born Catholic journalist, Logansport, Indiana, to Cardinal Gibbons, December 25, 1893, Denis O'Connell Correspondence, loc. cit., Box 9.

[83] Pahorezki, op. cit., pp. 137–68.

[84] Edward Osgood Brown to William J. Onahan, Easter Sunday, 1893, Onahan Papers, loc. cit.; Brown, "Labor and Capital," J. S. Hyland and Co., op. cit., pp. 46–52.

[85] M. T. Elder to William J. Onahan, June 6, 1893, Onahan Papers, loc. cit.; ibid., July 13, 1893; ibid., July 17, 1893; Elder, "Pauperism: The Cause and the Remedy," J. S. Hyland and Co., op. cit., pp. 179–83; "A Secular Showing of the Fallacies of M. T. Elder's Paper," *Pilot*, September 23, 1893; "The Question of Catholic Losses," ibid., September 30, 1893.

To most men and women of 1893 only social problems in an urban setting seemed worthy of serious attention. As against Miss Elder, who could see no relief in urban charity for the horrors of pauperism and crime, three experts on these subjects, Richard R. Elliott of Detroit,[86] and the Bostonians Thomas Dwight and Thomas F. Ring, insisted that solutions awaited only a vast expansion in the preventive and remedial agencies of Catholic charity. From the great humanitarian Catholic awakening they envisaged would come an army of competent lay workers for the charitable associations, especially the St. Vincent de Paul Society which, as Dwight said, "is the one that alone should do a large share of the work." [87] Ring informed the congress that in Boston the St. Vincent de Paul Society and non-Catholic charities had aided each other to mutual advantage. "Our danger does not lie so much in the antagonism of our Protestant neighbors as in the apathy of our Catholic selves," he believed. The key word in social service was "co-operation," he emphasized — co-operation "frankly and cordially with all our fellow-citizens for the common good of the community." [88]

In similar vein Bishop John A. Watterson of Columbus, Ohio, entertained the hope that all religious groups would unite behind the Pope's labor encyclical.[89] Several speakers studied the labor question in the spirit of Leo's "luminous exposition of the subject." With the Pope they accepted the wage system, insisting, however, that the remuneration be sufficiently large to support the worker and his family "in reasonable and frugal comfort." Besides an equitable contract between employers and employees, the speakers favored group insurance in order to lessen for workers the hazards of accident, invalidism, and old age. They believed that both insurance and the fair labor bargain would be won mainly through voluntary associations, aided if need be, however, by public authority. In papers of substantial factual content, J. P. Lauth of Chicago and E. M. Sharon of Davenport, Iowa, sketched in the labor aspects of the insurance picture. Both men were impressed by the

[86] "Public and Private Charities," J. S. Hyland and Co., op. cit., pp. 127–30.
[87] "Pauperism: The Cause and the Remedy," ibid., pp. 130–34.
[88] "Public and Private Charities; How Can They Be Made More Effective and Beneficial — A Catholic Layman's Experience," ibid., pp. 196–98.
[89] Ibid., pp. 42–44.

quantities of insurance available to workingmen in trade unions and fraternal organizations. Although the coverage was still small, not more than one twentieth of total workers, Lauth preferred the voluntary method "to the German policy of pensioning workmen." [90] Sharon, on the other hand, favored the compulsory principle. Since the state readily intervened to protect "the natural rights of individuals and the well-being of the society of which they form a part," it might, he thought, "exercise its paternal care for the benefit of wageworkers also, without transcending its legitimate and proper powers." Beginning with injured railway employees, the state should eventually insure all workers to the extent of half wages against sickness, invalidism, and old age.[91]

In behalf of a fair labor bargain the compulsory principle was even more strongly invoked. Of the four speakers on this phase of the program at Chicago, three were lawyers who entered strong pleas for state intervention. With "Pope Leo XIII on the Condition of Labor" as his subject, H. C. Semple, an Alabama judge, insisted that "the State should foresee and endeavor to remove all grievances which paralyze labor by strikes, often the result of injustice and the fruitful cause of strife and violence." If not paid wages sufficient for his support "appeal to the State for approval and protection." [92] The other lawyers, Robert M. Douglas [93] of Greensboro, North Carolina, a son of the "Little Giant," and John Gibbons [94] of Chicago, soon to become a judge of the city's circuit court, reached similar conclusions by way of legalistic analysis. Properly applied or extended, common law principles, they explained, would suffice to destroy the oppressive power of employing corporations. While the state could not "compel anyone to employ or work for a fixed price," it should use its "visitorial power," wrote Douglas,

---

[90] "Guilds and Fraternal Benefit Societies. Their Insurance Features Preferable to Pension Funds," ibid., pp. 168–72.

[91] "Life Insurance and Pension Funds for Wage Workers," ibid., pp. 172–76.

[92] Ibid., p. 137.

[93] "Trade Combinations and Strikes," ibid., pp. 150–53.

[94] "The Rights of Labor; the Duties of Capital," ibid., pp. 52–55; Onahan Papers, loc. cit.; cf. John Gibbons, "How Far Can Arbitration Be Made Compulsory Without Infringing on Private Rights?" in Industrial Committee of the Civic Federation, Chicago, *Congress on Industrial Conciliation and Arbitration* (Chicago, 1894), pp. 68–77.

to investigate and publicize through a bureau of corporations or some similar agency the causes of industrial conflict, the inquiry to examine not simply overt acts but wages, profits, and all other relevant factors.[95] Adept, like Douglas, at deriving industrial maxims from the common law, Gibbons reasoned that the standards adhered to voluntarily by humane employers should be "enforced as a legal duty in respect to those who regard their workmen as merchantable commodities." [96]

The fourth speaker, Frank J. Sheridan, an employee of the Department of Labor, opposed compulsory arbitration on the grounds that it would enslave the worker and establish state socialism "at the point of the bayonet." [97] Extolling voluntary arbitration, he urged his fellow delegates to establish a Catholic Association of the United States for the Promotion of Industrial Conciliation and Voluntary Arbitration. The Committee on Resolutions responding favorably, the congress constituted Cardinal Gibbons, Onahan, and Morgan J. O'Brien of New York a committee to organize the association on a national basis.[98] In strongly endorsing "the principles of conciliation and arbitration as an appropriate remedy for the settlement of disagreements between employer and employed," the congress did not restrict its approval to voluntary arbitration only.[99] Nor did it mention, either to approve or to condemn, compulsory arbitration or any other form of state intervention in industry. But in laying down moral standards legislation must meet in order to merit approval, the congress by implication sanctioned the interventionist program. Suggested remedies, varying "from the extreme of anarchical revolution to different types of state socialism," must fail, the Committee on Resolutions reported, "wherever they clash with the principles of truth and justice." In the light of Pope Leo XIII's teachings, the committee declared that "no remedies can meet with our approval save those which recognize the right of private owner-

[95] "Robert M. Douglas . . . at Catholic Congress," *Pilot*, October 7, 1893.
[96] "The Rights of Labor; the Duties of Capital," loc. cit.
[97] "Trade Combinations and Strikes," ibid., pp. 162–64.
[98] Ryan, "The Columbian Catholic Congress," loc. cit., p. 1023. This committee was also authorized to arrange for a third Catholic congress which was destined never to convene. Presumably the proposed arbitration association also failed to materialize.
[99] Hyland, op. cit, p. 199.

ship of property and human liberty." [100] The context of these statements clearly indicates that they were intended to moderate, but
not to destroy, the program of the state interventionists.

Whatever may have been its precise attitude on the role of the
state in economic matters, the congress achieved its main purpose
— that of enhancing Catholic prestige in the context of social reform. If chiefly it induced more Catholics to support the Church's
charitable and reformatory work in a more zealous manner, it also
contributed to the growing spirit of mutual respect among divergent reform groups. In concluding its comments on the congress,
the influential weekly paper, the *Congregationalist* of Boston, urged
Protestant clergy and people to study and support the Catholic social program after pointing out that nowhere had social questions
"been treated with greater skill, more moderation or with greater
appearance of thoroughness and candor than by members of the
Church of Rome." [101] But Catholics at the Columbian Exposition
did not rely upon their congress alone to soften the asperities of
religious conflict. They expected much from the World's Parliament
of Religions in which nearly every religious body in a spirit of mutual
forbearance and courtesy put its bid for universal acceptance. After
careful deliberation the archbishops decided to participate in this
"popular object lesson" in the comparative study of religions, sure
that the Catholic Church, having the plenitude of truth, might
without disadvantage stand "in the midst of all the old religions
which had preceded her and of all the bodies that had separated
from her unity." [102] In charge of Catholic participation, Bishop
Keane scoured the Catholic world for the most competent speakers
and writers to present the ripest fruits of Catholic scholarship in this
relatively new field.

If inevitably the Catholic apologia, with that of the other religions,
drew largely on philosophy and theology, the Parliament aimed
mainly to destroy the malignancy of religious rancor. Even partial
success on this score would at once ease the tasks of the Catholic
Church besides preparing the way for eventual reunion in Christen-

---

[100] Ibid., p. 198.
[101] "The Romanism of Today," October 26, 1893.
[102] "Bishop Keane on the World's Parliament of Religions," *Pilot*, October
14, 1893.

dom. Zealous social reformers discerned social significance in the
project. The World's Parliament of Religions would discover a "new
world of common activity," predicted the *Northwestern Chronicle*,
and urge "all to stoop together to lift up the drunkard and to wipe
dry the moistened face of pain." [103] In similar vein, Cardinal Gibbons told the Parliament that, while "we differ in faith, thank God
there is one platform on which we stand united, and that is the platform of charity and benevolence." [104] To Catholics less vitally interested in social questions, the Parliament presented a most unseemly spectacle. "Comedy of convocations!" exclaimed Pallen of
the *Church Progress*. "Think of putting a creed upon exhibition
at a Fair, as one might bring cattle to a show!" The appearance on
the same platform of paganism, heresy, and Catholicism implied that
each had the same claim on human faith and this further implied
the denial of Christianity altogether. "It is presumed," he explained,
"that everybody is right and nobody wrong, that man is not fallen
and perverse, but rather struggling upwards from lower conditions
(the evolutionary hypothesis) needing no redemption or regeneration from on high." [105]

If tradition-dominated Catholics accepted this logic, the more
liberal ones were also a bit dubious of the propriety and value of
mixed religious assemblies as a general practice. Only on condition that the Fair authorities provide for separate Catholic sessions
extending over a whole day did the archbishops consent to participate
in the Parliament [106] and, the experiment over, they quietly ar-
ranged with the Pope to dissociate Catholics from similar meetings
in the future.[107] But they were determined in ways not compro-
mising the Catholic faith to multiply contacts with folk outside the
Church.[108] One approach was through missions to non-Catholics
which distinguished converts, with the Paulist Walter Elliott at their

[103] "Parliament of Religions," April 14, 1893; *Church News*, September 16,
1893; *Catholic Review*, March 22, 1892.

[104] F. Tennyson Neely, *History of the Parliament of Religions and Religious
Congresses* (Chicago, 1893), pp. 45–46, 185–91.

[105] "A Religious Midway Plaisance," September 23, 1893.

[106] "The American Hierarchy and Abbé Charbonnel," ibid., February 8, 1896.

[107] *Western Watchman*, October 24, 1895.

[108] Rev. C. T. Patchell, "Christian Union in Bay City," *Independent*, March
21, 1895.

head, set in motion during the Exposition year. Beginning in Detroit, his home town, ex-lawyer Elliott explained Catholic doctrine uncompromisingly but charitably before audiences, largely Protestant, in secular buildings, generally public halls. Besides theology, Elliott and his helpers discussed social questions, notably intemperance, and urged Catholics to co-operate with their pastors to extend Catholic charities and to promote community welfare. Soon spreading to Cleveland and other dioceses, the movement found firmer support after 1896 in the formation of the American Catholic Missionary Union. Earlier, in 1895, the Pope informed the hierarchy that missions to non-Catholics were preferable to parliaments of religion.[109]

Meanwhile, Catholics were becoming more deeply involved in the social reform movement.[110] In New York City, Thomas J. Ducey, crusading pastor of St. Leo's Church, defied Archbishop Corrigan to support the Lexow Investigating Committee, whose startling revelations of complicity between organized crime and municipal officialdom resulted in Tammany's defeat in 1894.[111] Catholics were active elsewhere in the "civic renaissance." They helped the Union for Practical Progress, the *Arena* magazine editor's creation, to achieve its purpose "to unite all moral forces, agencies and persons for concerted, methodical, and persistant endeavor in behalf of the public good and especially for the abolition of unjust social conditions." [112] With support of clergymen from all faiths local branches of the

[109] "Catholic Missions for Protestants," *Pilot*, March 25, 1893; "Some Ways of Spreading Catholic Truth," ibid., October 27, 1894; "Editorial Notes," *Independent*, April 25, 1895; "America Catholic, So It Is Bound to Become, Says Father Elliott," *Church Progress*, May 4, 1895; "Cleveland Catholics Band Together to Convert Protestants," *Catholic Review*, September 28, 1895; "The Pope on Religious Congresses," *Review*, October 24, 1895.

[110] "The Pope's American Encyclical," *Independent*, February 7, 1895; "Editorial Notes," ibid., February 28, 1895; "Archbishop Ireland on Church and State," *Catholic Herald*, May 2, 1896; "True and False Liberalism," ibid., April 12, 1897.

[111] "Corrigan to Ducey, November 14, 1894," ibid., December 1, 1894; "Father Ducey's Answer," ibid.; "The Archbishop and Father Ducey," ibid.; "The Case of Father Ducey," ibid., December 22, 1894; Thomas J. Ducey to Denis O'Connell, July 30, 1894, Denis O'Connell Correspondence, loc. cit.; Miss A. M. Brown to Denis O'Connell, November 13, 1894, November 20, 1894, ibid.; "Editorial Note," *Catholic Review*, November 19, 1893.

[112] Abell, *The Urban Impact on American Protestantism*, pp. 103–6.

union fought not ineffectively a whole coterie of evils — municipal
corruption, child labor, the sweating system, and rotten tenements.
Catholic Charles J. Bonaparte was a member of the advisory board
of the national union and president of his local branch, the Baltimore Union for Doing Good, which, uniting some eighty churches,
societies, and labor unions, in 1893 concentrated its efforts against
child labor, the sweating system, and the circulation of obscene
literature. Its model bills on child labor and the sweating system
were adopted by the legislature. Anxious to retain Catholic support, the Union for Practical Progress resisted APA penetration.
"Instead of increasing the spirit of religious fanaticism, as the APA
is doing, the Union for Practical Progress," wrote its secretary, the
Reverend Walter Vrooman, "aims to destroy it by uniting Protestants, Catholics, Jews and atheists, all who" in the spirit of the
World's Parliament of Religions believed in "love and helpful-
ness." [113]

The welcome accorded socially liberal Catholics in the Union for
Practical Progress marked a milestone in their struggle for acceptance into the country's reform forces. But socially conservative Catholics found no cause for rejoicing in this development. They contended that when Catholics as Catholics affiliated with inclusively
constituted reform movements they encouraged the non-Catholic
participants "to be content with their present spiritual state," and
in this "neo-pelagian" manner fostered error at the expense of
truth.[114] Viewing reform in this light, the Reverend David S. Phelan
of St. Louis, the belligerent and fanatically anti-Cahenslyite editor
of the *Western Watchman*, opposed "union with Protestants on
the question of Sunday observance or any other religious question." [115] Particularly "neo-pelagian" in his opinion were James C.
Byrne, president of St. Paul's Seminary, and Bishop Keane, rector
of the Catholic University.[116] In a series of articles in the New

---

[113] "The A.P.A. Is the Enemy of Labor," *Pilot*, October 6, 1894.

[114] David S. Phelan, "The Roman Catholic Church," *Independent*, January
7, 1897.

[115] *Western Watchman*, October 24, 1895.

[116] Ibid.; "Pelagianism in the Northwest," ibid., August 22, 1895; "Tell
Them the Truth," ibid., October 24, 1895; "The Pope is Displeased," ibid.,
January 30, 1896; "Journalistic Indecency," ibid., January 8, 1897; *Independent*,
October 22, 1896.

York *Independent,* Byrne had explained that, while the Catholic Church possessed the full truth, other denominations already possessed some of it and were growing in wisdom and grace.[117] Keane had suggested that it would be desirable, pending permission to introduce Catholic teaching in all public schools, asylums, and penal institutions, to inculcate Protestant tenets. To Father Phelan, Keane's alleged motto, "If not the Priest, then the preacher," was preposterous heresy.[118] To Archbishop Ryan of Philadelphia, on the other hand, "the man who would see his child grow into an Ingersoll rather than a Gladstone ought to be locked up." [119]

The debate continued. But in its terms neither the content nor the technique of social reform was directly involved. For, anti-pelagian-like, the social liberals aimed to secure useful reforms mainly through associations of their own creation and independent direction. Apart from labor agitation, charity and temperance were the fields of endeavor in which the Catholic program as formulated by the lay congresses found clearest manifestation. Though not extensive, organization among laywomen for social service was significant in that it reflected the liberal social trend. Just as Protestant churchwomen in 1886 launched the remarkably successful King's Daughters movement,[120] so also in the years 1886-89 Catholic women in the St. Louis area developed the Queen's Daughters along both parochial and interparochial lines. Headed by Mary Hoxsey, a convert, the Queen's Daughters stressed primary instruction in religion and the household arts, providing sewing classes for young girls, a cooking school for older girls, and a well-equipped home for working women. Owing partly to its endorsement by the archbishops in 1896 and by Pope Pius X a decade later, this lay sisterhood for personal service grew steadily, having some sixty branches by World War I, fifteen in St. Louis and the remainder in cities from coast to coast. Known as was its Protestant counterpart for the broad and varied scope of its work, the Queen's Daugh-

---

[117] "A Plea for Christian Fraternity. Is It Possible Between Catholics and Protestants?" June 27, August 15, and September 19, 1895.

[118] "The Retirement of Bishop Keane (from the *Western Watchman*)," *Review,* October 15, 1896.

[119] *Northwestern Chronicle,* November 29, 1895.

[120] Abell, *The Urban Impact on American Protestantism,* pp. 219-22.

ters preferred to strengthen existing rather than create additional Catholic agencies.[121]

Of special importance were clubs for working girls to counteract the "dancing academies" and other questionable forms of recreation. Under the general direction of Grace H. Dodge, working girls' clubs drawing a large part of their membership from the Catholic population rapidly multiplied during the 1880s. Although Catholic women of refinement and leisure were welcomed into the management of these secular clubs, the arrangement only partially met the needs of wage-earning Catholic girls.[122] Distinctly Catholic clubs were appearing on the scene in considerable numbers by the time the Columbian Exposition opened in 1893.[123] Anxious to speed this and other forms of social service, the Women's Catholic Congress, meeting at the Fair on May 18 with Alice T. Toomy of California in charge, decided to launch the National League of Catholic Women.[124] As a body these women were encouraged to become "the messengers of mercy and love" by Cardinal Gibbons' great paper read to the World's Parliament of Religions. "It taught them the necessity," they said, "of organizing to aid the Church in her mission as the great philanthropic and charitable society of the world."[125] Lay women were bound, in honor, to do their part of the world's work in the world, argued the secretary of the new organization, Eliza Allen Starr, art teacher and lecturer, "since they decline, for social reasons, to do it in the cloister or under the protection of the religious habit."[126]

Designed to mobilize Catholic women in much the same way as the Women's Christian Temperance Union had aroused Protestant churchwomen, the new league displayed also a comparable "do-everything" attitude toward social service. In its view education,

[121] Mary V. Toomy, "The Work and Aim of the Queen's Daughters. A Society for the Improvement of the Home Life of the Poor and to Help the Unfortunate," *Catholic World*, LXVII (August 1898), 610–21; ibid., "The Queen's Daughters' Society," *Catholic Charities Review*, I (February 1917), 43–46; "The Queen's Daughters," ibid., V (March 1921), 90–91.

[122] "A New Field for Catholic Women," *Pilot*, May 19, 1894.

[123] "Catholic Girls' Clubs," ibid., February 4, 1893; "News Item on Working Girls' Clubs," ibid., April 1, 1893.

[124] Alice Timmons Toomy, "There Is a Public Sphere for Catholic Women," *Catholic World*, LVII (August 1893), 674–77.

[125] Mary Jane Burns, "Twenty-Five Years of the Catholic Woman's League of Chicago," *Catholic Charities Review*, II (December 1918), 308–10.

[126] "Our Fallow Field," letter to *Catholic Review*, July 8, 1893.

philanthropy, and the home and its needs deserved major attention.
The league proposed to promote education by spreading Catholic
doctrine; to promote philanthropy by encouraging temperance and
by forming day nurseries, kindergartens, protective and employment agencies, and clubs and homes for working girls; and to serve
the home and its needs by solving the domestic servant question
and by uniting the interests and tastes of the different members of
the family. In many Chicago neighborhoods the league flourished
and carried out much of its program; elsewhere it was slow in getting
a foothold.[127] Not in the beginning a federation of women's organizations, it never succeeded in its repeated efforts to become one.
Formed "without due consideration" of Catholic special needs, complained the Boston *Pilot*, the National League of Catholic Women
illustrated the deplorable tendency to imitate "every method that
had been successfully used in the Protestant or secular field of endeavor." [128]

Artificiality could not be charged against the "model" lay society,
the Society of St. Vincent de Paul, even though it was still unable
to enlist in its service a sufficiently large number of the Church's
ablest men.[129] But it did experience, as the Catholic congresses had
hoped, a remarkable expansion in organization and activities.[130]
In the attempt to keep pace with urban growth, in the newer cities
of the West as well as in the older sections of the country, the
number of local or parish conferences increased from 235 in 1883 to
428 in 1902.[131] During these years of mounting poverty and destitution, the society was sadly obliged to stress more than formerly its

[127] Kathryn Prindiville, "The Catholic Life of Chicago," *Catholic World*,
LXVII (July 1898), 484.

[128] "Catholics and 'Woman's Days,'" June 3, 1893.

[129] "St. Vincent de Paul," *Catholic Review*, January 17, 1891.

[130] For "foundations" and "developments" city by city, see Daniel T. McColgan, *A Century of Charity. The First One Hundred Years of the Society of St.
Vincent de Paul in the United States* (Milwaukee, 1951), I, 317–527; II, 1–
272.

[131] *Report of the Superior Council of New York to the Council General in
Paris, 1902* (New York, 1903), pp. 3–4; L. T. Jamme, "The Society in Amer-
ica," *St. Vincent de Paul Quarterly*, II (May 1897), 100; D. D. Donovan,
"Progress of the Society in New England for the Past Twenty Years," ibid., X
(May 1905), 137–38; Charles O'Donnell, "The Society in the West," ibid., I
(February 1896), 123; *St. Vincent de Paul Quarterly*, I (November 1895),
68, 85; ibid. (February 1896), 152–53, 157; ibid. (May 1896), 230–33; ibid.
(August 1896), 342–44, 349.

primary purpose of relieving the poor in their homes. So great was its reputation for efficiency in this respect that in periods of unusual distress, notably the depression of 1893–97, the society was chosen, in some cities, to aid in the distribution of public funds.

Apart from need and public favor, changes in methods of procedure contributed greatly to the expansion and perfection of the society's work. Realizing its inability properly to supervise the local bodies, the Superior Council of New York relinquished its powers of direction to regional groups — Central Councils operating on an archdiocesan basis. Beginning with Boston in 1889, such councils were established in Philadelphia, St. Paul, and various lesser places during the immediately ensuing years. Besides maintaining unity of management, Central Councils encouraged the formation of new conferences and the launching of "special works" for which the society was deservedly famous.[132] These much-needed forms of charity derived no little support from the conventions and journalistic efforts of the society. Aware by 1886 that the decision a decade earlier to hold decennial conventions did not afford sufficient opportunity to keep members abreast of the new needs and methods, the society convened in 1889, 1893, 1895, and annually thereafter.[133] In 1895 the society authorized the publication of a much-needed journal, the *St. Vincent de Paul Quarterly*. Intended primarily as a means of making the society an auxiliary of the clergy in their work of elevating the poor, the magazine also hoped to demonstrate "to the Catholics of America that our organization is something more than a mere relief agency and that our aims extend far beyond the mere food and clothing we give." [134]

The magazine certainly found much to record in the field of "special works." [135] Maintaining its earlier interst in child care, immigrant distribution, and boarding homes for working boys, the society perfected its efforts in these areas and sought new spheres of

[132] Ibid., I (November 1895), 8, 68–69; ibid., II (November 1896), 410–11; *Report of the Superior Council of New York to the Council General in Paris, 1902*, pp. 90–101.

[133] *Report of the Particular Council of Boston, 1886* (Boston, 1887), p. 14; *Catholic Review*, August 24, 1895; *St. Vincent de Paul Quarterly*, I (November 1895), 8–13, 76.

[134] Ibid., p. 4.

[135] For a summary, see *Report of the Superior Council of New York to the Council General in Paris, 1903* (New York, 1904), pp. 5–50.

usefulness. In the placing of destitute or orphaned children the
society now preferred home over institutional care. In order to put
this service on a systematic basis, the Particular Council of New York
set up in 1898 the Catholic Home Bureau.[136] Two years earlier the
same council had formed the Catholic Boys' Association, the purpose of which was to organize and sustain clubs for boys after the
example of the many attractive ones under Protestant auspices.
The association's first club, opened in December 1896, was well
equipped with playrooms, reading rooms, and a gymnasium. Within five years a dozen or more similar clubs graced the scene in New
York City. These, as well as the ones opened elsewhere, combined religious instruction with recreation.[137]

The members of the St. Vincent de Paul Society were tireless
in their efforts to find work for unemployed men, sometimes through
free employment bureaus established especially for the purpose.[138]
More and more the society, with the example of the Salvation Army
before it, displayed interest in homeless and outcast men. During
1895 William Downey and his fellow Vincentians established in the
nation's capital the Home of the Good Samaritan, whose conspicuous success assured wide support for this type of service in later
Catholic home missionary effort.[139] Not the least noble of the society's projects was attention to the needs of the deaf, dumb, and
blind.[140] Aware that while one half of these unfortunates in the
United States were Catholics they lacked systematic religious care,
the society decided to help the pioneer efforts being made in their
behalf, resolving in its convention of 1897 to "add the care of the

---

[136] Ibid., *1903*, pp. 12–15; McColgan, op. cit., I, 374–80.

[137] Ibid., pp. 367–68; *Society of St. Vincent de Paul, Eighth Annual Report
of the Central Council of Boston, 1896* (Boston, 1896), p. 19; I.E.R., "A
Catholic Boys' Club," *St. Vincent de Paul Quarterly*, II (February 1897), 29–
31; "First Annual Report of the Catholic Boys' Association of New York City,"
ibid., III (November 1897), 316–19; "The Catholic Boys' Club of New York,"
ibid., VIII (February 1903), 32–34.

[138] Edward T. Devine, "Relief and Care of the Poor in Their Homes," *Charities Review*, X (August 1900), 261–72; McColgan, op. cit., I, 331, 381, 393; II,
167, 211, 479–80; *St. Vincent de Paul Quarterly*, III (November 1897), 306–15.

[139] Ibid., II (November 1896), 416–17.

[140] Robert McGinnis, "Deaf Mutes and the Society," ibid., I (November
1895), 40–42; "The Catholic Deaf-Mutes Institutions," *Catholic Review*, September 4, 1897; F. A. Moeller, S.J., "The Appeal of the Deaf Mute," *First
American Catholic Missionary Congress, 1908* (Chicago, 1909), pp. 192–202.

deaf, dumb and blind to the Special Works of the Society."[141]

The society's most significant special work, the one most in favor at the Catholic congresses, was its co-operative ties with non-Catholic charities, specifically with the denominational and undenominational associations making up the charity organization movement.[142] Among the first to believe (from the early 1880s) that this movement was not ill disposed toward Catholics was Monsignor Thomas Preston, Vicar-General of New York, who counseled mutual understanding.[143] His opinions only half convinced Catholics, who generally believed that proselytism was a main purpose of organized charity. In the early 1890s, however, Thomas M. Mulry, a distinguished member of the society's New York Superior Council, discovered that only Catholic affiliation could prevent the incidental proselytism the movement practiced. Although some Catholics sneeringly proclaimed him the Protestant member of the St. Vincent de Paul Society, Mulry effected co-operation in fresh-air work during the summer of 1893.[144] When depression presently struck, Catholics and organized charity joined hands to launch tragically needed relief projects in Boston, Brooklyn, Philadelphia, Chicago, and elsewhere. In its historic convention of 1895 the society unanimously resolved that "it is advisable and necessary to co-operate freely and fully within the bounds prescribed by our general law, with all organized charities."[145] Action in accordance with this resolution would do more than tons of pamphleteering to promote Christian unity, asserted the *Catholic World*. "The relief of suffering humanity, whatever its creed or race," editorialized the magazine, "is a platform broad enough for all."[146] The *Independent* agreed, noting that the society's decision on co-operation was "in line" with the views on

[141] "Summarized Report of the General Convention, 1895," *St. Vincent de Paul Quarterly*, I (November 1895), 24.

[142] McColgan, op. cit., II, 364–81. "Editorial Comment," *Charities Review*, I (December 1891), 89.

[143] John F. Fenlon, S.S., "Grappling with Our Charity Problems," *Ecclesiastical Review*, LII (March 1915), 264–65.

[144] T. M. Mulry, "Outings for Poor Children," *St. Vincent de Paul Quarterly*, I (February 1896), 115–21.

[145] "Summarized Report of the General Convention, 1895," loc. cit., 24–27; "Outlook in Chicago," *Charities Review*, V (October 1896), 294; *Catholic Review*, November 20, 1897; Thomas M. Mulry, "Catholic Cooperation in Charity," *Charities Review*, VIII (October 1898), 383–86; Timothy D. Hurley, "Catholic Cooperation in Charity," ibid., VII (December 1897), 858–68.

[146] LXII (October 1895), 136.

Christian unity presented its readers recently by "a distinguished Catholic divine" — the Reverend James C. Byrne, whom his fellow priest, David S. Phelan, charged with pelagian heresy.[147]

The St. Vincent de Paul Society was also interested in the newest form of Catholic charity, namely, the social settlement in whose management lay folk of both sexes participated. The first thoroughly equipped Catholic settlement, for the benefit of Italian immigrants, was established in 1898 in connection with the Dominican parish of St. Catherine of Siena in New York City. Its head worker, convert Marion F. Gurney, was experienced in this field. In 1900 socially minded Catholics of Los Angeles founded Brownson House for the benefit mainly of Mexican immigrants. At about the same time the Paulists opened two settlements in New York City, one, the outgrowth of a boys' club, to aid youth to take advantage of the opportunities afforded by American liberty, and the other, a temperance settlement, to serve as a substitute for the saloon.[148]

In temperance work generally substitution, while endlessly extolled, was less widely practiced than in earlier days of the social movement.[149] Mainly, the agitation against intemperance conformed to the neo-puritan principles laid down in the Third Plenary Council and the Catholic congresses. As a phase of social liberalism, the Catholic temperance movement reached the crescendo of its power during the 1880s and 1890s. Stressing moral suasion, the Catholic Total Abstinence Union increased in membership from thirty-one to eighty thousand.[150] Able leadership, the affiliation of women, children, college students and seminarians, and an energetic

[147] "Editorial Notes," September 19, 1895; "Charity Organization Society of the City of New York," *Charities Review*, V (November 1895), 44; *Catholic Review*, November 20, 1897.

[148] *18th Annual Report of the Bureau of Labor Statistics of the State of New York, 1900*, pp. 396–98, 409–11; "The Paulist Temperance Settlement," *Catholic Review*, March 21, 1898; "Paulists' New Settlement House," *Church Progress*, July 16, 1898; Lawrence Franklin, "The Italian in America: What He Has Been, What He Shall Be," *Catholic World*, LXXI (April 1900), 18.

[149] Morgan M. Sheedy, "Suggestions to the Coming Total Abstinence Convention," *Catholic World*, LV (July 1892), 568–69; Patrick F. McSweeney, "Old-Time Temperance Societies," ibid., LXII (January 1896), 482–86; A. P. Doyle, "Economic Aspects of the Liquor Problem," ibid., LXVIII (November 1898), 250–54.

[150] "President Conaty's Report," *Lend a Hand*, III (September 1888), 516–18; "The Catholic Temperance Revival," *Independent*, August 9, 1894; Sr. Joan Bland, S.N.D., *Hibernian Crusade*, pp. 175–221.

publication bureau after 1891 were among the reasons why the membership rolls swelled "beyond all expectation." [151] Though refusing to endorse prohibition, the union favored the less drastic legislative remedies, singly or in combination. To this end the union's convention of 1895 voted to "co-operate with our non-Catholic fellow-citizens in every legitimate effort to restrict the evils of temperance." [152]

At this convention of 1895, staged in New York in honor of the union's silver jubilee, the saloon and temperance forces collided head on.[153] As Archbishop Corrigan said, the convention should "make the name of Catholic stand unmistakably for temperance." [154] The saloon interests, on the other hand, wished to enlist the union in a drive to nullify the state's restrictive laws. At the convention's mass meeting in Carnegie Hall, a Tammany politician, in order to test Catholic sentiment, suggested that after the next election the excise and Sunday closing laws would no longer be enforced. Hissed and booed by the vast audience, he "retired in complete discomfiture." The convention's attitude revealed, as the New York *Nation* reported, the existence of a great power on the side of law observance and a quiet Sunday.[155] The convention threw a white light "on the position of the Catholic Church in reference to whiskey and the beer business that will help," the *Catholic Review* thought, "to relieve the Church from unjustly inflicted odium on the part of non-Catholic Christians." [156]

Reforming Catholics did not confine their efforts in this direction to the legislative field. One bishop, John A. Watterson of Columbus, Ohio, withdrew approval in 1894 from all diocesan societies having liquor dealers or saloonkeepers among their officers. He further decreed that in the future liquor traffickers were ineligible for membership in the societies and that if they violated the civil law they

[151] A. P. Doyle, C.S.P., "A Study of the American Temperance Question," *Catholic Review*, August 15, 1896; *Pilot*, August 20, 1898; Michael P. Heffernan, "Our Boys," *Catholic World*, LXV (August 1897), 577–85; "The Future of the Total Abstinence Movement," ibid., LXVII (September 1898), 839–42.

[152] Joseph C. Gibbs, *History of the Catholic Total Abstinence Union of America*, p. 118.

[153] *Silver Jubilee Gathering of the Catholic Total Abstinence Union of America* (New York, 1895), esp. pp. 37–49, 94–102.

[154] "National Temperance Union," *Catholic Review*, July 13, 1895.

[155] "Catholics and the Saloons," August 15, 1895.

[156] August 17, 1895.

should be denied absolution in the confessional.[157] Satolli, the Apostolic Delegate, sustained Watterson's action as "being in harmony with the laws of the Church, and seasonable and necessary to the honor of the Church, especially in Ohio." [158] In the opinion of the New York *Voice*, a social reform journal favoring prohibition, Satolli's decision was "equivalent to an official condemnation of the saloon by the Catholic Church." [159] But the *Wine and Spirit Gazette*, also published in New York City, insisted that the ruling applied only to Columbus and dared Corrigan and his suffragan bishops to attempt its enforcement within their jurisdictions. The archbishop angrily announced that he accepted the Satolli principles "both in their spirit and in their letter," observing, however, that "acceptance of principles is not to be confounded with the blind application of the same, on all occasions and under all circumstances." [160] Despite these reservations, Corrigan's stand was a strong one which encouraged many priests and laymen, not only in New York but throughout the country, to redouble their efforts against the saloon power.[161]

Archbishop Ireland suggested, no doubt rightly, "that if other bishops" followed Watterson's example "their action will be sustained by the higher powers." [162] No bishop saw fit to do so. But several great Catholic societies, by refusing membership to liquor dealers, aided the enforcement everywhere of Watterson's decision. Thus acted in 1895 the Catholic Benevolent Legion and the Society of St. Vincent de Paul. "Think you," asked the latter society, "that a man, whose living depends on the sale of liquor, can visit the poor, and consistently advise them to refrain from drink?" [163] Congratulating the society, the *Catholic World* stated that "the relation of liquor selling to charity is that of cause and effect. The miseries which the St. Vincent de Paul Society tries to cure may often be traced, indirectly at least, to the pernicious trade with which it now

[157] *Outlook*, July 28, 1894.
[158] John Ireland, "The Church and the Saloon," *The Church and Modern Society*, I, 313.
[159] Quoted in *Catholic Review*, August 18, 1894.
[160] "An Insolent Defiance," *Catholic Review*, August 11, 1894.
[161] *Outlook*, August 4, 1894.
[162] "The Church and the Saloon," loc. cit.
[163] *St. Vincent de Paul Quarterly*, I (November 1898).

declares to have nothing to do. No peace is possible with such an enemy, that is, no peace with honor." [164]

If Catholics in sizable numbers resented the heavy involvement of their lay folk in the liquor traffic, they recoiled in horror at the sight of clergymen plying the trade. The issue centered on St. Vincent's Beer, brewed in the Benedictine abbey at Beatty, Pennsylvania, and sold in many parts of the world. Fortified by Pope Pius IX's permission to open the brewery, the monks easily braved the displeasure of successive local bishops and even the Third Plenary Council itself. But they could not long defy public opinion. As the anti-liquor crusade gained momentum in the early 1890s, its leaders heaped derision and scorn on "holy beer" — an incongruous concoction of grace and poison. The chief critics were the Reverend George Zurcher of Buffalo, an extremist social liberal, the Reverend Ferdinand Kittell of Loretto, Pennsylvania, onetime chancellor of the Pittsburgh diocese, and Martin I. J. Griffin, the fiery Philadelphia editor and reformer.[165] The Benedictine brewery inspired one of Zurcher's books, *Monks and Their Decline* (Buffalo, 1898), which speedily found a place on the Index of Prohibited Books.[166]

More effective because less extreme, Father Kittell in the *Catholic Citizen* and elsewhere after 1892 directed dart after dart of scornful mirth at the Benedictine brewers. He informed the public that 121 monks and their helpers at St. Vincent's consumed beer to the value of six thousand dollars a year. "How does it strike you, ye Catholics of America," he asked, "that 23,360 gallons of beer of which five per cent or 1,168 gallons are pure alcoholic poison, are required each year, at a cost of $16 a day, to slake the thirst of one religious community of the United States?" To many people this statistical blast seemed devastating. More damaging still was Kittell's revelation that the college students evaded the prohibition against drinking and appeared riotously drunk at religious picnics and other events connected with the life of the community. He

[164] "Editorial Notes," LXII (October 1895), 136.
[165] "Editorial Notes," *Independent*, August 31, 1893; ibid., December 19, 1895; "The Catholic Church and Total Abstinence," ibid., August 15, 1895; "Beer Monks to Go," *Voice*, December 26, 1895; "St. Vincent's 'Holy Beer' Brewed by Papal Authority," ibid., April 21, 1898; "Monastic Beer and Teetotalist Fanaticism," *Church Progress*, July 16, 1898.
[166] *Independent*, June 30, 1898; *Western Watchman*, September 22, 1898.

cited the mother "who curses the day she sent her sons to St. Vincent's College. They are now men gone to destruction, and she traces their downfall to that brewery." [167] Kittell and others pointed out that St. Vincent's Abbey as well as Princeton and Yale might well follow the example of the University of Notre Dame, which prospered without the aid of "holy beer." [168] Just as public opinion forced Yale and Princeton to close their liquor-dispensing inns, so also it obliged St. Vincent's Abbey, in 1899, to dismantle its monastic brewery.[169]

However impressive its victories, the Catholic temperance movement failed to continue its momentum into the twentieth century. Not only the users and venders of alcoholic beverages but also the guardians of Catholic teaching interposed objections. Critics charged that the more zealous agitators had lost sight of the Church's teaching that only immoderate drinking was sinful and aimed to ban all intoxicants. The fact that a goodly number of Catholics embraced prohibition lent some justification to this fear. Not a few Catholics wished to direct zeal for temperance into labor reform. Clearly indicative of this purpose was the mass meeting in March 1897, at Lenox Hall, New York City, under the auspices of the Archdiocesan Union of Temperance Societies. Presided over by Archbishop Corrigan, the convention, with the "social betterment of the masses" as its object, discussed not temperance but Leo XIII's great encyclical on the condition of labor, the salient features of which were thoroughly explained and liberally interpreted.[170]

As the century neared its end, the social liberals were pleading for the concentration of Catholic missionary and social effort on the needs of the new urban masses, the rapidly mounting Catholic immigration from southern and eastern Europe. Poor, unskilled, and largely illiterate, these immigrants were also spiritually destitute in the sense that many of them, the Italians notably, were slow to seek the usual ministrations of church or school. In all the large cities after 1897, laity and clergy in sizable numbers sensed the seriousness of the situation. Their mouthpiece was Humphrey J. Desmond,

[167] "Beer Monks to Go," loc. cit.
[168] "No Use for 'Holy Beer' at Notre Dame," ibid., May 12, 1898.
[169] "The End of a Scandal," *Review*, April 6, 1899.
[170] W. H. Thorne, "Betterment of the Masses," *Globe*, VII (June 1897), 217–30.

editor of the Milwaukee *Catholic Citizen* and publisher and director of the *Northwestern Chronicle* of St. Paul, the *New Century* of Washington, D.C., and other journals also.[171] Desmond contended that only by the "well considered methods" of the social settlement and its adjuncts could the Church carry the blessings of faith to the millions of new immigrants flooding the country. In order to make available sufficient funds and personnel for carrying forward the new work, the Desmond newspaper chain suggested that laymen and religious turn over to the state most of their "pathological" charity — hospitals, foundling asylums, reformatories, and homes for the indigent, the aged, and the insane.[172] No longer should the state "be allowed to sponge on the generosity of the Catholic community" through a charity system which was suitable only "to the economy of church-and-state countries." [173]

The social liberals expected the emerging federation movement to incorporate the whole of the Church's social program. In the wake of the APA crusade, numerous Catholics representing nearly every faction in the Church resolved to mobilize the whole Catholic body against "un-American bigotry." To the old grievances, among which were double taxation for school purposes, unfair treatment of Catholic Indian schools, and refusal of political parties and administrative agencies to extend consideration to Catholics in proportion to their numerical strength, were now added the new ones, namely, the unwillingness of the federal government to accord American Catholics an adequate voice in decisions affecting the Catholic Church in the overseas possessions. In midsummer 1897 Arthur Preuss wrote in the New York *Independent* that Catholics must thoroughly organize for the defense of their constitutional rights, and for once the liberal *Northwestern Chronicle* of St. Paul agreed with him.[174] The fifty-odd Catholic societies, it was widely believed,

---

[171] "The Italian Question," *Northwestern Chronicle*, November 26, 1897; "The Italian Immigrant Problem," *Church Progress*, December 4, 1897; "More Help for the Italians," ibid., January 29, 1898.

[172] Desmond, *Chats within the Fold: A Series of Little Sermons from a Lay Standpoint* (Baltimore, 1901), pp. 116–22.

[173] "Our Charities," *New Century*, July 28, 1906; "A Charity Question," ibid., October 12, 1907.

[174] "Catholic Organization," *Northwestern Chronicle*, August 13, 1897; ibid., *Review*, August 19, 1897; "The Lack of Catholic Public Life in the United States," ibid., IX (No. 43, 1902), 682.

should draw more closely together, and at their convention in June 1899 the Knights of St. John formally proposed a federation and appointed a committee to forward the realization of the project.

The Knights of St. John and others friendly to federation desired a Catholic pressure group, not a Catholic political party. This was most emphatically the attitude of Bishop James A. McFaul of Trenton, whose writings and speeches raised him to a position of commanding leadership in the movement.[175] Only one outstanding figure, Arthur Preuss, desired an American Catholic party on the model of the Center party in Germany. Even if the federation movement did not terminate in a Catholic political party, its "grievance" program seemed to many equally dangerous, involving, as the Reverend Thomas H. Malone, editor of the *Colorado Catholic*, insisted, a drive "for political unity along religious lines." [176] Besides being dangerous, the proposed federation, social liberals charged, ignored the truly vital problem, namely, the social and educational betterment of the Catholic masses. "It is not the Indians, nor the Philippines, nor the soldiers, who furnish the larger questions for the Catholic public," editorialized the *Northwestern Chronicle*. "The larger questions are found in the way Catholic immigration from Italy and other parts of Europe is being lost to the Church; in the way the home life of the poorer Catholic classes in our cities is being neglected"; and finally, the paper concluded, "in our unscientific treatment of such important matters as Catholic charities and Catholic higher education." [177] In this newspaper's view, nine tenths of the Catholic task in America lay outside politics.[178]

But federation gained momentum mainly as a grievance movement. In striking contrast to its attitude on most issues, the Catholic press, as the *Midland Review* of Louisville reported, was "practically a unit in advocating federation." [179] The idea strongly appealed to German-American Catholics, partly because of its conserv-

[175] "Catholic and American Citizenship," *North American Review*, CLXXI (September 1900), 320–32; ibid., "Catholic Rights and Needs," *Donahoe's Magazine*, XLIV (September 1900), 268–71.
[176] "Catholic Citizens and Constitutional Rights," *North American Review*, CLXXI (October 1900), 594–99.
[177] "The Federation Idea Again," September 22, 1900.
[178] "Keep Politics Out," ibid., July 27, 1901.
[179] "Progress of the Catholic Federation Movement," October 26, 1899.

ative overtones, but mainly because they now realized they could no longer live religiously isolated from other Catholics in America. As the German population, immigrant and native-born, rapidly Americanized, successive Roman rulings, the last one in 1897, granted parishioners liberty to leave German- and to join English-speaking congregations.[180] With the discontinuance of the Priester-Verein in 1898, German Catholics openly acknowledged the passing of Cahenslyism.[181] Moreover, German immigration was dwindling — a fact making the maintenance of an independent position increasingly untenable.

French-Canadians and some others, still ethnic and minority-conscious, showed little interest in plans for federation. Even the societies favorably disposed moved slowly while awaiting guarantees of their autonomy in the proposed organization. At the first meeting of the federation committee, in September 1899, only seven delegates appeared. Not until Thanksgiving Day, 1900, did a meeting widely representative of Catholic societies assemble at the Fifth Avenue Hotel in New York. Steering away from politics, this conference declared the purposes of federation to be: "the cementing of bonds of fraternal union among the Catholic societies of the United States," "the fostering of the works of piety, religion, education, and charity," and "the state and conditions of our social life and the dissemination of truth." [182] This social emphasis may have mirrored, to some extent at least, the views of Bishop (later Archbishop) Sebastian G. Messmer, who after Bishop McFaul was the most active prelate in the federation movement. Some weeks before the New York meeting, Messmer formulated a comprehen-

[180] Gerald Coghlan to Denis O'Connell, Philadelphia, July 23, 1897, loc. cit., Box 12; "A New Roman Decision," *Review*, May 27, 1897; Romanus, "True Import of the Recent Ruling of the Prefect of the Propaganda," ibid., June 3, 1897; "Bishop Messmer's View," ibid.; "A German Pastor's View," ibid., June 10, 1897; "Our French-Canadian Confreres," ibid.; "Exchange Comment," ibid.

[181] Joseph J. Wahlen, "Seventy-five Years of Catholic Action," *Diamond Jubilee Celebration and 74th Annual Convention of the Catholic Central Verein of America* (Baltimore, 1930), p. 46.

[182] "For Catholic Federation: The Project Discussed at a Meeting Held in New York," *Catholic News*, December 1, 1900; "Catholic Federation Going Slow," *Northwestern Chronicle*, December 15, 1900.

sive program under three headings: religious, social, and civil. Conceding that Catholics must insist on their rights, he urged them to attend first of all to their duties, especially to promoting the welfare of the poor and warring on political corruption. In words reminiscent of the Catholic congresses, Messmer stated that "our work is not to be 'sectarian' in a narrow, bigoted sense, which would not exclude in principle all co-operation with non-Catholic organizations or individuals." A glance at the proposed program would show, he said, "the many points of contact where Catholics can work together with Protestants toward a happy solution of the burning social questions. . . ." [183]

Indirectly, the plea of Messmer and others for a social program had its effect on the federation movement. After some more harassing delays the committee in charge finally effected a temporary organization for the American Federation of Catholic Societies in a meeting in late August 1901 at Long Branch, New Jersey.[184] On December 10, 1901, three hundred delegates representing six hundred thousand Catholics convened in Cincinnati to approve a constitution and survey the field of operations. "Partisan politics," read one clause in the constitution, "shall not be discussed in any meeting of this Federation or of its subordinate bodies; nor shall this body or any of its subordinate bodies endorse any candidate for office." Nor did the convention draw up a list of grievances, being content with generalizing resolutions on fraternity in Catholic societies, filial devotion to the Holy See, patriotic love of country, need for study of the papal encyclicals, and encouragement of a sound Catholic press, literature, and education.[185] Although five prelates — Elder, Horstmann, McFaul, Messmer, and Maes — attended the convention, it did not request endorsement by the hierarchy or make clergymen eligible for official positions in the organ-

[183] "Catholic Federation," ibid., September 24, 1900; S. G. Messmer, "A Program for Federation," *Review*, November 15, 1900; "Bishop Messmer's Plan," New York *Freeman's Journal*, November 24, 1900.

[184] "The Catholic Federation: Bishop McFaul's Instructive Letter on the Project," *Catholic News*, May 18, 1901; T. B. Minahan, "The Federation Convention: What Citizens Expect from It," *Donahoe's Magazine*, XLVI (November 1901), 430–32.

[185] "The Cincinnati Convention and Catholic Federation," *Review*, January 9, 1902.

ization.[186] For its first president the convention chose Thomas B. Minahan of Columbus, Ohio, who forthwith demonstrated his social liberalism by lecturing on temperance in Washington Gladden's First Congregational Church of his native city.

[186] On the early progress of the movement, see Anthony Mitre, "Catholic Federation — Its Missions and Results." *Dominicana,* III (December 1902), 411–12; James A. McFaul, "The American Federation of Catholic Societies," *Donahoe's Magazine,* LII (July 1904), 87–90.

CHAPTER V

Not Socialism—but Social Reform,
1900–17

By the second decade of the present century, reform — commonly known as Progressivism — had pushed its way to dominance in the nation's economy and politics. The "social unrest" which in earlier decades had affected mainly farmers and wage earners now enveloped vast sections of the urban middle class.[1] By scores of thousands ambitious men, anticipating satisfying rewards for ability and personal effort employed in business and the professions, found the avenues to success monopolized by industrial and financial combinations whose growth and ramifications after 1896 hampered small- and medium-scale business enterprise and threatened to deliver the country into the clutches of a plutocracy. Their hopes frustrated, their sense of justice and propriety outraged, the propertied and educated middle classes embraced reform, becoming the driving force in Progressivism, a great political movement directed to economic and social ends.

The Progressives saw the main evil in the sinister alliance between great business interests and servile party machines. They would then, first of all, rehabilitate democratic government with the aid of primary elections, the initiative and referendum, and other instruments of direct popular rule. With plutocracy eliminated, corporate wealth could be controlled and economic opportunity assured to all the people, be they business and professional men, farmers or wage earners. Speaking for labor, Samuel Gompers predicted in 1911 that, with "the transferral of the power of political machines to the voters of the industrial communities," the "entire toiling producing class, including the farmers, will concentrate their strength in suppressing the grosser forms of national monopoly."[2] From a

[1] Richard Hofstadter, *The Age of Reform* (New York, 1955).
[2] "Dr. Gladden on Trade Unionism," *American Federationist*, XVIII (August 1911), 601–2.

religious viewpoint, Progressivism marked the triumph of the social gospel: if the Protestant social reformers of the 1880s and 1890s had failed to draw the working people into their churches, they had succeeded in predisposing their vast middle-class constituency to social reform.[3] Catholic reform interest of the late nineteenth century continued without a break into the twentieth. Archbishop Ireland "is certainly a conservative" on public issues, observed editor Humphrey J. Desmond in 1907; "nevertheless, the tendency of American Catholics," he maintained, "is strongly towards liberal and radical ideas in American politics." While the large Catholic admixture in the labor unions of the country "holds the situation against Socialism," he happily noted, "it has no such predilection against radicalism or populism, so called." But this highly influential journalist was too candid and forthright not to emphasize that many Catholics were political corruptionists. "So far as Catholic activity in city politics is respectable," he summarized, "it is mostly of the radical and anti-corporation kind; so far as it is discreditable, it is of the grafter and corporation kind." [4]

More than in curbing monopoly or democratizing politics, reforming Catholics were interested in the social justice side of the Progressive movement. During this period some forty states either passed new laws or radically amended older ones pertaining to the working conditions of women and children. Whereas the earlier statutes had applied only to factories, the new or amended ones covered all non-agricultural work places — stores, restaurants, hotels, offices, and communications. The best of these laws limited women's work to eight or nine hours a day, forced all children under fourteen to attend school, abolished night work for all boys and girls under sixteen, and reduced their daily working hours to eight in a six-day week. In order further to protect women and children thirteen states (and the District of Columbia), beginning with pioneering Massachusetts in 1912, secured minimum wage enactments by 1919. Three years earlier Congress, in an effort to raise standards everywhere to the level of the advanced states, outlawed

[3] Henry F. May, *Protestant Churches and Industrial America* (New York, 1949), pp. 263–65.
[4] "Are We Liberals?" *New Century*, April 13, 1907.

child labor from interstate commerce. All but five states in the years 1911–19 passed laws obliging employers to insure their employees against industrial accidents.

These measures were secured mainly by humanitarians and social workers of middle-class affiliation bringing pressure to bear on lawmaking bodies through a half dozen effective agencies of education and propaganda. The oldest of these, the General Federation of Women's Clubs, dating from 1889, stressed social reform and labor legislation after 1904. Dedicated to the same ends were the National Consumers' League (1898), the National Women's Trade Union League (1903), and the National Child Labor Committee (1904). More important for the future was the American Association for Labor Legislation, an outgrowth in 1906 of the American Economic Association, whose legislative program, formulated in the decade before the nation's entry into World War I, foreshadowed and helped to usher in the social security measures of the New Deal.[5] Environmentalist in outlook, Progressive reformers were primarily interested in the prevention of human distress, only incidentally in relief and rehabilitation. Indicative of this attitude was the conviction of the National Conference of Charities and Correction (National Conference of Social Work after 1917) that "industry should be subjected to certain tests of social efficiency and should measure up to standards demanded by public health and safety."[6] Among these demands were minimum wage laws, public guarantee of low-cost housing, and compulsory social insurance. When society assured to all persons the minimum of comfort and welfare, then — and only then — could social workers temper and supplement justice with charity.

By and large reforming Catholics approved the crusade for protective legislation, especially the minimum wage laws, deemed essential to the realization of the "living wage" program of Popes Leo XIII and Pius X. They took exception, however, to the excessive emphasis on environment which undoubtedly motivated many champions of human welfare. In some attempts to stamp out

[5] A. I. Abell, "Labor Legislation in the United States: The Background and Growth of the Newer Trends," *Review of Politics*, X (January 1948), 35–60.
[6] *Proceedings, 1912*, 376–436.

evils, notably prostitution, the theory was advanced that sin and virtue were caused by low and high wages respectively. While devoted to the reform cause, the *Catholic World*, Paulist monthly, never tired of attacking the "insolent" proceedings of the various public and private social vice investigating committees which it charged with undermining the sense of personal accountability in the moral realm.[7] Catholics also regretted the growing secularist outlook which was to find one of its expressions in a campaign against religious charities, particularly child-caring institutions.[8]

But the environmental extremism most offensive to Catholics was socialism, with which they were preoccupied during the whole of the Progressive era. In America during this period international socialism ceased to be the exclusive possession of doctrinaire Marxian immigrants and took on the form of a nationally orientated political movement of great potential strength. Under prodding from Eugene V. Debs, Victor L. Berger, Morris Hillquit and their followers, the principal Socialist factions coalesced in 1901 into the Socialist party of America, "a broad political organization representing all shades of leftist conviction." [9] Its revolutionary aim — the establishment of a co-operative commonwealth — the new party planned to attain by peaceful and evolutionary means, pinning its faith on political and parliamentary action. Confident of eventual success, these Socialists boldly challenged the older parties at the polls. Unable to score in the Electoral College — although presidential candidate Debs rolled up nearly nine hundred thousand votes in 1912 — the party elected more than a thousand local officials, including

[7] "With Our Readers," XCVII (April 1913), 142–43; ibid., XCVIII (March 1914), 851–52; ibid., C (February 1915), 715–16. See also "Vice Investigation That Begins Wrongly," *Extension Magazine*, VII (May 1913), 4; James Fitzgerald, "The Wage Question and the Catholic Girl," ibid., XI (June 1916), 16, 37.

[8] "Studies and Conferences," *Ecclesiastical Review*, XL (June 1909), 756–62; John O'Grady, "State Aid to Catholic Institutions," ibid., LIII (November 1915), 501–7; John J. Dunn, "The New York Charities Investigation: A Campaign of Calumny — What's Behind It All?" *Extension Magazine*, XI (August 1916), 26; George Eisenbacker, "The Social Problem of the Dependent Child," ibid. (October 1916), 19, 33; Robert Briggs, "The Policy and Practice of Catholic Institutions in Receiving, Caring for and Discharging Children," *St. Vincent de Paul Quarterly*, XXI (November 1916), 314–21.

[9] David A. Shannon, *The Socialist Party of America: A History* (New York, 1955), p. 6.

two congressmen and mayors of Milwaukee and several lesser cities.

Not all supporters of the Socialist party wished really to destroy capitalism. They were for the most part reformers who voted Socialist in order to rebuke the old parties for failing to speed up the Progressive program. Before 1911, it is to be remembered, few remedial laws were enacted by the various state legislatures. By voting for Socialist candidates impatient reformers drawn largely from middle-class and trade union intellectuals hoped to get the Progressive movement off dead center. At an early date the Western Federation of Miners and the United Brewery Workmen, along with several lesser unions, endorsed socialism. Radicals with waning faith in political action launched in 1905 the Industrial Workers of the World (IWW) whose propaganda against the "wage system" by means of sensational strikes, picturesque "free speech" encounters with the police, sabotage, and other "direct action" techniques, aroused no little class consciousness among low-paid, exploited workers — immigrants in Eastern cities as well as farm hands, miners, and lumberjacks in the Far West.

Although the IWW and the Socialist party were bitterly opposed by the ruling groups in the American Federation of Labor, Socialist-orientated class feeling, though not doctrinaire Marxism, grew steadily among trade unionists of the rank and file. Chiefly responsible was the renewal on the industrial front and in the courts of the "open shop" campaign which greatly impaired the ability of workers to secure their ends through trade agreements and collective bargaining. Unable to win a satisfactory enlargement of constitutionalism in industry, workers in the Progressive period "increasingly responded to the gospel of socialism, especially in its milder versions," concludes Professor Philip Taft from the perspective of history.[10] As they observed their scene, some Progressives were no doubt unduly impressed by the Socialist impact. One of these, economist John Curtis Kennedy, wrote in 1907 that "the day of business unionism is rapidly passing." He pointed out that the trade unions "are becoming more class-conscious, they are going into politics, and they are beginning to demand collective ownership and management of capital." He did not think it rash to predict that "in the course of a few years the situation now prevailing in

[10] *The A.F. of L. in the Time of Gompers* (New York, 1957), 255.

Wisconsin will become general throughout the United States: 'The trade-union movement will be the economic wing, and the Socialist Party the political wing of the labor movement.' " [11]

In striving to make this prediction a reality, the Socialist party was anxious to isolate its economic program from unpopular causes of a cultural and theological character. In questions involving the merits or demerits of free love and theism, the party had no interest, its leading spokesmen affirmed. "The Socialist Party is primarily an economic and political movement," read its platform of 1908. "It is not concerned with matters of religious belief." This pronouncement mirrored the views of the Christian Socialist Fellowship, an organization formed in 1906 by left-wing Protestant ministers who firmly insisted that "the Socialist party stands for economic and in no sense whatever for religious or anti-religious propaganda." [12] Noting that these Christians stood for "straight, uncompromising socialism," John Spargo contended that the Socialist movement had entered a new phase: it had thrown off its earlier associations with atheism and crude materialism. "When," he concluded,

> a bishop of the Protestant Episcopal church in America can carry the red card of membership in the socialist party, and when, as at the last convention in Chicago, delegates to the national convention of the socialist party, as loyal Catholics, without any shame or apology to any of their comrades, can go directly from mass to the work of shaping the policy of the socialist party, it is obvious that we are in the presence of a new socialism of a quality and temper undreamed of by Marx and Engels. [13]

As if not to be outdistanced by their Protestant "comrades," the Catholic Socialists of Chicago organized in 1909 a Catholic Socialist Society in close though unofficial affiliation with the Socialist party and the Christian Socialist Fellowship. Within five years, predicted *Wilshire's Magazine* (Socialist), "the Socialist movement

---

[11] "Socialistic Tendencies in American Trade Unions," *Journal of Political Economy*, XV (October 1907), 487–88.

[12] Eliot White, "The Christian Socialist Fellowship," *Arena*, XLI (February 1909), 47.

[13] "Christian Socialism in America," *American Journal of Sociology*, XV (July 1909), 20. See also his *The Spiritual Significance of Modern Socialism* (New York, 1908), reviewed at length in B. O. Flowers, "Socialism as a Philosophy of Practical Idealism," *Arena*, XLI (February 1909), 91–99.

within the Catholic Church . . . will be one of the great forces of the Socialist party." [14] While this prophecy failed to materialize, some Catholics were drawn into the movement, acquiescing in Socialist propaganda in the trade unions, joining the Socialist party, and supporting its candidates for public office. In some predominantly Catholic communities Socialists scored electoral triumphs in the face of direct opposition from the Church authorities. Studiously refraining from attacking the Catholic religion, these successful candidates promised Catholics an improvement of their material interests — "more of the product of their hands, shorter hours and better conditions, *here and now*." [15]

The relatively few Catholics who voted Socialist were no doubt variously motivated. In the opinion of some observers, these Catholics preferred Marx to the Great Galilean. "Are they good Catholics? Are they Catholics at all?" queried the economically conservative New York *Independent* of the Polish Catholics who helped sweep the Milwaukee Socialists to victory in the 1910 elections.[16] If Catholic leaders asked the same questions, at least some of them answered that most Catholic Socialists did not want a co-operative commonwealth but economic reforms which in no sense conflicted with faith or morals. Catholics desiring economic socialism lacked clerical leadership and support. The two priests, Thomas J. Hagerty and Thomas McGrady, who were prominent in the Socialist movement early in the century, lacked the necessary patience and tact to win ecclesiastical approval for their cause. Hagerty was more interested in defending left-wing unionism than in performing his pastoral duties in the Chicago, Dallas, and Santa Fe jurisdictions, while in the same years, 1895–1902, McGrady, pastor of St. Anthony's Church in Bellevue, Kentucky, expounded socialism with surpassing eloquence in lecture tours to all parts of the country. In 1902 Hagerty gave up his clerical assignment to become editor, in Chicago, of the *Voice of Labor*, organ of the American Labor Union, an agency through which the battle-scarred Western Federation of miners sought to spread industrial unionism of the Socialist type.

[14] Quoted in *Catholic Fortnightly Review*, XVI (July 1, 1909), 402.

[15] Fred D. Warren, *The Catholic Church and Socialism* (Girard, Kan., 1914), 7.

[16] "Editorial," April 14, 1910; for comment, see M. Kenny, S.J., "Catholics and Socialists," May 7, 1910, and "What Socialism Is and What It Is Not," *La Verita*, July 16, 1910.

Hagerty was one of the seven men who prepared the groundwork for the organization in 1905 of the IWW, whose confidence and support he was to enjoy to the end.

Unlike Hagerty, McGrady was not closely identified with radical unionism. Yet Catholic workingmen coming under the spell of his eloquence were, in the words of George Rybrook, Premonstratensian and brilliant philosopher, "just crazy about him," lending a ready ear to his teaching: "If we had a just economic system, the laborer could have all the luxuries for two hours' work a day." [17] Although in common with many Americans McGrady feared that the growing discontent would terminate in bloody revolt,[18] he deplored violence, pointing out that socialism, as taught in America, advocated "the gradual absorption of industries by the government" through constitutional amendment.[19] "If here and there some dull-witted Socialist, made sullen by poverty and pain, cries out for vengeance, his violence," McGrady contended, "is no more to be attributed to Socialism than the savage cruelty of a Torquemada is to be imputed to Catholicism." Nor did socialism "beget Atheism any more than chemistry begets infidelity." The early Fathers of the Church "were, as a rule, Socialists," he believed, "and they showed no tendencies toward Atheism." [20]

Although he claimed that socialism was an economic science, not a religious creed, he was not content to discuss economic issues only; he associated free thought with socialism, openly praising Darwin, Zola, Renan, and other anti-theistic writers. By so doing he played into the hands of his religious superior, Bishop Camillus P. Maes of Covington, who was less tolerant of modernist thought than of socialism, and called for a public retraction. Against the advice of Socialist friends who wanted him to remain in the Church, McGrady refused to meet the bishop's demands, which implied, he reasoned, that "a Catholic would be guilty of heresy if he praised the Declaration of Independence which," he wrongly thought, "was

[17] "The McGrady Scandal," *Review*, VIII (November 21, 1901), 538–39.

[18] "A Singular Catholic Volume," *Midland Review*, IV (June 8, 1899), 6–7.

[19] "What Is Socialism?" *Christian Socialist*, II (August 15, 1905), 5.

[20] "To the Rev. L. W. Mulhane, Literary Editor of *The Catholic Columbian*, Columbus, Ohio," *Wilshire's Magazine*, No. 41 (November 1901), 12–14.

written by an infidel." [21] On McGrady's death five years later (in 1907), the widely read Socialist journal, *The Appeal to Reason*, stated that the ex-priest acted unwisely in voluntarily leaving the Church. He should have remained in the Church, preaching "the truth as he understood it, with patience and love, as long as the hierarchy would permit." Perhaps he could have escaped expulsion; if not, he "could have made his trial a magnificent opportunity for effective propaganda." [22] The feeling that McGrady had let down the cause, along with envy of his ability and success, explains why some Socialists portrayed him as a "sky pilot," "grafter," and "fakir." Envious Socialists, as his friend Debs observed, had hounded McGrady, an "absolutely honest man," into a "premature grave." [23]

In his disillusionment with socialism McGrady conceded shortly before his death that the Catholic Church favored social reform. "She preaches justice to all," he wrote. While she defends the right of private property in the instruments of production and distribution, at the same time "she denounces the trusts and the illegitimate acquisition of wealth and sanctions the unions, and thereby gains the confidence and esteem of the middle class and the army of toilers." [24] Similarly "A Leading Socialist," also once Catholic, noted that the Catholic Church through Irish workers had become closely affiliated with labor unionism.[25] The popular strength derived by the Church from this relationship would be jeopardized by the advance of socialism, especially in view of its equivocal stand on revealed religion. The leading Catholic student of American socialism, the Reverend William J. Kerby, professor of sociology at the Catholic University of America, generalized Progressive Catholic opinion on this issue.[26] The Catholic Church must oppose social-

[21] "Father McGrady Resigns," ibid., No. 54 (January, 1903), 34–37.
[22] "The Catholic Church and Socialism," *Christian Socialist*, V (February 1, 1908), 4.
[23] "Rev. Father Thomas McGrady, A Glowing Tribute by Eugene V. Debs," ibid., V (January 1, 1908), 2–3.
[24] "The Catholic Church and Socialism," *Arena*, XXXVIII (July 1907), 27.
[25] "Why the Catholic Church Opposes Socialism," ibid., XXXVII (May, 1907), 523–24.
[26] See his penetrating analysis "Socialism," *Dolphin*, IV–V (November, December 1903; January, February, March 1904), 513–21, 674–88; 50–61, 134–45, 269–78.

ism, he stated in 1904, "for it is a menace, immediately, to our institutions, and remotely to our faith." [27]

Kerby reported that many American Socialists, perhaps a majority, expected religion and marriage to continue undisturbed in the future co-operative commonwealth. But the doctrinaire Marxists, teaching "a philosophy, not a voluntary policy," were less reassuring, not knowing or claiming not to know "what the future will bring" concerning marriage, family, and Church.[28] Kerby discovered that many Socialist leaders and a considerable portion of the party press "are atheistic and that a theory of economic determinism, which logically destroys religion, is widely accepted. But," he hastened to add, "this theory is not logically worked out in many minds." [29] To John A. Ryan the American Socialist movement seemed "to be largely if not predominantly anti-Christian." [30] If perhaps "many of the socialist leaders are not hostile, but merely indifferent to religion," the fact remains, he said, "that a vast number of them conduct their propaganda in such a way as to identify socialism with irreligion." [31] Kerby's and Ryan's comments may have been based partly on the experience and testimony of two brilliant New England ex-Socialists, David Goldstein and Mrs. Martha Moore Avery, the former a trade unionist and the latter a middle-class intellectual. On the refusal of the Socialist party in Massachusetts in 1902 to adopt their resolution repudiating atheism and free love, they withdrew from the party, joined the Catholic Church, and entered actively into the anti-Socialist crusade. In their book, *Socialism: The Nation of Fatherless Children* (Boston, 1903), they quoted Socialist writers from Marx to Spargo to show that the movement aimed to abolish not only capitalism but all existing institutions, including Christian marriage.[32]

[27] "Socialism," *The Washington Conference, Being the Mind of the Missionaries Associated with the Non-Catholic Mission Movement in the United States* (Washington, D.C., 1904), p. 173.

[28] "Socialism," *Dolphin*, IV (December 1903), 678–79.

[29] Ibid., p. 683.

[30] Quoted from *Catholic Review of Pedagogy*, I, 261, by An American Priest of Dutch Birth [presumably George Rybrook], "The Anti-Strike Laws and the Recent Social Crisis in Holland," *Review*, X (May 28, 1903), 333.

[31] "A Catholic View of Socialism by a Catholic Priest" [Unmistakably Ryan's literary style], *New Century*, March 22, 1902.

[32] Pp. vii-x, 1–7, 244–96.

Social liberals among Catholics agreed with Father Kerby that few Catholic workingmen were "inclined to Socialism, even in its purely economic form," [33] but that many would embrace it if genuine reforms were not forthwith instituted, and try at the same time to retain their Christian faith.[34] Actually, as Kerby saw it, social reform was the only effective defense against the Socialist crusade. Arguments against it, though true, were wasted on the masses, who made "comfort and contentment" their test of "democratic institutions." [35] In the absence of "practical reform work" resolutions against socialism availed little and were unworthy of priests who expected "to direct public opinion." If they should look upon socialism as the arbitrary creation of lawless men or as chiefly a form of atheism, they would be guilty of inexcusable error. For socialism stemmed from the despair induced by corrupt government, dishonest and inhumane industry, and the inordinate power of wealth. "You may say that Socialists are lazy, or idle, or intemperate, or vicious. I care not," he stated. "I wish to insist mainly on this point: that Socialism is an effect, natural, necessary, unavoidable in present historical circumstances." Priests should "take hold of the conditions which produce it." Nor did he fail to remind them that in the encyclical *Rerum novarum*, Pope Leo "gives to Socialism only secondary attention, while the main force of that splendid document is directed to reform." [36]

In similar vein wrote William Stang, scholarly bishop of Fall River, Massachusetts, and a leading figure in the American Catholic Missionary Union which Father Walter Elliott had launched in 1896 to sponsor missions to non-Catholics. Only a few American Catholics had "joined the ranks of real Socialists," Stang consolingly reported in his book, *Socialism and Christianity* (New York, 1905), an excellent commentary on the history of the Catholic social movement and Leo XIII's labor encyclical. Nevertheless, he was distressed to find that "some of our Catholic workingmen unconsciously have imbibed principles and opinions on civil authority, property, individual rights, which would hardly bear the test of orthodoxy." [37]

[33] "Socialism," *Dolphin*, V (January 1904), 60.
[34] Ibid., (February 1904), 141.
[35] Ibid., p. 145.
[36] "Socialism," *The Washington Conference* . . . , pp. 172–74.
[37] Pp. 140–41.

Aside from more genuine religion, morality, and honesty, he pinned his faith on social reform to check socialism. In the manner of the typical Progressive, he attributed to corrupt politics the country's backwardness in labor legislation, which was the crying need of the hour. "A sound insurance system, indemnifying not only against accidents, but against reverses of life, such as sickness, loss of work, old age, would give the laboring classes," he thought, "what at the present time they need the most, security of existence, and would keep them from drifting into Socialism." [38] The Fall River bishop favored a limited amount of public ownership along with effective trade unionism making use of apprentice limitation and the primary boycott.[39]

Less optimistic and liberal was Stang's fellow worker, Paulist missionary William S. Kress, who headed the Mission Band in Cleveland, one of the major units in the American Catholic Missionary Union. The union included lapsed Catholics within the scope of its work, and in the course of conducting a religious census in Cleveland, Kress and his helpers discovered in Irish and German Catholic neighborhoods a degree of "leakage" which they regarded as "not only disquieting but absolutely alarming." [40] Suspecting that social discontent was the cause, the Mission Band in the spring of 1903 instituted a series of lectures which considered several relevant topics in the light of Leo XIII's labor encyclical, namely, social ills, socialism's remedy, the single-tax remedy, the trade union remedy, Christianity's remedy, the living wage, and strikes and state intervention.[41] Noting that the audiences were most interested in socialism, Kress had recourse to the question-box technique. To the queries of both Catholic and non-Catholic Socialists, he essayed the laborious task of framing satisfactory answers. In 1905 he published these questions and answers in a booklet entitled *Questions of Socialists and Their Answers* which the *Ecclesiastical Review* pronounced the most "appropriate response to captious critics" since Father Lambert's reply to Ingersoll.[42]

[38] Ibid., p. 70.
[39] Ibid., pp. 49–53, 66–68.
[40] "Editorial Notes," *Catholic World*, LXXIV (December 1901), 414.
[41] W. S. Kress, "Fighting Socialism," *Ecclesiastical Review*, XXX (March 1904), 309–14.
[42] "Criticisms and Notes," XXXIV (February 1906), 214; "Literary Chat," ibid., XXXIX (December 1908), 724.

Kress was disturbed to find many Catholics who believed that "every one who opposes Socialism is not a friend of the working-men." For this reason Catholics who ordinarily were deferential and submissive to ecclesiastical authority questioned the priest's right "to say what is false or true, right or wrong." They had dared him to a debate with them. They had attacked him in the press, "once by means of a scurrilous circular, more times by the modern medium of the telephone. . . . " Kress referred to the Sicilian women in Colorado, one of whom had recently cut off a priest's ear with a cleaver because he dared challenge their opinions regarding the current coal strike. In the pages of the *New Nation* a Catholic Socialist had just repelled the Jesuit Thomas E. Sherman's charge that Socialists meant to steal "with the naïve remark that Socialists will do only what is lawful; for when they confiscate property it will be in obedience to laws passed by a majority." Kress held out a ray of hope in his observations that not all who called themselves Socialists were Socialists in reality and that "only too often the evils they aim to correct have a very real existence." [43]

Some Catholics were even less hopeful than Kress that working-men would distinguish between Socialists and morally permissible reform. The remarkable advance in trade unionism at the turn of the century was viewed by various German Catholic spokesmen as synonymous with the march of "socialism and anarchy." Asserting that the "labor unions are all based on the principles of socialism," the Green Bay bishop (later Archbishop of Milwaukee), Sebastian G. Messmer, predicted that the "day is fast coming when the question whether" Catholic workingmen "may consistently join labor unions will have to be answered in the negative." [44] Among German-American Catholics the suggestion in the second Cahensly Memorial that Catholics organize trade unions of their own took on a new lease of life as Socialist propaganda gained the upper hand in several national unions having a large minority of Catholic workers. In one of these, the United Brewery Workmen, the Buffalo, New York, local forced its membership, largely German Catholic, to subscribe to its organ, the *Arbeiterzeitung*, which was violently revolutionary and anti-Christian in character, attempting also

[43] "The Apostolate in Relation to Public Questions," *The Washington Conference* . . . , pp. 166–71.

[44] "Points of View," *New Century*, June 18, 1904.

to boycott opposing newspapers and to drive them from the workers' homes. Vehemently, the German Catholic daily, the *Volksfreund*, fought back; Buffalo Catholics mobilized and brought the controversy to the attention of the whole country. In an Open Letter, early in 1902, Bishop James E. Quigley (later Archbishop of Chicago) roundly denounced Social Democracy, a "recent importation from Continental Europe," as a movement marked "by unbelief, hostility to religion and hatred of the Catholic Church." Urging study and support of *Rerum novarum*, Quigley declared that, while a Catholic could be a good union man, no Catholic could be a Social Democrat.[45]

He did not, as Socialists claimed and extremist Catholics wished, favor the formation of Catholic trade unions. "We do not tell you to leave the unions," he informed Catholic workingmen in no uncertain terms. "The enemies of religion and society would be glad if you were out," he explained, for then they "could ply their nefarious business unchallenged. We want you to stay there to guard the unions against the influence of the enemies of Christian labor." [46] Most Catholics echoed Quigley's sentiments, holding that the labor unions of the country were "conducted on a Christian basis" as laid down by Cardinal Gibbons and Pope Leo XIII. No greater service could be rendered the Church, wrote Professor Charles Rivier of St. Bernard's Seminary in Rochester, New York, "than to give up that uncompromising tendency of which the plan of purely 'Catholic labor unions' is but another and, alas! a too significant example." [47] Even Arthur Preuss, a strong advocate of Catholic labor unions,[48] conceded that Catholics might rightly belong to secular labor unions "that are not in opposition to Catholic teaching." These were competent to adjust wages and to improve economic conditions. But supplementary Catholic labor unions or associations were "the only means," he argued, to make the secular

[45] "Social Democracy: Bishop Quigley Strongly Condemns It," *Northwestern Chronicle*, March 8, 1902; "For a Catholic Social Movement," *Review*, IX (No. 11, 1902), 167–69; Rev. W. Thurston Brown, "Socialism and the Church," *Wilshire's Magazine*, No. 46 (May 1902), 37–47.

[46] "Catholic Labor Unions," *Review*, IX (No. 21, 1902), 330–31.

[47] "Labor Unions Once More," ibid. (July 10, 1902), 417–20.

[48] "On the Necessity of Catholic Labor Unions," ibid. (February 13, 1902), 81–83.

ones "a leaven fit to regenerate the working classes and effectively ward off Socialism." [49]

While this strategy, as outlined by Preuss, was popular in German Catholic circles, only a handful of Catholic workingmen associations were actually formed — and these mostly on a parish basis. More direct attempts to soften the impact of labor unionism on Catholic workingmen also largely failed. In Milwaukee the local Catholic Federation as late as 1904 included in its proposed resolutions against socialism a clause on "ways and means to protect non-union workingmen." The clause was dropped on protest from delegates who were also trade unionists, one of whom strongly insisted that "the question of union and non-union is entirely outside the sphere of this organization . . . does not form part of the question of Socialism. If we are going to fight Socialism, let us," he suggested, "fight Socialism and not the Unions," which would not in his opinion stand dictation from an organization like the federation.[50]

These were also the sentiments of all Catholic social liberals, whose most authenic mouthpiece was Humphrey J. Desmond in his newspaper chain. In a manner reminiscent of Cardinal Gibbons' memorial on the Knights of Labor, Desmond insisted that it was "unwise and useless" for the Church or Catholic societies to "interfere in all the details of the industrial conflict." The task of repressing violence and illegal acts in the course of strikes was by and large well handled by the courts and the labor leaders, notably John Mitchell. Predicting that labor itself would "find its own Moses," the editor suggested that "the useful practical expedients are apt to come, not from men trained in seminaries, but from men close to the working conditions, and grappling with all the complex actualities of the great modern industrial problem." [51] The Church would act wisely if it maintained a sympathetic attitude toward Catholics in unions to the extent even of tolerating their efforts to eliminate the "scab" worker.

On this issue many Catholic leaders took a socially liberal position: the veteran defender of labor organization, Archbishop Ire-

[49] "Catholic Labor Unions," loc. cit.
[50] "Don't Antagonize Labor," *New Century*, June 11, 1904.
[51] "Facing a Problem," ibid., June 21, 1906.

land, upheld the right of unions to use moral suasion, though not physical violence, on non-union workingmen. He was conservative in the sense that he opposed further extensions of public ownership. "Let all be on guard," he warned. "Common ownership in one direction leads readily to common ownership in another — all the more so," he added, "when the purpose really held in mind is to grasp wealth without much personal effort, to despoil others to make up for one's own deficiencies." [52] Not all Catholics, certainly, shared the archbishop's view that the adoption of moderate forms of socialism must terminate in total socialization. "Obviously, we know how to distinguish," wrote the *New Century*, in its comments on Catholic Edward F. Dunne's election as Mayor of Chicago in 1905 on a platform calling for municipal ownership of the city's railways. Dubbed "the socialistic candidate for mayor" by conservative interests, Dunne was nevertheless elected, largely by Catholic voters, who failed to perceive anything "in the encyclical *Rerum novarum* which inhibits an Amercian city from buying a street car." [53] Noting that not all forms of socialism were "anti-Christian, anti-family, anti-property, and anti-justice," John A. Ryan believed that "the moderate Socialism that has obtained a strong foothold among the labor publicists of the United States" is "not necessarily wrong if it can be made practicable." Inasmuch as socialism demanded the abolition of private property in capital goods, but not necessarily in consumer goods, the problem was to guarantee men the secure possession of the latter. If that were done, they might forgo private property in capital goods without endangering their livelihood and freedom.[54] Yet in his widely hailed study, *A Living Wage* (New York, 1906), Ryan ignored socialism except in a footnote to exclude it from the methods of state activity which in addition to private activity were necessary to actualize the minimum wage principle.

If, for the most part, the social liberals did not esteem even moderate socialism to be necessary or practicable, they conditionally approved it in order to emphasize the dire need of less radical re-

[52] "The Social Unrest as Archbishop Ireland Sees It," *Independent*, December 13, 1906.

[53] "A Socialistic Mayor," *New Century*, April 22, 1905.

[54] "A Catholic View of Socialism. By a Catholic Priest," loc. cit., *"The Union and Times* vs. A Catholic Priest," ibid., April 19, 1902.

forms. They noted with regret that many fellow Catholics crusading against socialism were silent on other evils — uncontrolled trusts, railway rebating, food adulteration, the stealing of public lands, the looting of insurance funds, and political corruption. "What we want," wrote the *New Century*, "is evenhanded justice — the rich sinner and the poor sinner held up as equally in the wrong." The journal suggested that trusts "constitute a kind of moral evil and social injustice which ought to be rapped from the pulpit equally as hard and equally as often as Socialism."[55] The *New Century* directed much of its fire against the rapidly growing American Federation of Catholic Societies. This organization, it was said, minimized reform while fulminating against anarchy, socialism, and liberalism and wasting its energies airing Catholic "grievances," high among which were alleged unfairness toward parochial schools and unjust treatment of Catholics in the overseas possessions. The rabidly Americanist newspapers in the Desmond chain charged that the federation was dominated by neo-Cahenslyites in the Central Verein. "The Central Verein meets first," as the *New Century* pointed out; "and the resolutions it adopts are afterwards translated into English and then passed by Catholic Federation."[56]

In Desmond's view — which was widely shared — crusading against socialism ought not to have priority over urban mission work for the spiritual and social welfare of the Catholic masses.[57] These were drawn largely from the so-called "new immigrants" flooding the country at an average rate of over a half million a year by the early twentieth century. Unskilled, largely illiterate, and desperately poor, the new immigrants were also in marked degree spiritually destitute. Many of the newcomers, notably the Italians, refused the ministrations of immigrant priests, suspecting, among other things, that these men were more interested in money than in souls. In order to provide acceptable clergy, American bishops increasingly sent seminarians and newly ordained priests to Europe to acquire familiarity with the languages and customs of the lands sending immigrants in large numbers. On their return home these priests either manned

[55] "Even-Handed Justice," June 4, 1904; "A Supposed Case," ibid., June 30, 1906.

[56] "Do We Want a Catholic Party in Politics?" June 18, 1904; "History 'As She Is Wrote,'" ibid., November 3, 1906.

[57] "Saving Society," ibid., August 25, 1906.

new churches and missions in urban immigrant colonies or assisted in older English-speaking parishes within whose boundaries new immigrants had penetrated.[58] By 1907 a parish of this kind in the Hartford diocese dispensed religion in ten languages.[59] Although this was a wise method of clergy recruitment, it did not in itself solve the immigrant religious problem. Early in the century the Jesuit magazine, the *Messenger of the Sacred Heart,* published Thomas F. Meehan's statistical studies which showed that only a handful of the nearly four hundred thousand Italians in New York City was reached by the Catholic parishes while Protestants were scoring impressive gains through the humanitarian adjuncts attached to their churches and missions. "It is evident," commented the *New Century,* "that the Protestant denominations are drawing very large numbers of the Italian children from the Church by methods with which we Catholics have made no attempt to compete." [60]

The better to assure to new immigrants the blessings of religion, Catholics, it was now argued, must broaden the base of their manifold charities. These had served mainly the helpless members of society, the orphaned, the sick, the aged, and the dying; the time had come to serve more intently the unprivileged masses — persons and families who with proper training and counsel would be able to take care of themselves. More than reformatories for incorrigible boys, houses of the Good Shepherd, asylums for the feeble-minded, "and a dozen other classifications of Catholic charity" — "end houses," as Desmond called them — society needed "half-way houses" of prevention and rehabilitation, such as temperance and fraternal societies, young men's clubs, homes for working girls and women, employment bureaus, and social settlements in the tenement districts.[61] Always the militant reformer, Miss M. T. Elder also called upon

[58] Marshall I. Boarman, S.J., quoted in "Catholicity in the West," *ibid.,* September 16, 1905.

[59] J. T. Roche, "From the Front," *Extension Magazine,* I (January, February, March 1907), 14–15; same author, "A Practical Solution of the Immigrant Problem," *ibid.,* I (May 1907), 10.

[60] "What of the Italians?" March 28, 1903.

[61] Humphrey J. Desmond, *Chats within the Fold,* pp. 116–17; "A Broader Charity," *Northwestern Chronicle,* February 16, 1901; "Rightly Ordered Charity," *ibid.,* September 15, 1900; "To Promote — To Prevent," *New Century,* September 16, 1905; "Editorial Notes," *ibid.,* December 18, 1909.

the Church to serve living no less than dying men. After recalling that during a vicious New Orleans race riot in the summer of 1900 a priest risked his life to give absolution to a dying policeman, she queried why there should be "heroic priests to console the men who are dying — and no priests (very few) to govern and guide the men who are very much alive!" In Catholic New Orleans three Protestant institutions — a seamen's bethel, a house for homeless men, and a rescue mission — "were concerned about men — primarily young laboring men. . . . And not one Catholic institution of the kind," she exclaimed, "among the countless Catholic institutions of this much institutionalized city!" [62]

If the new requirements in social service were to be met, money and personnel must be forthcoming. One way to release Catholic resources for the new work would be for the state and local governments fully to subsidize Catholic institutions of the "pathological" type — hospitals, foundling asylums, reformatories, and homes for the indigent, the aged, and the insane.[63] The public authority failing to do this, the Church should, in Desmond's view, relinquish these charities and oblige governments to shoulder directly the enormous burden.[64] Pending a final decision on this issue, Catholics should allocate existing funds and personnel between the two kinds of charity on a rational basis. This end could be achieved through the formation of diocesan charity boards with recommendatory and supervisory powers.[65] The main task of the boards would be to persuade the sisterhoods to accept the new responsibilities. If some of them, suggested the *New Century*, "would adopt the social settlement idea, open their houses to the children of the poor in the midst of poor neighborhoods, instruct both parents and children in better methods of living, a new field of usefulness would be entered upon." [66]

[62] M. T. Elder, "Letter to Editor, July 31, 1900," *Northwestern Chronicle*, August 11, 1900; "Miss Elder's views," ibid.; "Letter to Catholic Citizen," November 10, 1900, quoted in George Zurcher, *The Apple of Discord*, pp. 492–93.

[63] Desmond, *Chats within the Fold*, pp. 121–22; "A Charity Question," *New Century*, October 12, 1907; "Dearth or Redundancy," ibid., May 2, 1908.

[64] "Our Charities," ibid., July 28, 1906.

[65] "Diocesan Charity Boards," ibid., November 14, 1908.

[66] "Wanted: A Social Settlement Sisterhood," August 4, 1906.

Although the problems of finance and co-ordination were important, the difficulty lay deeper: Catholics, even those with the means and the disposition to help the poor, did not fully grasp the meaning and possibilities of the social settlement idea. In their view, as an anonymous student of the question reported, the social settlement was not a social reform center, only a new technique, "another agency in the Church through which pious and unsophisticated young Catholics can work off their youthful zest and energy, and get some experience in practical charity." Not even educated Catholics saw in settlement work a religious vocation demanding more self-sacrifice than either almsgiving or the seclusion of the cloister.[67]

To some extent, these misconceptions were removed through organized missionary effort. Two groups, the American Catholic Missionary Union and the Church Extension Society, directed attention to the home mission field. As previously noted, the American Catholic Missionary Union was formed in the mid-1890s to promote missions to non-Catholics and was viewed approvingly by Leo XIII as a substitute for parliaments of religion. The union grew steadily, having by 1908 thirty diocesan mission bands or apostolates whose members had conducted nearly five thousand missions. A third of the union's work was aimed mainly at Catholics in country districts of the South and West too poor to supply their own religious needs. Among the able leaders were the Paulists, Walter Elliott, the founder Alexander P. Doyle, and William S. Kress, and the bishops-to-be, Joseph S. Busch, Thomas F. Cusack, and William Stang. In a convention at Winchester, Tennessee, in 1901,[68] these men and their close associates took steps to set up a Mission House for Home and Colored Missions to prepare young priests, as Stang reported, "for their diocesan apostolates or as volunteers for the missions of the South or West." [69] The Apostolic Mission House, located on the grounds of the Catholic University, opened its doors

[67] "Educated Catholics and the 'Social Settlement' Question," *Dolphin,* VI (December 1904), 703–5.

[68] William L. Sullivan, C.S.P., "The Winchester Conference of Missionaries to Non-Catholics," *Catholic World,* LXXIV (October 1901), 90–96; William Stang, "The First National Congress of Missionaries to Non-Catholics," *American Ecclesiastical Review,* XXV (October 1901), 331–38.

[69] "The Proposed Seminary for the Home and Colored Missions," ibid., XXVI (January 1902), 75–77.

in the spring of 1904.[70] In the hope of convincing Protestants that the Catholic Church was not tied up with "the saloon and low politics," the union continued to stress the social virtues as well as Catholic doctrine in its integral fullness.[71]

The Church Extension Society was founded in 1905 by a small-town Michigan priest (later bishop), Francis C. Kelley, with strong backing from Archbishop Quigley of Chicago and other prelates. Kelley had discovered that Protestants attributed their strength in rural and small-town America largely to the work of their denominational home missionary and church extension societies.[72] Determined to win similar success for the Catholic Church, Father Kelley, who combined missionary zeal and business ability, raised substantial sums with which to subsidize the erection of churches among weak, scattered congregations in almost all parts of the South and West. By 1920 the society had bestowed gifts, generally of five hundred dollars, on nearly two thousand churches, more than half of the total number of new Catholic church structures erected during these years.[73] In some places, particularly where industry and mining penetrated into agricultural communities, the society's church building benefited the new immigrant.[74] The Church Extension Society expended little, if any, money on churches for urban immigrants. It emphasized, however, that as Catholics nurtured in rural churches moved cityward they would reinvigorate urban Catholicism in its unequal struggle against the mounting forces of worldliness and paganism. In line with this view Kelley surmised that Protestants would contribute more to the strengthening of Christian civilization if they should divert the money and effort spent on city missions for Catholic immigrants to the expansion of their country churches.[75]

70 Henry F. Wyman, "The New Laborers in the Vineyard," *ibid.*, XXXI (November 1904), 454–59.

71 Professor W. Robinson, "Hour to Reach the Devout New Englander," in *The Mission Movement in America, Being the Mind of the Missionaries Assembled in the Third Washington Conference at the Apostolic House* (Washington, D.C., 1906), pp. 28–31.

72 Francis Clement Kelley, *The Bishop Jots It Down* (New York, 1939), pp. 106–42; same author, *The Story of Extension* (Chicago, 1922), pp. 1–61.

73 Kelley, *The Story of Extension*, pp. 252–62.

74 B. Hilgenberg, "Echoes from the Coal Fields," *Extension Magazine*, VI (March 1912), 5–6.

75 "Protestantism's Rural Claim," *ibid.*, VII (February 1913), 3; "The Woes of the 'Country Church,'" *ibid.*, VIII (September 1913), 20, 24.

As a supplement to their main work, church extension leaders considered plans to secure a "wiser" distribution and location of the incoming population. Estimating that Catholics in search of desirable farm land numbered fifty thousand at all times, Paul P. Rhode, Auxiliary Bishop of Chicago (later Bishop of Green Bay), proposed in 1908 that a colonization agency, operating along national rather than ethnic or regional lines, be set up to serve primarily as "an informative, directive and protective bureau to the prospective Catholic settler." In this way many Catholics could be located in communities already supplied with churches and pastoral care. In Rhode's view, colonization was "a very natural, somewhat necessary adjunct of Church Extension work." Guided as it was by "an intelligent charity," the Church Extension Society "will find it preferable," sooner or later, he predicted, "to give a parish members than to give it money." [76] The Catholic Colonization Society, incorporated in July 1911, with Archbishop John J. Glennon of St. Louis as president and Archbishop Sebastian G. Messmer of Milwaukee as chairman of its executive committee, embodied the essentials of the bishop's plan.[77] Rhode believed that a colonization agency should function in the industrial as well as the agricultural field. The Association of Belgian and Netherlands Priests, formed in 1907 at the suggestion of the Reverend Charles L. Steur of Mishawaka, Indiana, covered both fields. The association's missionary band sought out and ministered to churchless Belgians and Hollanders in all parts of the country. By means of its annual guidebook, published in Flemish and Dutch, the association supplied prospective immigrants with information about cities, towns, and rural regions containing Dutch or Flemish parishes. By 1913 the association had located 134 Belgian or Dutch groups whose members it urged immigrants to augment.[78]

Although the missionary bodies stressed rural work, their conventions and publications studied the broader field as well. At its sec-

[76] "Colonization," *First American Catholic Missionary Congress, 1908* (Chicago, 1909), pp. 148–54.

[77] S. G. Messmer, "The Catholic Colonization Society, U.S.A.," *Salesianum*, VII (April 1912), 36–44.

[78] "Association of Belgian and Holland Priests," *First American Catholic Missionary Congress, 1908*, pp. 472–76; ibid., *Second American Catholic Missionary Congress, Official Report, 1913* (Chicago, 1914), pp. 270–78.

ond and third conventions, held at the Apostolic Mission House in 1904 and 1906, the Catholic Missionary Union brought into view nearly every religio-social issue facing American Catholicism in the early twentieth century. Discussion continued on a more comprehensive plane in the two magnificent missionary congresses, sponsored by the Church Extension Society, the first one in Chicago, in 1908, and the second, in Boston, in 1913. Viewed from the missionary angle, the Chicago meeting was truly, as the New York *Independent* observed, "the first assemblage of the Catholic hosts in the history of the country." [79] Inasmuch as earlier in the year Pope Pius X had removed the Catholic Church in America from the jurisdiction and tutelage of the Sacred Congregation for the Propagation of the Faith, the congress was symbolic of a growing determination among American Catholics to shoulder their full share of missionary responsibilities in the Universal Church. The frank earnestness with which specialists searched for facts and meanings in missionary situations lent weight to Father Kelley's assurance that the warnings of Miss Elder and others would no longer go unheeded. In the future Catholic lay leaders, Kelley urged, should involve themselves less in nationalist movements abroad and devote their major energies to the solution of religious and social problems at home.[80] Here, certainly was no lack of opportunities. As one cleric wagged, the Pentecostal order was no longer, "Go, teach all nations," but, "Stay, all nations are coming to you to be taught." [81]

The procedure of the missionary conventions was to discuss and evaluate the new techniques and agencies, not to list or describe them. Some exceptions were made, notably of institutions for "down-and-out" homeless men, a large part of whom were baptized Catholics. Not quite reached by parish effort or the St. Vincent de Paul Society, this class constituted perhaps "the most serious leakage in the Church in America." [82] The Catholic pioneer in this branch of rescue, William F. Downey of Washington, D.C., informed the third convention of the Catholic Missionary Union that five thou-

[79] "Two Great Meetings," December 3, 1908.

[80] "Church Extension," *First American Catholic Missionary Congress*, 1908, pp. 95–110.

[81] J. S. M. Lynch, "Introductory Remarks on Immigrant Question," ibid., p. 271.

[82] "The Most Appalling Leakage," *Missionary*, XXIII (August 1910), 12–15.

sand destitute men — unemployed, discharged prisoners, and convalescents — had received free food, clothing, and shelter at his Home of the Good Samaritan during its eleven-year history. Hundreds of these men had resumed the practice of their religion. Downey preached the lay sermon at the opening early in 1906 of the Holy Name Mission on the Bowery, whose founder was the Reverend Daniel J. Cunnion, a member of the New York diocesan mission band. Appealing to cheap lodging-house dwellers, the Holy Name Mission enjoyed the support of neighboring St. Andrew's parish and the good wishes of the Salvation Army, whose officers assured Cunnion that "if there is any power on earth to raise up these men it is the priesthood of the Catholic Church." [83] The most popular and widely known of homeless-men benefactors was the Reverend Timothy Dempsey, the colorful and dynamic pastor of St. Patrick's Church in St. Louis. Cheap lodging houses having invaded his parish by 1906, he sought to exert an uplifting influence by establishing a substitute institution, Father Dempsey's Hotel. Rooms were ten cents a night and meals from five to fifteen cents apiece. For the penniless, accommodations were free. The hotel also functioned as an employment agency. Archbishop Glennon and a generous body of laymen sustained "Father Tim" in this and other measures for the moral and social improvement of the community.[84]

As for the new immigrants, scarcely a million of the six million non-English-speaking Catholics were receiving "the blessings of religion," Roderick A. McEachen of Barton, Ohio, told the missionary conventions.[85] A multilingual missionary to Slovak and Hungarian workingmen in a vast coal mining region, McEachen employed every resource of the spoken word — the comprehensive philosophic view of the problem, the apt phrase, the quick summary of facts and trends — to depict the religious and social condition of the new immigrants. "Their very mission to America," the struggles and hardships attendant upon it, and "their all too frequent disappointment at not finding here the promised land flowing with

[83] William F. Downey, "The Apostolate among the Poor and the Dependent Classes," *The Mission Movement in America*, pp. 100–7.

[84] Harold J. McAuliffe, S.J., *Father Tim* (Milwaukee, 1944), pp. 1–76.

[85] "The Apostolate of the Immigrants," *The Mission Movement in America*, pp. 93–99; "Our Five Million Immigrants," *First American Catholic Missionary Congress, 1908*, pp. 272–77.

milk and honey makes them malcontents," McEachen contended, "and prepares their minds for socialism and its most dangerous principles." Their utopian expectations not realized, immigrants easily became embittered and concluded that all who seemingly prospered were their natural enemies — "the rich, the government, the priest, the Church, and even God." Though the immigrant was generally "honest, virtuous, strong-hearted, industrious and religious," he was misunderstood by the average American, being contemptuously styled a Dago or Bohunk and pronounced the "scum of society and a curse to the land." "He is a stranger in the House of God largely," McEachen thought, "because he has not been called thither by the tender tones of his mother tongue." He could find his language spoken in "the hotel, in the factory, in the money bank and in the saloon, but not in the Church." In consequence, the immigrant "day by day" is "becoming a castaway to the faith, infidel, anarchist, atheist, or Protestant."

In fact, non-Catholic churches, McEachen reminded his hearers, were "bending every energy" to win over the immigrants, "supporting hundreds of men and women who speak the necessary languages to labor amongst them." The methods employed by these well-supported missionaries were "logical and effective. They approach the immigrant with an act of charity, offering him something for his neediness, a coat for himself or shoes and sweet-meats for his little ones. This is often," McEachen by implication reproached his clerical brethren, "the first expression of sympathy the poor exile has experienced; his heart is moved. His children are then invited to a basket of delicacies and a chapter of Protestant teaching, and they generally go." If the immigrant was not to become a Protestant on the one hand or a firebrand of "socialism and anarchy" on the other, the American priest must become his friend, "be despised with him, share his sorrow . . . help him to bear his burdens . . . entreat him, compel him to come in" — in short, "prove that he is not a mercenary, but a good shepherd."

Although he was greatly distressed by the virtual absence of immigrant priests, McEachen did not believe that the foreign priest was best fitted to serve his countrymen in America. "Ignorant of the conditions about him, he first makes mistakes, then shortly his mistakes turn to abuses." Only American priests familiar "with the dangers and struggles of American life" and hardened "against the enticements of American gold" could save the immigrant. Those clergymen who mastered one or more of the appropriate foreign languages could render immediate help. In order to solve the problem, however, the Church should raise up a priesthood from among the immigrants in America themselves. McEachen was amazed that the colleges and seminaries failed to teach the languages which were the sole means of intercourse for more than six million Catholics. "It seems self-evident then," he concluded, "that the only true solution of the immigrant problem consists in the establishment of an institution or institutions in which young men can be trained for the priesthood, and at the same time given a thorough and practical knowledge of the language spoken by their fathers." [86] In reply to the "much esteemed" *Ave Maria*, which questioned the wisdom of "perpetuating in this country the languages of the different countries from which the converging tide of immigrants reach us," McEachen answered that he was interested only in the preservation of the languages for a few years, not in their perpetuation.[87]

Besides a multilingual clergy, McEachen pleaded for more fine churches, schools, and charitable institutions. The results achieved in "a few hundred places serve only to show," he suggested, "what should be done in thousands of cities and towns throughout the land." [88] Other speakers stressed the need for social service. At the second Missionary Congress Peter J. Muldoon, Bishop of Rockford, insisted that Catholics must "adopt in a large measure the seemingly attractive instrumentalities that the designing outside the Church are using to allure the Catholic immigrant from the Church." [89] More pointedly, Andrew Shipman, perhaps the leading Catholic authority on immigration, urged Catholics to help newcomers "to get and keep the opportunity of earning a living." Both men commented at length on the eagerness with which Protestant mission workers adopted the external forms of Catholic worship and

[86] "The Immigrant Problem — Its Solution," *Extension Magazine*, II (August 1907), 11.

[87] "The Mother Language in Religion," ibid. (December 1907), 6.

[88] "Our Five Million Immigrants," loc. cit., p. 273.

[89] "Immigration to and the Immigrants in the United States," *Second American Catholic Missionary Congress, Official Report, 1913*, pp. 132–46.

established day nurseries, clubs, and other social services to win the friendship of aspiring immigrants. "The loss to the faith," stated the precisely informed Shipman, "through the lack of such opportunities is simply incalculable." He reminded his fellow Catholics "that missionary work can be done more effectively sometimes in the indirect manner, and that the Church must supplement its direct worship and teachings by an appeal to the other qualities of men and women." Above all else, social service kept growing youth from running into evil ways and from "abandoning or becoming indifferent to the ancient faith or losing its heritage of Catholicity." [90]

Some attention was given to the social settlement movement in the missionary conventions. After urging his brethren to emphasize the urban mission field, the Reverend James B. Curry, pastor of historic St. James' parish in lower New York, pointed out that, while living wages were the basic need, the Catholic social settlement would be of great help to the crowded districts of great cities. It would put an end to the non-sectarian club, tend to encourage Catholic in place of mixed marriages, and counteract "the poor man's club," namely, the saloon.[91] The model Catholic settlement, as well as one of the earliest, was St. Rose's, opened in 1898 by Clement M. Thuente, O.P., pastor of the church of St. Catherine of Siena, in a thickly populated Italian section in the central part of New York City. From the outset this settlement was a well-equipped and wisely led institution. Besides its clubs "and other popular gatherings for the development of social life," St. Rose's had "classes in Christian doctrine for public school children and for the instruction of the ignorant and neglected, whether children or adults." For the latter, a night school offered instruction in English and the simple religious duties. Moreover, there was constant visiting in the homes of the sick and poor.[92] A similar course was followed by the other settlements, numbering twenty-five hundred by 1915, which were mostly supported and managed by Catholic settlement as-

[90] "Emigration," ibid., pp. 154–71.
[91] "Settlement Work," *First American Catholic Missionary Congress, 1908,* pp. 155–65.
[92] Laurence Franklin, "The Italian in America: What He Has Been, What He Shall Be," *Catholic World,* LXXI (April 1900), 18; *18th Annual Report of the Bureau of Labor Statistics of the State of New York, 1900,* pp. 396–98.

sociations, missionary groups, women's leagues, or other variously named lay-clerical organizations.[93]

The settlements were at great pains to make clear that they expected only to supplement, not supplant, the Catholic parish and school in needy neighborhoods. That settlement workers could do for the people in their homes what no single priest or ten priests could do "is no reflection on the old system which the settlement movement is intended to supplement and aid," explained Archbishop Patrick J. Ryan, as he approved and helped launch in 1904 the Catholic Missionary Society of Philadelphia. "The adopted system of the Church is justified by centuries of experience," he stated, "but the great and unexpected success of the settlement plan in New York shows that it should be a success here." [94] It was realized, moreover, that, apart from its religious value, the settlement helped the "ambitious poor" to surmount class barriers. "Settlement work," as Father Doyle, Paulist founder of two settlements,[95] claimed, "offers children of the less-favored classes the opportunities of lifting themselves above their station in life." [96]

Mainly, however, the Catholic settlements were founded to help the Church rehabilitate the religious faith of Italian immigrants. If they all achieved success, some attained extraordinary results. At the Angel Guardian Mission in "Little Italy," Chicago, the Reverend E. M. Dunne (later Bishop of Peoria) launched a great enterprise, the heart of which was a Sunday School Association whose 120 lay teachers, drawn from all parts of the city, instructed three thousand children and carried on "continuous social work" terminating in elaborate club features for youth of both sexes.[97] In Philadelphia

[93] John O'Grady, *Catholic Charities in the United States*, pp. 287–99. See Robert Biggs, "What We Are Doing in Settlement Work," *St. Vincent de Paul Quarterly*, XIX (November 1914), 237–45, for the list to that date.

[94] "To Aid the Neglected Italians," *New Century*, December 3, 1904.

[95] "The Paulist Temperance Club," *Catholic Review*, May 21, 1898; "Paulist New Settlement House," *Church Progress*, July 16, 1898; *18th Annual Report of the Bureau of Labor Statistics of the State of New York*, 1900, p. 409.

[96] Ibid., p. 411.

[97] Mary Berger, "Catholic Settlement Workers," *Extension Magazine*, IV (June 1909), 7–8, 27; W. H. Agnew, S.J., "Pastoral Care of Italian Children in America," *American Ecclesiastical Review*, XLVIII (March 1913), 257–67; E. M. Dunne, "Memoirs of 'Zi Pre,'" ibid., XLIX (August 1913), 192–203.

the Missionary Society, also a city-wide, predominantly lay organization, supported and operated, under professional guidance, two fully equipped settlements, Madonna House, opened in 1904, and L'Assunta House five years later, each primarily for Italians, but ultimately for all Catholic people needing aid or sympathy. The effectiveness of Madonna House was enhanced by neighboring St. Paul's School, at the settlement's disposal for catechetical and chapel purposes.[98] In 1915 Philadelphia lay folk relinquished these settlements into the hands of nuns — the Servants of the Immaculate Heart of Mary.[99]

By this date several sisterhoods were taking up the new work after the example of the Cincinnati Sisters of Charity whose Santa Maria Institute was one of the earliest and best Catholic settlements. Convert Marion F. Gurney, organizer and head worker of St. Rose's Settlement, founded a new order in 1908, the Sisters of Our Lady of Christian Doctrine, which under her direction as Mother Marianne of Jesus scored a brilliant record in settlement work on New York's lower East Side.[100] Laywomen were chiefly responsible, however, for Catholic settlement work in the years before World War I.[101] With the fortune of her deceased brother at her disposal, Annie Leary, an experienced social worker, opened in 1906 an Italian Settlement House on Charlton Street in New York City, which provided recreation and stressed the fine arts as well as the more useful ones.[102] Mary J. Workman was head worker at Brownson House in Los Angeles, while Grace O'Brien supervised a half-dozen settlements, chiefly for Italians, in Brooklyn. In the nation's capital, invalid Mary V. Merrick incorporated many settlement features into

[98] "The Madonna House in Philadelphia and Its Splendid Work among the Italians," *New Century*, February 29, 1908; John T. McNicholas, O.P., "The Need of American Priests for the Italian Missions," *Ecclesiastical Review*, XXXIX (1 December, 1908), 677–87.

[99] Edward J. Lying, "Catholic Missionary Society of Philadelphia," *Catholic Charities Review*, VI (September 1922), 236–39.

[100] Elinor Tong Dehey, *Religious Orders of Women in the United States, Catholic*, pp. 768–71.

[101] See John O'Grady, *Directory of Catholic Charities of the United States* (Washington, D.C., 1922), pp. i–iv, for the list of women's organizations.

[102] "To Teach the Italians," *New Century*, April 28, 1906; "Miss Leary's Work in New York," ibid., June 9, 1906.

the Christ Child Society which she founded in 1891 to supply Christmas toys to indigent children.[103] In 1906 Josephine Brownson of Detroit founded Weineman Settlement as part of her successful plan to mobilize public school teachers into the Catholic Instruction League to teach catechism to immigrants.[104]

In Pittsburgh the Catholic Women's League, dating from 1904, established a social service center, the De Paul Institute, raising large sums for this and other agencies of the new charity. Under the direction of "a competent salaried secretary," the league members worked through the Associated Charities, the National Consumer's League, and the National Child Labor Committee as well as supervising the new Catholic agencies. The accomplishments of the league "permit the Church," claimed Bishop Canevin, "to hold a place of honor in the social movements of the day." [105] In most urban communities, both large and small, Catholic women after 1905 formed leagues, clubs, or guilds in order to promote human welfare. Through their "chain of city-wide organizations," these women "did for the new immigrants," thinks Monsignor John O'Grady, "what the St. Vincent de Paul Society did for the older immigrants." [106] The experience gained in their various societies enabled some laywomen to participate fruitfully in the crusade for social justice. The conspicuous example was Caroline Gleason of the Catholic Women's League of Portland, Oregon. The league was formed in 1908 under the direction of Edwin V. O'Hara, who was destined as priest and bishop to exert a powerful influence on the Catholic social movement in both its urban and rural aspects. In the league's behalf Miss Gleason investigated labor conditions in Portland. Her findings led the Oregon legislature in 1913 to pass a compulsory minimum wage law for women, the first in the nation.[107]

[103] O'Grady, *Catholic Charities in the United States*, pp. 295–97, 324–26; "The Laetare Medal Awarded to Miss Mary V. Merrick, Washington, D.C.," *St. Vincent de Paul Quarterly*, XX (May 1915), 127–29; *Catholic Charities Review*, I (January 1917), 32; "The Christ Child Settlement House of St. Paul," ibid., I (March 1917), 87; "Progress of Christ Child Society," ibid., V (September 1921), 232–33.

[104] Monica Weadock Porter, *Josephine Van Dyke Brownson, Alumna* (New York, 1948).

[105] "Fine Work," *Catholic Columbian-Record*, March 21, 1913.

[106] *Catholic Charities in the United States*, p. 324.

[107] "Catholic Activity," *Extension Magazine*, V (January 1911), 4; *Catholic Charities Review*, I (January 1917), 23; J. G. Shaw, *Edwin Vincent O'Hara, American Prelate* (New York, 1957), pp. 1–62.

Women in growing numbers carried on social work as auxiliaries of the St. Vincent de Paul Society. They served mainly as volunteer helpers. In its endeavor to improve its family relief work, the society increasingly felt the need of professional assistance, male and female. The society's particular council in Baltimore pioneered the way, setting up in 1908 a central office with a salaried staff under the direction of Grace L. Wellmore.[108] If women aided the St. Vincent de Paul Society, that body in turn facilitated the work of the women's organizations, especially their efforts to attain a comprehensive view of the social service field. After repeatedly failing to form a federation of their own, the various clubs, leagues, and guilds welcomed the invitation of the St. Vincent de Paul Society to send representatives to its annual convention of 1908.[109] This joint meeting laid the foundation for the National Conference of Catholic Charities, formally organized two years later at the Catholic University of America. While leaders of the St. Vincent de Paul Society and priests eminent for their study and direction of Catholic charities formed the conference and thereafter headed it, laywomen attended the meetings (biennial until 1920) more widely than men and fruitfully participated in the discussions. At its first convention in September 1910 Grace O'Brien of the Catholic Settlement Association in Brooklyn read a valuable paper on "Social Settlements" while Mrs. P. T. Toomey, active in the St. Louis Queen's Daughters, discussed "Schools of Philanthropy." In a session of their own, "the most vital and remarkable held," the two hundred women delegates listened to the excellent paper of the Reverend P. Mueller-Simoni of Strassburg, Germany, on the work of the International Association for the Protection of Young Girls, and discussed the reports of city committees showing that low wages as well as midnight joy rides and lack of parental supervision caused moral shipwreck.[110]

The conference as a whole sounded the keynote that urban poverty and crime stemmed mainly from bad industrial conditions. Speaker after speaker called for remedial measures of a preventive character.[111] "The man or woman," stated Robert Biggs, eminent

[108] McColgan, *A Century of Charity*, II, 351–57.

[109] Ibid., pp. 294–312.

[110] William J. White, "The First National Conference of Catholic Charities," *Survey*, XXV (October 1910), 94–95.

[111] M. F. McEvoy, "First National Conference of Catholic Charities," *Salesianum*, VI (October 1910), 33–39.

Baltimore leader of the St. Vincent de Paul Society, "who has no other conception of charity work than the mere giving of material relief should stay out of the work or learn new methods. Time and thought and not almsgiving," he insisted, "are the real factors that should inspire every worker." The delegates applauded Michael F. Girten, municipal court judge of Chicago, who demanded "that the merchant prince who pays criminally low wages with one hand, while making large public subscriptions with the other, be boycotted and that a ban be placed on underpaid labor." Another speaker insisted that charity workers "must initiate or take part in movements that have for their object the material well being of the workingmen." He exhorted the delegates to take an interest in the Consumers' League, the Child Labor Committee, the anti-tuberculosis crusade, and other movements for the betterment of the poor. The platform on which the delegates stood, reported Monsignor William J. White, distinguished superintendent of Catholic charities in Brooklyn, "includes organization, co-operation, and a war on the causes of poverty whether that cause is a disease germ lurking in a dark corner or a merchant prince grown rich on defrauding laborers of their wages." [112]

On the Church's social mission these delegates, Father Kerby believed, were "nearly as progressive as Leo XIII or Pius X" — popes not behind the age but in advance of it. But the charities the delegates represented were "not as active in promoting social movements as many of the secular charities are." Catholics lacked a "vigorous, technical literature of charity" and schools for the training of leaders in charity and social movements.[113] Catholics, especially laymen, must speedily acquire more social interest and knowledge, Paulist Joseph McSorley told the delegates. The working people "will not submit much longer to the rules that now control the distribution of wealth," he argued, and Catholic laymen should be ready to guide the discontented army "along legitimate ways" and "to prevent violent revolution" by wise and just reform.[114]

All but the ignorant or indifferent recognized, as the first decade

[112] Op. cit., 93–95.
[113] "The National Conference of Catholic Charities: An Interpretation," *Catholic World*, XCII (November 1910), 145–56.
[114] "The Catholic Layman and Social Reform," ibid., 187–95.

of the present century passed into history, that social discontent was becoming dangerously prevalent. Some informed Catholics — the number is indeterminate — attributed the growing unrest mainly to Socialist agitators. Representative of this viewpoint was Father Kress of the Cleveland Apostolate, who as late as 1912 could see no valid reason for social discontent in the United States. There was little destitution "and of what there is much has been self-inflicted through shiftlessness or intemperance, or both combined." The squalor of tenement-house living was more the result of the herd instinct of recent immigrants — a moral defect in Kress's view — than of poverty, unemployment, or landlord profiteering. Kress noted that the needy could get "abundant relief" through private and public channels, that depressions were becoming rarer and milder, that occupational mobility was still a reality, and that democratic institutions could facilitate reform. "If the community at large is agreed that a correction should be made, it can make its will effective," he believed.

Yet, in spite of the steadily improving condition of the laboring classes, they were bitterly dissatisfied, "and the discontent," Kress lamented, "is being industriously fanned by Socialist agitators." [115] Not a few Catholics who saw no excuse for socialism heaped frenzied abuse on its leaders. "The Saints of Socialism," editorialized Charles J. O'Malley of the Chicago *New World*, "should be haloed with the hell-pots of seething steel," [116] while a Brooklyn priest, John L. Bedford, wrote in his parish paper that the Socialist agitator "is more dangerous than cholera or smallpox — yes, he is the mad dog of society and should be silenced, if need be, by the bullet." [117] This sort of vituperation was more likely to extend than to weaken Socialist influence among the downtrodden masses. Editor Arthur Preuss complained that "the unintelligent, brutal attitude of a portion of our Catholic press" placed "weapons" in the hands of Socialist propagandists. Not "infrequently," as the Socialists were quick to point out, Catholic newspapers upheld the "robber trusts" and suppressed "the really salient passages" in Leo XIII's labor encyclical "for fear

[115] *The Red Peril* (Cleveland, 1912), pp. 42–43.
[116] "A Great Pity," *Christian Socialist*, VII (January 1, 1910), 5.
[117] Quoted from the *Catholic Tribune* in "A Foolish Priest," *Christian Socialist*, IX (May 16, 1912), 5–6.

of offending their capitalistic readers and advertisers!" Preuss hoped that Socialist journals would keep on "ribroasting Catholic editors" until they stopped "boosting robber trusts," informed themselves "on the underlying principles of the great social question," and took "a hand in working for its practical solution." [118]

With more restraint but no less emphatically, John A. Ryan indicated that a more tolerant attitude toward the Socialist economic program would be good strategy. "If our opposition to Socialism were concentrated more upon its philosophical, religious, and revolutionary aspects, and less upon its economic features, except when these are certainly and evidently immoral, we should be more successful," he thought, "in keeping Catholics out of the movement and convincing them that the Church is not opposed to genuine and legitimate industrial reform." The "very many" American Catholics who called themselves Socialists desired the essentials of economic socialism, or semi-socialism, which did not, he believed, fall "under the condemnation of either the moral law or the Church." For socialism of this type permitted all that the moral law as expounded in Leo's encyclical called for, namely, "that the rights and opportunities of private ownership be sufficiently extensive to safeguard individual and social welfare." Socialism upheld private ownership in "stable and permanent possession" with regard to food, clothing, furniture, and all other goods of consumption. Socialism would convert only the means of production, and not all of these, into common property: it would permit the individual to own shares in co-operative industries and to enjoy the full benefit of all land improvements.[119]

A more intimate acquaintance with medieval conceptions of labor and industry would compel us "to realize," Ryan said, "that the spirit and traditions of the Church are much less favorable to the current claims and pretensions of wealth and capitalism than the uninformed reader would be likely to infer from a study of many contemporary Catholic writers" — authors who understate the amount of truth in the claims of the Socialists "and overstate the rights of property and the advantages of the present system." [120] Ryan con-

[118] "Fighting Socialism with Boomerangs," *Catholic Fortnightly Review*, XVL (November 15, 1909), 647–48.

[119] "May a Catholic Be a Socialist?" ibid. (February 1, 1909), 70–71.

[120] "Notes and Comments," *Christian Socialist*, January 5, 1911, quoting a book review by Ryan in Preuss's *Catholic Fortnightly Review*.

cluded that the Catholic "who can see no adequate remedy for present industrial ills except in some moderate form of economic Socialism, has a right to as much moral freedom as other Catholics with respect to other theories and practices." [121]

But Catholics were not morally free, Ryan insisted, to affiliate with the Socialist party of America because the movement it represented was inherently anti-religious. Editor Preuss, among others, was of the same opinion, informing Socialist John Spargo that, while many Catholics shared his economic views, "we are deterred from making common political cause with 'Socialism' because we do not feel we can trust its influence in the moral and religious field." True, Catholic timidity was "unfortunate for the cause of economic reform," but it was justified. "Tell us," Preuss asked Spargo, "if we were to put you and yours in power, would you confine your activity strictly to the economic territory, speaking no word and lifting no hand against the moral principles, doctrine truths, or religious institutions that we hold sacred?" [122] To these questions the American Socialist movement never returned satisfactory answers. The party's resolution of 1908 that socialism was "not concerned with matters of religious belief" was not accepted by Catholics at face value. They noted that in the vehement debate on the resolution the more uncompromising Socialists damned the proposal as a monstrous lie and that the plank finally carried by only one vote. Ryan not incorrectly observed that the circumstances surrounding the plank's adoption "strongly suggested that some of the members voted for the resolution solely as a matter of good tactics." [123]

If in fact most Socialists, irrespective of their personal religious views, hewed to the line of the party's official statement, several "comrades," especially those in close touch with the rural middle class, openly attacked the "Romanist political machine" in APA fashion. The leader of the anti-Catholic Socialists was J. A. Wayland, whose widely read *The Appeal to Reason*, published at Girard, Kansas, denounced Catholicism with scarcely less vigor than capitalism itself.[124] Over the protest of religiously tolerant Socialists,

[121] "May a Catholic Be a Socialist?" loc. cit.
[122] "Social Reform vs. Socialism," *Catholic Fortnightly Review*, XVII (1910), 356–57.
[123] "May a Catholic Be a Socialist?" loc. cit.
[124] "The Appeal to Reason and the Catholics," *Christian Socialist*, November 15, 1908.

notably the men and women in the Christian Socialist Fellowship, Wayland persisted in his course, shortly before his death, by his own hand, in 1912, launching the notorious *Menace*, which was forthwith recognized as the leading organ of the new Know-Nothingism.[125] The Christian Socialists also lost the "Barnes Case," involving J. Mahlon Barnes, "a proved and self-confessed adulterer," who was dismissed as national secretary of the Socialist party only to be designated Socialist campaign manager in the presidential election of 1912.[126]

These new twists to Socialist practice confirmed Catholic apprehensions and rendered co-operation between the Church and the Socialist movement more unthinkable than ever. Happily, socialism's value as a social irritant declined as old familiar agencies, including the major political parties, were pushed by public sentiment into the reform current after 1910. With social betterment in prospect, reforming Catholics spelled out the details of their own program. The Catholic workingmen did not want socialism, asserted *La Verita*, a Catholic Italo-American newspaper published in Philadelphia, but a "living wage" which "his Church declares he should have and should use all just means to acquire." [127] In his epoch-making book, *A Living Wage* (New York, 1906), John A. Ryan had demonstrated that employers were duty bound to supply workers with the necessary minimum income. He increasingly laid stress, however, on the various "indirect methods" of augmenting wages through legislative action. These included the eight-hour day; restriction on the labor of women and children; legalization of picketing, persuasion, and boycotting; conciliation and arbitration by state and national boards with compulsory powers; and relief of unemployment by state employment bureaus, labor colonies, and social insurance. Likewise provision should be made against accidents, illness, and old age. Finally the state should launch a housing program, not only condemning and preventing unsanitary housing and congestion, but erecting decent habitations for the poorer classes,

[125] "Socialists Launched the Filthy Menace," *Live Issue*, December 27, 1913; "The New Know-Nothingism," *Extension Magazine*, VII (November 1912), 3.
[126] "Editorial Comment," *Christian Socialist*, September 28, 1911; "Deep Disgrace of the Socialist Party," ibid., June 6, 1912; Shannon, *The Socialist Party of America*, pp. 69, 73–76.
[127] "The Catholic Workman and Socialism," March 5, 1910.

to be rented or sold — preferably sold — on easy conditions. Besides assuring to the laboring classes a reasonable minimum of wages and other economic goods, the state should protect the consuming public against extortionate prices. To this end, Ryan favored public ownership of natural monopolies, including mines and forests; rigid control of monopolies not based on natural advantages; progressive income and inheritance taxes; taxation of future increases in land values; and prohibition of speculation on the exchanges.[128]

Through these proposals, which anticipated the course of social legislation in the New Deal as well as the Progressive period, Ryan hoped to put the influence of the Catholic Church on the side of "economic democracy." He called attention to the fact that the broad movement for economic democracy, of which socialism was the spearhead, "shows, even in our country, a strong tendency to become secular, if not anti-Christian." Should the clergy remain unable and unwilling "to understand, appreciate, and sympathetically direct the aspirations of economic democracy, it will inevitably," he warned, "become more and more unchristian, and pervert all too rapidly a larger and larger proportion of our Catholic population." Ryan ventured the opinion in 1909 that on matters of social teaching and social works (the new philanthropy) the bishops "who have made any pronouncements . . . could probably be counted on the fingers of one hand, while the priests who have done so are not more numerous proportionately." [129]

So far as organization was concerned, the bishops and priests participating in social justice movements before World War I did not operate under the direction of the Catholic hierarchy but through laymen-led Catholic societies. Many of the major societies were loosely united in the American Federation of Catholic Societies, whose program gained steadily in positive social content. By 1907 the federation was ready to champion "social justice," as defined by Leo XIII in *Rerum novarum*, conceding now that "some of the practical demands advocated by Socialists for the betterment of the condition of workingmen are quite reasonable and just," while pointing out that "these reforms and demands have for years been

---

[128] "A Programme of Social Reform by Legislation," *Catholic World,* LXXXIX (July, August 1909), 433–44, 608–14.
[129] "The Church and the Workingman," ibid. (September 1909), 781–82.

championed by Christian economists, and are by no means the distinctive program of socialism." The federation promised to "encourage all reasonable endeavors of workingmen by organized effort to promote their moral and material well-being," and to "heartily support any legislation beneficially regulating labor hours, factory conditions etc." The federation leaders urged "upon Catholic workingmen who belong to labor unions to use their utmost efforts to protect those organizations from being used by unprincipled demagogues as instruments of political and social revolution." Alongside the regular or secular trade unions the federation recommended "the formation of Catholic workingmen's societies wherein our Catholic workingmen may be well grounded in the Christian principles of social justice, as set forth by Pope Leo XIII in his Encyclical on the Condition of Labor." [130]

In this same year, 1907, the Central Verein, not unexpectedly, also took action, appointing a committee to investigate the field of social reform and to outline a program. In its convention the next year the Verein voted to transform this committee, one of whose members was Frederick P. Kenkel, into a permanent agency of social propaganda, the expense to be borne not by a per capita assessment "but by the voluntary contributions of those who believe in the movement." In the *Catholic Universe* of Cleveland, Father Peter E. Dietz, soon to be second only to Ryan as a Catholic leader, penned interpretative comments on the Central Verein's new course of action. Its leaders now realized that in order to combat socialism, and to "have a determining influence on the progress of humanity," something more than the passing of resolutions was called for. The Central Verein did not recommend the formation of separate Catholic trade unions, as in Germany, but rather the grappling with socialism in existing unions. "Since there is danger," as Dietz explained, "that the advocates of radicalism will succeed in obtaining a parliamentary control of the labor unions, every Catholic Unionist must regard it as his sacred duty to be present at the meetings of his trade union and to represent with manly ability the Christian point of view." Workers would not be able to do this unless they "were well aware of the issues and sufficiently instructed to be a

[130] "Federation's Attitude Towards Socialism: Pronouncements at National Convention," *Catholic Columbian-Record*, December 16, 1910.

match for their opponents." For this reason the Central Verein intended to give the Catholic workingman "an adequate preparation for his vocation." [131]

The Central Verein, as the liberal *New Century* admitted, "is really digging deep for results worth having. We shall watch the sequel with interest — and sympathetically." [132] Alongside the Central Bureau for the Promotion of Social Education, headed by Kenkel, the Verein established a German-English magazine, *Central-Blatt and Social Justice*, exclusively devoted to social advancement. At its convention of 1909, the Central Verein formulated in specific terms a notably constructive program, calling especially "for the promotion of more progressive labor legislation." Calling also for the better enforcement of existing labor laws, the Verein promised to support "all legislation in the interests of the workers' health, life and limb." "We condemn child labor," one resolution read, "and acclaim every legislative provision for the physical and moral safeguarding of the young." Realizing that "under the given economic conditions woman's work in the domain of industry and general business cannot be done away with," the Verein demanded rigid regulation of such work in factories and workshops and recommended "the introduction universally of the eight-hour day for woman workers." It also decided to agitate for the abolition of all unnecessary Sunday work. In keeping with the spirit of the era's Progressivism, the Central Verein was interested also in political reform. "As there is a marked demand all over the country for improved methods of municipal government, via the Initiative, Referendum and Recall, the Commission Plan of Municipal Government . . . we recommend the thorough-going study of these new administrative measures." [133]

In order effectively to advance these many reforms, the Verein promoted social education and the labor union movement. Catholics were ineffectual in social reform, the Verein realized, because they lacked information and knowledge. Not until a large number of

---

[131] "Worth Observing," *New Century*, October 17, 1908; see Central-Vereins, *Offizieller Bericht*, 1908, pp. 19–21, and "Sociale Frage," ibid., 1910, pp. 76–77.

[132] "Worth Observing," loc. cit.

[133] "The Aftermath of the Indianapolis Convention," *Central-Blatt and Social Justice*, II (October 1909), 7–9.

Catholics came to realize and accept the Church's solution of social problems could they hope to convince the American people of its justice and wisdom. Accordingly, many local societies, under the direction of the Verein's Central Bureau, built up social libraries and established social study circles. The Verein provided scholarships for several men to study the Catholic Social movement in Germany; held in 1912 two social-study summer schools, one at Spring Bank, Wisconsin, and the other at Fordham University; and agitated for the establishment of a Catholic School of Social Science (to be called Ketteler House for Social Studies) to train the Church's leaders in the social field. This ambitious project barely failed of success and the attempt was not without influence on the universities and seminaries. The Verein's educational policy, if followed by other Catholic organizations, should within a decade, predicted John A. Ryan, provide men "able to justify Catholic opposition to both the abuses of capitalism and the excesses of Socialism" and with "the ability and the courage to defend plans of positive social reform." [134]

The Central Verein also recognized that the success it hoped for must rest upon organized labor. While conceding "that organized labor in the trade union movement has at times made mistakes," the convention of 1909 "unhesitatingly" endorsed "the right of organization" and recommended "faithful co-operation with the American Federation of Labor, guided as it is by conservatism, with the National Civic Federation, with the American Association for Labor Legislation and kindred organizations." The Verein denounced the powerful open-shop campaign as "tantamount to a denial of the workingmen's right to organize." Strategic considerations partly accounted for the sympathetic attitude of the Verein toward organized labor: "it is only with the co-operation of the laboring classes generally that we Catholics shall be able to compel the national, State and municipal authorities to adopt a rational programme of social reforms and to carry it out consistently." [135] So anxious were the leaders of the Central Verein to put the Church

[134] "Two Important Points in the Social Program of the Central Verein," *Catholic Fortnightly Review*, XVI (March 1, 1909), 130–32.
[135] "A Catholic Social Reform Movement under Way," ibid. (November 15, 1909), 642.

in the good graces of the labor movement that they formed Catholic workingmen's associations in several cities, "not in competition with the labor unions," as the *Central-Blatt and Social Justice* wrote, "but to fit the Catholic workingman for his proper sphere in the trade-union." [136]

Although the Central Verein influenced mainly Catholics of German antecedents, its social program was adopted by nearly all Catholic societies, largely because of the persistent efforts of one of its members, the Reverend Peter E. Dietz. Born in New York City in 1878 of Bavarian immigrant parents, Dietz prepared well for the priesthood and after ordination in 1904 devoted his splendid organizing talents to conforming American Catholics to the social teachings of Leo XIII. The scenes of his pastoral labors were in Ohio and Wisconsin, beginning at the Chapel of the Sacred Heart at Oberlin. Defending organized labor from the outset, he first attracted national attention through the pages of the *Central-Blatt and Social Justice*, whose English section he launched and for a short time edited. In this journalistic venture he revealed social zeal, profound knowledge of American industrial conditions, and realization of the momentous task facing his fellow Catholics. "Leadership, discipline and organization work focused steadily upon definite objects in view is business-like," he said, "and bring results. Nothing else will do." [137] Facile of speech and pen and above racial prejudice and "foreignisms," Dietz won all types of Catholics to the cause of organization for social service. Just as John A. Ryan was the academician, so Peter E. Dietz was the organizer, of the American Catholic social movement.

Convinced that the Church must establish a closer relationship with organized labor, Father Dietz discovered, as he studied the religious scene, that Protestants were evolving orderly procedures to aid workers and to reconcile them to the various churches. He was particularly impressed by the success of the recently founded social service commissions of the leading denominations and of the Federal Council of the Churches of Christ in America [138] in developing

[136] II (July 1909), 9.

[137] "The Present Outlook," ibid. (February 1910), 11–12.

[138] For an excellent account of these commissions, see Charles Howard Hopkins, *The Rise of the Social Gospel in American Protestantism, 1865–1917* (Yale Studies in Religious Education, XIV, New Haven, 1940), pp. 280–317.

a "quasi-working relation with the trade-union movement." Attending the Toronto convention of the American Federation of Labor in 1909, Dietz was told by Catholic trade union delegates that the Prostestant churches through the Reverend Charles Stelzle, fraternal delegate from the Federal Council's Commission on the Church and Social Service, "were doing a wonderful amount of good . . . and that the Catholic Church was not officially putting herself on record in the matter of the American Federation of Labor. . . ." [139] His suggestion that the American Federation of Catholic Societies, now nearing the peak of its numerical strength, send a fraternal delegate to future conventions resulted in his own designation as the official Catholic representative to the St. Louis convention of the American Federation of Labor in 1910. In his address to the assembled delegates, Dietz assured them of the Church's support of conservative trade unionism. During the convention he brought Catholic trade union officials together in a permanent organization, the Militia of Christ for Social Service.

In building up mutual understanding and sympathy between the Church's social program and that of organized labor, the Militia of Christ devoted its major efforts (largely of a personal, informal character) to combating extremists in both camps. Members of the society, mostly Catholics in key positions in labor unions, helped conservative trade unionists, "the pure and simplers," to thwart the continuous endeavors of the Socialists to capture the American Federation of Labor. The Militia of Christ must have been effective, it was said, or it would not have come under steady Socialist fire and "have inspired so much Socialist rhetoric." [140] More important was its work in refuting those Catholics who exaggerated Socialist strength in the American Federation of Labor. "The Militia of Christ . . . has no patience," said Dietz, "with the pessimistic view . . . entertained by many well-wishers of organized labor as such." He was sure that the imperfections could be remedied "by the growing sense of Catholic responsibility and consequent activity." [141] As executive secretary and as editor of the short-lived

[139] "Protestantism and the Workingman," *Central-Blatt and Social Justice*, II (December 1909), 9–10.

[140] American Federation of Catholic Societies, *Bulletin*, VII (November, 1913), 7.

[141] "Trade Unions and Catholics," ibid. (March 1913), 6–7.

magazine, *Social Service*, Dietz tirelessly worked to carry Christian ethics into the trade union field by lifting Catholic thought and activity from the haphazard of individualism to the effective level of systematic, organized effort. Only less influential was Peter W. Collins, secretary-treasurer of the Electrical Workers of America, who as lecturer for the Militia of Christ bespoke earnest approval of organized labor as the surest way of thwarting socialism — the greatest potential danger, he thought, to the workers' welfare.[142]

The Militia of Christ's labor program began exerting a vast influence in the Church's life when in 1911 the American Federation of Catholic Societies, meeting at Columbus, Ohio, established a Social Service Commission to promote "the further amelioration of conditions among the working people for the preservation and propagation of the faith." [143] In statements and resolutions approved in successive conventions after 1910, the federation declared its sympathy with the aspirations of the workers to better their conditions by organized effort in conservative trade unions, endorsed collective bargaining and trade agreements, and urged employers to recognize the fundamental right of workingmen to organize. The federation pledged its support to all legislative action for the elimination of unnecessary labor on Sunday, a living wage, reasonable hours of labor, protection of life and limb, abolition of child labor, just compensation for injury, and proper moral and sanitary conditions in the home, shop, mine, and factory.[144] The newly created Social Service Commission was to promote this program by having Leo's labor encyclical "systematically circulated, studied and applied." [145]

Besides the indefatigable Dietz, who served as its secretary, the

[142] But Collins insisted that Catholics not overestimate Socialist strength. See his "The Labor Movement and Socialism," *Central-Blatt and Social Justice*, II (February 1910), 7–10, in reply to Joseph Husslein, S.J., "Socialism and the American Federation of Labor," *America*, November 13, 1909.

[143] "Catholic Federation Resolutions," *Catholic News*, September 2, 1911; "The American Federation of Catholic Societies," *Extension Magazine*, VI (October 1911), 4.

[144] "Views of Catholic Societies," *Survey*, XXIX (October 19, 1912), 84; "Resolutions of the Catholic Federation," *America*, IX (August 23, 1913), 479; John J. Burke, "The Catholic Federation Convention," *Outlook*, CXIII (August 30, 1916), 1030–32.

[145] "Catholic Federation Resolutions," loc. cit.

members of the commission were the most Reverend Peter J. Muldoon, Bishop of Rockford, the Reverend John Cavanaugh, president of the University of Notre Dame, James Hagerty, professor of economics at Ohio State University, and Charles I. Denechaud of New Orleans. Bishop Muldoon was a truly progressive prelate who, as chairman of the commission and later in a similiar post on the National Catholic War Council and the National Catholic Welfare Conference, championed constructive social action. "We are ready with our condemnation of this and that dangerous tendency, but unless we go out into the open and do something practical for the solution of our pressing problems," he warned his fellow Catholics, "our condemnations will react upon us." [146] Denechaud, who became president of the federation in 1913, considered social service its most important work, while Professor Hagerty displayed special talents in arranging for economic discussions at the yearly conventions of the commission — a form of social action foreshadowing the postwar Catholic Conference on Industrial Problems.

Though retaining its organization and special interest in trade unionism, the Militia of Christ closely affiliated with the Social Service Commission. Collins and Dietz were the lecturers and secretaries respectively of the two bodies. The *Bulletin*, official organ of the federation, gave over half its space to a social service section, edited by Father Dietz who, as has been seen, had launched a magazine of similiar name for the Militia of Christ. This suggests that the Social Service Commission was essentially an enlarged Militia of Christ as also do its preoccupation and sympathy with the efforts of workers to wrest from employers better pay and recognition of unions.[147] In its weekly economic newsletter for the Catholic press and its pamphlet literature, the commission promoted the trade union cause alongside many specific moral and legislative reforms. The commission also explored the whole problem of social work in its bearing on the successful handlings of immigrants. The

[146] "Social Service," *America*, VII (May 18, 1912), 136–37.

[147] Thus Dietz in the commission's name demanded that employers in the upper regions of Michigan recognize the Western Federation of Miners. "Big Strike in the Copper Region of Michigan," *Bulletin*, VIII (January 1914), 7–8; "A Catholic View of the Copper Miners' Strike in Upper Michigan," *Survey*, XXXI (January 31, 1914), 521–22.

discussions made clear that modern "scientific social work, and especially work of a preventative kind . . . is the imperative need of our immigrant parishes." [148] The Social Service Commission and its work mirrored a "general awakening of social consciousness on the part of American Catholics," observed *America*, the new Jesuit weekly, and heralded "future organization . . . to help the Church in her divine progress and to make of her an ever more important factor in the social regeneration of our country." [149] During the same year, 1912, the non-sectarian *Survey* similarly commented, pointing out that the formation of the National Conference of Catholic Charities, the Militia of Christ, and the Social Service Commission marked "a new advance in Social Service in the American Catholic Church." [150] These organizations were not alone: various small groups composed largely of Catholic intellectuals discussed social questions and urged reforms. Thus the Common Cause Society, formed in Boston in 1912, studied to "advance the cause of equity within the sphere of economics upon the basis laid down by Pope Leo XIII" and "to bring forth by argument and given facts the falsity of Socialist principles and their treasonable use of the ballot." The society held public debates on Boston Common and elsewhere and sponsored the *Common Cause*, a monthly magazine. The society also had the support of *Live Issue*, a widely read weekly newspaper (1912–14), published by the New York Social Reform League, an outgrowth of the Laymen's League for Retreats.[151] Advocating Christian social reform as against revolutionary socialism, the *Live Issue* sought to popularize "co-partnership and co-operation in industry" as well as trade unionism, social insurance, and protective labor legislation.[152] In 1913 college graduates and professional people in the New York City area organized the American Eunomic League (well-lawed league) for "the discussion and scientific examination of those social problems which demand the immediate attention of thinking Catholics." With Richard Dana Skinner as

[148] Frederic Seidenburg, "The Immigration Problem," *Bulletin*, X (October 1915), 1, 4.
[149] "Social Service," VII (May 18, 1912), 136–37.
[150] "Views of Catholic Societies," loc. cit.
[151] *Live Issue*, March 28, 1914.
[152] "Declaration of Principles," ibid., November 15, 1913.

president, the league published the *Eunomic Review,* a four-page magazine.[153]

The minor organizations, even more than the major societies, stressed social study with a view to more fruitful social action. Before World War I only three theological schools, St. Paul Seminary, St. Francis Seminary near Milwaukee, and the Divinity School at the Catholic University, provided systematic instruction in social and industrial ethics. The more pressing need, however, was for professionally trained social workers, lay and clerical. In an address before the American Federation of Catholic Societies in 1915, Father Kelley of the Church Extension Society noted that "Catholics have not gone seriously into social work," and urged them to put a higher estimate on salaried service. "We need in this day of specialists, some specialists of our own," he said. If preachers of the gospel lived "by the gospel," charity workers should "receive at least enough remuneration to live." [154] In an effort to meet the new requirements, Frederic Seidenburg, S.J., recently returned from several years of social study in Europe, founded in 1912 a lecture bureau under the auspices of Loyola University in Chicago. Its comprehensive lecture courses being heavily attended by serious students, the bureau was reorganized in 1914 on a permanent basis as the Loyola University School of Sociology. Similarly, the Fordham University School of Philanthropy and Social Service, in full operation by 1917, was the outgrowth of a lecture series, the "School for Social Studies," inaugurated as early as 1911 by the Laymen's League for Retreats.[155]

In 1913 the Catholic Charities of Boston established a social service school. In this area, as in so many others, Father Dietz pioneered. Sharing in the growing conviction that successful social work required a trained personnel, he founded in 1915 the American

[153] "Literary Chat," *American Ecclesiastical Review,* XLVI (May 1912), 635–36; Abell, "The Reception of Leo XIII's Labor Encyclical in America, 1891–1919," loc. cit., 492–93; "Common Cause Society Starts Indoor Meetings," *Live Issue,* December 13, 1913; Fox, *Peter E. Dietz,* pp. 36–37.

[154] "Hour to Assist the Poor and the Immigrant," *Bulletin,* X (November 1915), 1.

[155] "A Catholic Lecture Bureau," *America,* VIII (October 12, 1912), 16; "Catholic Courses of Social Philanthropy," ibid., X (October 18, 1913), 40; *St. Vincent de Paul Quarterly,* XIX (August 1914), 185–92; ibid., XXI (November 1916), 322–27; *Catholic Charities Review,* I (February 1917), 60, 62; ibid., III (September 1919), 215–16; ibid., V (April 1921), 128; ibid. (October 1921), 274.

Academy of Christian Democracy for Women. As soon as the school demonstrated its usefulness he moved it from Hot Springs, North Carolina, its original site, to Cincinnati where opportunities for field work abounded. In the eight years of its existence the institution provided its hundreds of graduates with a most satisfactory social education which enabled them to assume positions of leadership in almost every major Catholic community.[156]

As the graduates of the social service schools penetrated the charity field, they stepped up the expansion of Catholic social service and by the same token provoked opposition and resentment.[157] Some Catholics, unable to comprehend how a person could legitimately earn a money income helping others, considered the professional social worker "as a sort of cold-blooded mercenary." [158] The extent and character of the opposition alarmed and distressed social workers; one of their number, Margaret Tucker, widely known settlement leader and teacher in Dietz's school, suggested a compromise system, namely, the semi-cloistered deaconess institution. This arrangement, she felt, would allay suspicion that the social worker was motivated by worldly considerations without impairing her lay freedom and usefulness.[159]

Not alone professional social service but the new social legislation was called into question. Mothers' pensions and child labor laws violated "social liberty," contended an editorially approved article in the *Catholic Standard and Times* of Philadelphia.[160] "It is astonishing," the author wrote,

> how many good Christians are beguiled by this pitiful plea against child labor. Stop and think: freak, childless women shedding crocodile tears for the God-loving children of the poor! Who has ever heard any

[156] Fox, op. cit., pp. 146–72.

[157] The tension between the Conservatives favoring "volunteers" and the Progressives who championed paid "experts" is well brought out in Henry Somerville, "National Conference of Catholic Charities," *Catholic World*, CV (August 1917), 587–97.

[158] Margaret Tucker, "Catholic Settlement Work — An Analysis," *Catholic Charities Review*, II (December 1918), 306.

[159] Ibid., III (January 1919), 18–21; Tucker, "Cross Currents in Catholic Charities," ibid., VI (March 1922), 78; "Two Letters on Social Service," ibid., III (September 1919), 204–5; "A Religious Community of Professional Social Workers," ibid., V (April 1921), 124–27.

[160] Edward J. Maginnis, "The Outlook: Signs of the Socialistic State," December 27, 1913.

considerable number of parents blessed with large families decrying child labor? And yet why shouldn't they have some say on the question? How in the name of common sense is the poor workingman (whom we shall have always with us) to rear a large family under present conditions if his children are denied the right to employ their hands at labor?

The *Live Issue*, in behalf of the Common Cause Society, was quick to retort that one "of the good Christians" who had been "beguiled" by the plea against child labor was the "memorable" Archbishop of Mainz, Emmanuel von Ketteler. This John the Baptist of Pope Leo XIII had branded child labor in factories as "a monstrous . . . cruelty committed against the child by the spirit of the age and the selfishness of parents." [161]

Coming to bat for his contributor, the editor of the *Catholic Standard and Times* excoriated the advocates of social legislation as "posturing busybodies" intent on applying the principles of Rousseau's *Social Contract*.[162] The *Live Issue* editors countered with crushing force that Rousseau was a rank individualist whose principles applied "to the domain of political economy led to the *laissez-faire* policy," to unrestricted freedom of competition, to industrial concentration, to the isolation of the defenseless masses, "in short, to those present-day abuses that are censured in the Labor Encyclical of Pope Leo XIII." The state had the right, *Live Issue* contended, "to regulate by legislation the conditions which put the working class at the mercy of capitalistic exploitation." [163] No Catholic reformer could deny the correctness of this position. By 1914, however, some Progressives feared that reform was being pushed forward with undue rapidity. "Too easily," thought the Central Verein, "are the representatives of authority influenced . . . by an unreasonable zeal to make thoughtless attempts at unstable reforms which are often prompted only by party politics and selfish motives." [164]

But the leading Catholic reformers, including Ryan and Dietz, were undeterred by timidity and caution; on the contrary, they

[161] "Individualism and Collectivism," January 10, 1914.
[162] "Socialism in Charity," December 27, 1913.
[163] Ibid.
[164] Central-Vereins, Resolutions of the 58th Annual Convention, 1913, *Offizieller Bericht*, p. 169.

labored to step up the progress of the reform drive. In his famous debate with Morris Hillquit on *Socialism: Promise or Menace?* (New York, 1914),[165] Ryan argued that "every indication points to a great acceleration of all movements for specific reforms." The many social improvements of the previous quarter century would be extended, through increase in social knowledge, the awakening of the social conscience, "and the enlarged intelligence, determination, and power of the less fortunate classes," until all our people were provided "with abundant food, clothing and housing." The existing system, "radically amended," would provide the necessary diffusion of income. Through legislative measures of the type previously elaborated by Ryan and already partially enacted, wages would be raised and unearned fortunes abolished. In his tussle with Hillquit, Ryan emphasized for the first time the need of wider distribution of capitalist ownership in the absence of which the other reforms would be powerless to insure the necessary stability.[166] "No nation can endure," he averred, "as a nation predominantly of hired men." [167] Ways must be found, he insisted, "through which the majority of the workers will gradually become owners, at least in part, of the instruments of production." [168] The transition to the new order would be effected mainly by co-partnership and co-operative societies.[169]

As a step in this direction, Ryan helped Colonel Patrick H. Callahan in 1912 to draw up a profit-sharing plan for his Louisville Paint and Varnish Company. Profits in excess of a living wage and six per cent interest on investment were divided equally between the workers and management. Modified from time to time to meet changing conditions, the arrangement was widely acclaimed, continuing until the plant was totally destroyed by fire in 1937, a few years before the founder's death.[170] As for Ryan, he was mainly concerned, in the field of practice, during the Progressive era, as in later years, with labor legislation, notably the enactment of

[165] Brilliantly reviewed by moderate Socialist William English Walling in *American Journal of Sociology*, XX (January 1915), 534–37.
[166] Hillquit-Ryan, *Socialism: Promise or Menace?*, pp. 39–41.
[167] Ibid., p. 41.
[168] Ibid., p. 249.
[169] Ibid., p. 42.
[170] A. I. Abell, "Patrick Henry Callahan," *Dictionary of American Biography*, XXII, 86–88.

minimum wage laws. He drafted the Minnesota statute, enacted in 1913, which empowered a specially created commission to guarantee working women and minors wages sufficient to maintain health "and the necessary comforts and conditions of reasonable life." Making "comfort" as well as "health" the test of a living wage, the Minnesota measure was more generous, Ryan thought, than the pioneer Oregon law with which Caroline Gleason and Father Edwin V. O'Hara were prominently associated.[171]

Father Dietz showed less interest in labor legislation as his career developed. Nor did he have much faith in profit-sharing or other forms of co-partnership, which would be used, he feared, to defeat wage justice. This attitude stemmed in large part, no doubt, from his increasingly close connections with the American Federation of Labor, which minimized legislation and co-partnership schemes.[172] Dietz wished above all to see that Socialists in the trade union movement "really get the education they need."[173] To this and other ends, he memorialized the Executive Council of the American Federation of Labor early in 1915. Recalling that the American Federation of Catholic Societies had sent a fraternal delegate to AFL conventions since 1910, Dietz proposed that the relation between the two groups be made "more vital, definite and progressive." The two bodies should set up joint committees to work out specific measures respecting strikes, industrial education, social service, and related matters, their guiding principle to be "that the state should not do for associations and unions what they ought to do for themselves without state aid." In its courteous reply the Executive Council explained at length that it was not within the province and power of the AFL to accept the proposal but that "sympathetic co-operation" could be maintained without entering into any agreement.[174] In later years, it is to be noted, the AFL and

[171] Ryan, *Social Doctrine in Action. A Personal History* (New York, 1941), pp. 120–23; Shaw, *Edwin Vincent O'Hara*, pp. 38–62.

[172] Abell, "Labor Legislation in the United States: The Background and Growth of the Newer Trends," loc. cit., 42–43; Taft, op. cit., pp. 289–300.

[173] "Catholics in the Trade Union Movement in the United States," *Live Issue*, April 18, 1914; "Something to Think About," ibid., December 27, 1913; "Dr. John A. Ryan's Views on Right of Associations, and Some Comments," ibid., January 31, 1914; "The International Secretariat and the Militia of Christ," ibid., February 7, 1914.

[174] Fox, op. cit., pp. 118–20, 272–75.

several of its affiliated bodies helped Dietz financially to transform his social service school into a genuine labor college.[175]

Unlike Ryan or Dietz, most Catholic Americans who supported the Progressive movement — undoubtedly a vast number — were mainly interested in secular and political objectives. But many were motivated in some degree by essentially religious considerations. They saw in the progress of social reform the most effective means of arresting the growth of socialism, which they deemed to be, even in its moderate American manifestation, inherently irreligious. Only in the context of opposing socialism does the Catholic social movement have significant meaning in the two decades before Ameirca's entry into World War I. To be sure, other motivations were present, not the least of which was the desire to disarm nativist attacks. When another of these recurrent crusades threatened after 1908, Catholic leaders reaffirmed the civic and social liberalism of the late nineteenth-century Americanists. The Knights of Columbus assumed direction of the movement by setting up in 1914 a Commission on Religious Prejudices under the chairmanship of the Louisville industrialist, Patrick H. Callahan.[176]

With fifty thousand dollars at its disposal the commission over a three-year period conducted a painstaking investigation. The commissioners found that not all the bigotry was on the Protestant side: some Catholics, chiefly editors, cruelly misrepresented Protestant intentions. Apart from its unfairness, this attitude invited Protestant retaliation.[177] While Catholics did not owe the Pope political allegiance or oppose the public school system, as Protestants persistently alleged,[178] they were, indeed, deficient in social action, that is, "slow" to endorse "certain civic reforms being proposed and agitated in current times." Since other citizens, "and not always a minority," often displayed the same fault without incurring suspicion, "Catholics ought not to be singled out," the commission thought, "because they are not wiser than their generation." The commission pointed out that there was no political question on which Catholics "are not divided and no political movement in which they are not found."

[175] Ibid., pp. 141, 180–81, 189–92.
[176] *Report of Commission on Religious Prejudices*, 1915, pp. 1–6.
[177] Ibid., pp. 18–19.
[178] Ibid., 1916, pp. 39–42.

Catholics were a "body" only with respect to what the Church teaches, namely, "faith and morals, not civics." [179] Even so, the commission, "aware of the part which social conditions play in preparing a field for the cultivation and growth of prejudice," urged Knights of Columbus and Catholics generally "to become more intimately acquainted with social problems and more closely identified with right movements looking to their solution," and "as a body" to join actively "with those of all other creeds . . . for the betterment of public morals, the furtherance of social justice and the very best in citizenship." [180]

In some measure at least Catholics by 1917 were prepared to act "as a body" in the social field. In the previous decade and a half several first-rate religio-social leaders had appeared on the scene — Patrick H. Callahan, Peter E. Dietz, James E. Hagerty, William J. Kerby, Frederick P. Kenkel, Peter J. Muldoon, Edwin V. O'Hara, and John A. Ryan — all of whom were to figure prominently in the years ahead. These men worked through the agencies at hand — Catholic Charities, institutions of higher learning, and the various societies loosely united in the American Federation of Catholic Societies. In the great task of social education, only just begun by World War I, persons and societies alike did not yet enjoy the support and direction of the Catholic hierarchy and could make little further progress, as was widely recognized, without full episcopal approval. To this important phase of the Catholic crusade for social justice we now turn.

[179] Ibid., p. 39.
[180] Ibid., 1915, p. 30.

CHAPTER VI

Social Reconstruction in the Wake of World War I
— the Bishops Take Command

Not until America's entry into World War I did the Catholic bishops of the country assume in measurable degree direct responsibility for thought and action in the social field. During the "Americanist" or social-liberal crisis of the previous generation the bishops all but unanimously concluded that most current efforts at economic reform, notably labor unionism, were in harmony with the demands of justice and charity. They had accordingly extended to Catholics generally full liberty to participate in reform movements, confident that leaders and people would avoid taking extremist positions. The success with which the Catholic body in the prewar decades resisted the inroads of organized socialism, while supporting many beneficent reforms, seemed to justify the hierarchy's essentially hands-off policy.

Yet for the greatest Catholic effectiveness in an age of growing complexity something more was required of the hierarchy than abstention or neutrality. Among the first to call for "positive declaration and guidance" were Father Dietz and Catholic labor leaders in the Militia of Christ. In a letter to Cardinal Gibbons in 1912 these leaders urged the Committee of Archbishops to draw up an official document on trade unionism, its "norms," and its proper relationship to legislation, the courts, and society in general. In their struggle for the betterment of human conditions laymen were often "discouraged" or "demoralized," Dietz pointed out, "because of the lack of moral support by the Church. . . ." At the cardinal's request Dietz listed topics for treatment in the proposed pastoral. Although the Committee of Archbishops considered the matter, it issued no report. Father Kerby surmised that the committee would delay until the Commission on Industrial Relations completed its work. "The hierarchy would have to make a national document . . .

practical, not merely speculative," he wrote Dietz. "It will hardly venture to do so without national knowledge of facts. The federal investigation promises the information needed." [1]

The hearings and reports of the Industrial Commission, whose chairman was Frank P. Walsh, a leading Catholic social liberal, did not move the hierarchy and its Committee of Archbishops to action; only the shock of war would suffice to overcome timidity and caution. Within a short time after the outbreak of the World War in 1914, its impact on the American economy created or intensified social problems of vital importance to the Catholic Church. As industry set out to supply the war needs of the Allied Powers, workers and their families were drawn into war-industry areas, in many of which housing and living needs were woefully inadequate. Conditions became particularly acute in Bridgeport, Connecticut, the nation's chief munitions center. Appalled by the social disintegration of the mounting population, three fourths of which was Catholic of many nationalities, Bishop John J. Nilan of Hartford established in December 1915 the Catholic Charitable Bureau of Bridgeport, a case-working organization. One of the first Catholic agencies of this type, the bureau with Marguerite Boylan, a professional social worker, as executive secretary, largely succeeded in co-ordinating Catholic activities and correlating them with the over-all social service of the community. In all its work, carried forward through five departments, the bureau stressed family aid and rehabilitation. [2]

Similar action was taken in other cities, whose problems resembled those in Bridgeport, especially after the nation entered the war in April 1917. [3] In specific Catholic war work the Knights of Columbus scored the most conspicuous record. [4] The Knights proposed to provide enlisted men with recreational and religious facilities

[1] Fox, *Peter E. Dietz, Labor Priest,* pp. 69–73.

[2] "The Catholic Charitable Bureau of Bridgeport," *Catholic Charities Review,* I (March 1917), 86; Marguerite Boylan, ibid., III (May 1919), 151–154; same author, *Social Welfare in the Catholic Church* (New York, 1941), pp. 52–55.

[3] See *Catholic Charities Review,* I (February 1917), 50–51; ibid. (March 1917), 86; ibid. (April 1917), 120; ibid. (May 1917), 149; ibid. (June 1917), 192; and M. J. Scanlan, "Diocesan Charities and Their Organization," ibid., II (December 1918), 297–301.

[4] For an extended though uncritical account, see Maurice Francis Egan and John B. Kennedy, *The Knights of Columbus in Peace and War* (2 vol.; New Haven, 1920), 201–378.

in a manner roughly similar to services already extended to soldiers of the Regular Army and the National Guard at the Mexican border. When war was declared against Germany the board of directors of the Knights of Columbus promptly offered the services of the order to the War Department. On the recommendation of its semi-civilian Commission on Training Camp Activities, the War Department accepted the "generous proposition" of the Knights "in regard to the erection of buildings for social purposes in the army training camps of the United States." The commission's chairman, Raymond B. Fosdick, in his letter to Supreme Knight James A. Flaherty accepting the offer, pointed out that many of the camps would contain from forty to sixty thousand men and that "the need for social and relaxational facilities" in these "sizable cities in themselves" is going "to tax the efforts of all those of us who are interested in providing a sane, well-rounded life" for the servicemen. Fosdick welcomed the "strong position" which the Knights had "always taken in regard to the moral hazards surrounding a young man's life" and was confident that the order's influence in the camps "will add much to their general tone." [5]

Catholics viewed the situation the more urgently in that most of the camps were to be located in the South where regular religious provision was virtually non-existent. With the nationally known and highly respected Patrick H. Callahan as the first chairman of their committee on war activities, the Knights planned to support volunteer chaplains as well as to provide entertainment and creature comforts in their halls or buildings. Prodded by Cardinal Gibbons, the bishops released priests for war service while helping the laity of both sexes to gather in the necessary funds. Its original assessment of a million dollars proving ridiculously insufficient for its work "of gigantic and rapidly expanding proportions," the Knights launched several independent war drives which yielded by Armistice Day over fourteen million dollars. With this financial backing the Knights opened in the course of the war some three hundred sixty recreational centers in the home camps and an almost equal number of service stations overseas. These operations were managed by nearly two thousand secretaries. The brilliancy of the Knights' war effort owed much to Callahan's organizational abilities, which included

[5] Ibid., 220–21.

a flair for public relations. The war activities of the Knights of Columbus were a striking exhibition of his thesis that the Church's gain in public estimation was commensurate with its participation in community projects. President Wilson, Secretary of War Baker, and Secretary of the Navy Daniels praised the manner in which the Knights of Columbus, the Y.M.C.A., and lesser service groups worked in co-operation to maintain the morale of soldiers and sailors.[6]

In the course of the war the work of the Knights of Columbus was correlated with that of the Church's general agency, the National Catholic War Council.[7] Recreation for the armed personnel was only one of many "incidental" war needs. In order to meet the many heavy and ever changing demands for aid and counsel an organization broadly representative of the whole Catholic body was deemed necessary. Accordingly, Cardinals Gibbons, Farley, and O'Connell called a General Convention of Catholics to meet August 11–12, 1917, at the Catholic University of America. Representing sixty-eight dioceses, twenty-seven national Catholic organizations, and the whole of the Catholic press, the convention endorsed the Knights of Columbus war work and created the National Catholic War Council "to study, coordinate, unify, and put in operation all Catholic activities incidental to the war." [8] The heads of the American Federation of Catholic Societies and the Knights of Columbus and a clerical and lay appointee of each of the fourteen archbishops comprised the executive committee of the new organization. This provision suggests that the hierarchy at first was only slightly more willing to assume responsibility for the direction and control of the National Catholic War Council than it had been of the influential prewar but now largely defunct American Federation of Catholic Societies. Soon sensing, however, that the executive committee was unwieldy and inefficient, the archbishops in November 1917 con-

---

[6] See John B. Kennedy's two articles, "The Work of the Knights of Columbus," *Extension Magazine*, XII (April 1918), 8, 32; and "Where the K. of C. War Work Stands," *National Catholic War Council Bulletin*, I (June 1, 1919), 4.

[7] Michael Williams, *American Catholics in the War. National Catholic War Council, 1917–1921* (New York, 1921), a vivid narrative and documentary account.

[8] John J. Burke, C.S.P., "Special Catholic Activities in War Service," *Annals of the American Academy of Political and Social Science*, LXXIX (September 1918), 213–20; John M. Cooper, "The National Catholic War council," *Ecclesiastical Review*, LIX (December 1918), 607–17.

stituted themselves the National Catholic War Council and placed its administration in the hands of four bishops — Patrick J. Hayes of New York, William T. Russell of Charleston, Joseph Schrembs of Toledo, and Peter J. Muldoon of Rockford. Muldoon and Schrembs had been prominently identified with the American Federation of Catholic Societies.

As was predicted, the hierarchy's action resulted in "a speeding up of the organization in all parts of the country." [9] The on-the-spot direction of the council's work devolved upon the Reverend John J. Burke, editor of the Paulist *Catholic World*, who was appointed chairman of the Committee on Special War Activities. Zealous and businesslike, Burke mobilized millions of Catholics through seven subcommittees: on finance, on men's activities, on women's activities, on chaplains' aid, on Catholic interests, on historical records, and on reconstruction and after-war activities. The subcommittee on chaplains' aid supplied army and navy chaplains with Mass outfits and religious articles — New Testaments and prayer books in several languages, rosaries, scapulars, and the like — for distribution among fighting personnel. The Catholic Army and Navy Chaplain Bureau in charge of Bishop Hayes was hard pressed to fill the Catholic quota of eleven hundred fifty priests.

In close touch with public and voluntary war agencies, the National Catholic War Council was in a position to furnish guidance to nearly fifteen thousand Catholic societies, most of which engaged in some form of war work. The subcommittee on men's activities, headed by Charles I. Denechaud of New Orleans, established twenty-two service clubs and subsidized nearly four hundred others in which soldiers and sailors on leave or in transit could find housing and recreational facilities. This subcommittee also opened and operated fifteen "Everyman's Clubs" for workingmen in need of a substitute for the vanishing saloon. Even more impressive was the work of the women's societies, whose chairman was Father William J. Kerby. Catholic women were active in Red Cross work, in chaplain aid, and in the sale of Liberty Bonds and War Saving Stamps. They provided no little housing and protective care for women workers in war industry. In some of the war camps the subcommittee

[9] "The National Catholic War Council," *Survey*, XXXIX (December 8, 1917), 296.

on women's activities established visitors' houses in which nearly a million and a half friends of soldiers were entertained. In order to help meet the desperate need for trained social workers this sub-committee opened the National Catholic Service School for Women at Clifton in the nation's capital.

Inasmuch as America's participation in World War I was of relatively short duration, the National Catholic War Council's major effort was made after the Armistice. Not until August 1918 did the War Department recognize the council as an official agent of the government in war welfare work. While continuing its recognition of the Knights of Columbus, the government decided, in the words of Secretary Baker, "to recognize not only the child but the parent of the child." Henceforth the council was in every sense the Catholic counterpart of the War Time Commission of the Federal Council of Churches and of the Jewish Welfare Board. With six other service organizations (the Y.M.C.A., the Y.W.C.A., the Jewish Welfare Board, the American Library Association, the War Camps Community Service, and the Salvation Army) the council participated in the United Fund Drive which yielded over a hundred seventy million dollars.[10] The council allotted most of its share of the funds, thirty million dollars, to its overseas units and to the Knights of Columbus, reserving only about five million dollars for reconstruction and after-war activities.

The council put these funds to good use. It set up two schools for the rehabilitation of wounded illiterate veterans, one in Washington, D.C., for men wishing urban jobs, and the other at Leonardtown, Maryland, for the training of farm workers.[11] In this as in virtually all its after-war social service, the National Catholic War Council co-operated with the appropriate government and community agencies. This was true of the council's thirty-nine unemployment bureaus, located in cities from coast to coast, which helped to secure jobs for thousands of returning veterans. In close association with the Red Cross, the War Risk Insurance Bureau, and the Federal Board

[10] "A National War Chest Campaign," ibid., XL (September 14, 1918), 674–75; "Financial Report," *National Catholic War Council Bulletin*, I (March–April 1920), 25–26.

[11] "Training Disabled Fighters," ibid. (June 1919), 16; Michael Williams, "Re-making Uncle Sam's Broken Heroes," ibid. (July 1919), 6–8.

for Vocational Education, the council opened in fifteen Catholic hospitals outpatient and social service departments for the aftercare of discharged veterans and their families. More spectacular, although not necessarily more important, were the twenty-eight community houses set up and operated by the subcommittee on women's activities. While a few of these houses were for women and girls only, most of them were neighborhood or community centers which functioned in the hope that the discontent stirred up by the war and its aftermath might be turned from "radicalism and anarchy" into "the ways of American liberty and freedom." [12]

The community centers were one phase of the War Council's participation in the Americanization Crusade. This was a broadly social and political movement, prewar in origin, designed to promote mutual understanding between native Americans and the new immigrants. Leaders assumed that in return for fair and just treatment the immigrant would learn English more readily, accept naturalization, and shoulder the responsibilities of citizenship. The need during the war for national unity and the fear during the postwar period that the immigrants might embrace Bolshevism led people and government to adopt the Americanization program.[13] Following the Armistice, Americanization agencies under the direction of the War Civics Committee, the joint creation of the War and Interior Departments, determined "to test the effects of concerted effort in the big drive for higher citizenship and social betterment. . . ." [14] Attention centered on East St. Louis, Illinois, whose appalling race riots early in the war still lingered in the public memory. Mainly a railway and stockyards center, the city had experienced a phenomenal growth after 1914, drawing in large masses of Negro and non-English-speaking peoples. Inasmuch as many Negroes had come to East St. Louis as strikebreakers, their presence served only less to embitter industrial relations than to intensify ethnic tensions. On this socially sick and disorganized city were brought to bear the recreational, health, and educational agencies of the federal

---

[12] "Our Post-War Responsibilities," ibid., 30.

[13] See Edward George Hartman, *The Movements to Americanize the Immigrant* (New York, 1948), pp. 7–104.

[14] "Co-ordinating a Community," *National Catholic War Council Bulletin*, I (July 1919), 15, 29–30.

government and of the seven religious war service organizations. At a cost of two hundred seventy-five thousand dollars the National Catholic War Council built a community house in which a recreational and civil program of far-reaching scope was carried forward.[15]

As its special contribution to postwar Americanization, the War Council launched a nationwide Civic Education Program. The subcommittee on reconstruction and after-war activities, whose chairman was sociologist John F. O'Grady, entrusted the direction of the campaign to John A. Lapp and Charles A. McMahon, experts in adult education. Lest subversive radicalism make undue headway the Catholic effort centered necessarily on recent immigrants "who have had," Lapp regretfully observed, "no instruction in democracy or any experience in its operation." To be sure, the native-born, as Lapp stressed, had not been adequately instructed because civics was not widely taught in the elementary schools, the only schools attended by the "great majority" of the country's youth. For the time being, however, priority would be given to the immigrants. For these the subcommittee projected entertainment programs in the course of which were to be interspersed "brief lessons and instruction in civics" along with "inspirational addresses by immigrants as well as by Americans." [16]

In the months following the Armistice civics programs were speedily set up in all communities heavily populated with foreign-born. At twenty dollars apiece the Community Motion Picture Bureau of New York furnished sufficient film to provide a civic education center with an evening's entertainment of some ninety minutes' duration. The injected short talks or lectures on American democracy, civics, and vocational opportunities were given first in the appropriate foreign language and then repeated in English. While most centers preferred a short course of six weekly entertainments, some demanded the year's program of twenty-four meetings.[17] The lecture material was prepared mainly by Lapp, who wrote sev-

---

[15] "Opening of East St. Louis Community House," ibid. (September 1919), 12–14; "Our House in East St. Louis," ibid. (May 1920), 21–23.

[16] "The Campaign for Civic Instruction," ibid., I (July 1919), 11–12.

[17] "Moving Picture Citizenship Campaign," ibid., 24; "Citizenship Taught Through Motion Pictures," ibid. (August 1919), 9–13; Charles A. McMahon, "Education and Good Citizenship," ibid. (March–April 1920), 14–17; Frederick A. Sweet, "Putting Over a Civic Education Program," ibid. (August 1920), 10–11.

eral books and pamphlets on citizenship, beginning with *The Fundamentals of Citizenship*, a simple textbook of civics, and *Co-Builders of Our America*, which played up the contribution of immigrant leaders to the growth of American democracy. Translated into thirteen languages, Lapp's works merited their wide circulation of over a million copies.[18] His writings, in the opinion of the Providence *Journal*, were "the most noteworthy documents that have been published bearing on questions of citizenship and the historical background of American life." [19] The *Journal of Education* pronounced *The Fundamentals of Citizenship* to be historically clear, civically sound, educationally illuminating, patriotically impressive, and personally wholesome. The journal found it "refreshing to have a religious organization with millions of loyal adherents . . . emphasizing most manfully the duty of naturalization with specific reference to the ways and means of achieving citizenship." [20]

From the outset the council sought to develop a program that "fits the spirit of the immigrant as well as the spirit of our institutions." Relying on persuasion alone, Lapp and his associates at no time subscribed to the dictum of the superpatriots and red-baiters "that every person should be forced to learn English and become a citizen, or leave the country." They also bemoaned the attempt (only partially successful) to turn the Americanization campaign against social reform and organized labor. This brand of Americanization repelled the immigrant who was wont to associate American patriotism and citizenship with the great ideals of truth, justice, and human brotherhood. "Social justice and fair play," Lapp argued, "must be at the basis of all attempts at Americanization which hope to succeed." [21] Even apart from strategic considerations, "no plan short of complete social justice should be held as a goal in programs for good citizenship or Americanization." [22]

---

[18] "Text Book on Civics," ibid. (June 1919), 16; Charles A. McMahon, "The N.C.W.C. Program for Better Citizenship," ibid., III (July 1921), 6; Lapp, "Unit Courses in Civic and Social Problems," ibid., V (September 1923), 7–9; " 'Civic Duty' Radio Topic of Dr. Lapp," ibid., VII (November 1925), 7–8; Elizabeth B. Sweeney, "Discharging the Duties of Citizenship," ibid., X (June 1928), 28–29.

[19] McMahon, "The N.C.W.C. Program for Better Citizenship," loc. cit.

[20] "The Fundamentals of Citizenship," ibid., I (November 1919), 22–24.

[21] "Bringing Immigrants into Citizenship," ibid., III (July 1921), 2–4.

[22] Lapp, "Bogus Propaganda: Dollar Mark Shows in Attempts to Control Americanization Program," ibid., I (June–July 1920), 9–10.

As its leaders anticipated, the Civic Education Program scored its greatest success among native-born youth in the sense that most parochial schools introduced civics instruction, often using, especially at first, Lapp's various textbooks. In addition to the immigrants, other adult groups, including leaders in diocesan charity organization, were influenced by the council's civic work. Besides helping to finance a community house in Des Moines, Iowa, the War Council aided the bishop of the diocese, Thomas W. Drumm, to systematize its social service. A small but representative diocesan board was established to lay down general policies and to handle "the larger financial projects," while a more numerous body, the Catholic Community Council, was formed to "co-ordinate all Catholic activities and to promote interest in social welfare work." This group functioned through several departments or bureaus: parish centers, social service, legal aid, medical aid, information, public morals, education, and recreation — all designed to make primarily "for better citizenship and loyalty to American ideals." The Catholic Community Council of Des Moines expected to exert its "most far-reaching" influence among later immigrants. "Even now," it was reported in early 1920, "a deeper community feeling has been observed among them and they have shown that they appreciate what America and American ideals mean. The red radical," it was confidently predicted, "will find poor soil for his propaganda in the neighborhood of the Community House, or wherever Catholic social action has shown its influence." [23]

The desire to counteract Bolshevism partly inspired, no doubt, the War Council's social survey work in Pittsburgh and New York. The Ordinaries in these jurisdictions wished to secure an over-all picture of the local charity situation with a view to improving, expanding or curtailing, and above all co-ordinating diocesan charity activities. They sought advice and direction from social service experts in the National Catholic War Council. Immediately on becoming Archbishop of New York early in the year 1919, Patrick J. Hayes commissioned the experienced John A. Lapp to help a specially designated committee of New York priests and laymen to

[23] "National Catholic War Council's Organization in Des Moines," ibid. (February 1920), 20–23; "Our Community Work at Des Moines Wins Public Support," ibid., II (December 1920), 12–13.

make a complete survey. The committee accomplished its stupendous task with thoroughness and dispatch, presenting its findings and recommendations in a report of more than two hundred thousand words. Hayes promptly accepted the committee's proposal for the creation of a central organization to be designated the Catholic Charities of the Archdiocese of New York. The arrangement as outlined and put into operation provided for an executive council and advisory council to the archbishop, the head of the organization; a secretary for charities, as the executive director; and six divisions: relief, children, general administration, health, protective care, and social action.[24]

As for social action in its industrial aspects, Catholics everywhere were to find inspiration and guidance in the War Council's document, "Social Reconstruction: A General Review of the Problems and Survey of Remedies." Written by John A. Ryan largely to counteract the Socialist influence of the Social Reconstruction Program of the British Labor party, the manuscript was originally intended for delivery before the Knights of Columbus in Louisville. Too detailed and lengthy for such an audience, the discarded speech was presented by Father O'Grady, chairman of the War Council's Reconstruction and After-War Activities Committee, to the Administrative Committee of Bishops, who made a few verbal changes and published it as their own pronouncement on Lincoln's Birthday, 1919.[25] This "Bishops' Program," as it is generally referred to, was destined to become more widely known than any of the other sixty-odd proposals for postwar social reconstruction.

Many were amazed at the spectacle of representative Catholic bishops, presumed to be extremely conservative if not reactionary, publicly proclaiming a desire, as one journalist put it, not only to "make Capitalism good, but to make it less." [26] The attractiveness

[24] "With Our Readers," *Catholic World*, CXI (April 1920), 138–40; Lapp, "Catholic Social Work," *Survey*, XLIV (May 22, 1920), 280–81; same author, "Survey of the Field of Catholic Social Work: A Statement of the Purpose, Scope and Results of Diocesan Social Studies," *National Catholic Welfare Council Bulletin*, IV (September 1922), 3–5; Patrick J. Hayes, "The Unification of Catholic Charities," *Catholic World*, CXVII (May 1923), 145–53.

[25] Ryan, *Social Doctrine in Action*, pp. 143–45.

[26] William Hard, "The Catholic Church Accepts the Challenge," *Metropolitan Magazine* (January 1920), quoted in Ryan, *Social Reconstruction* (New York, 1920), p. 18, and in *N.C.W.C. Bulletin*, I (January 1920), 16.

of the program stemmed largely, no doubt, from the felicity with which it related immediate and more remote objectives. Correctly judging that the people generally were opposed to "revolutionary changes," the bishops confined their attention "to those reforms that seem to be desirable and also obtainable within a reasonable time, and to a few general principles which should become a guide to more distant developments." The desirable immediate reforms would aim, through legislation to the extent necessary, to actualize the family living wage while the "more distant developments" referred to those "ultimate and fundamental reforms" whereby the majority of workers should "become owners, at least in part, of the instruments of production." In the light of these two principles, the bishops surveyed the postwar industrial situation and proposed a wide variety of reforms.[27]

The bishops introduced their discussion with pertinent remarks on reconstruction as viewed by the British Labor party, the American Federation of Labor, the British Quaker employers, the executive officials of the United States Chamber of Commerce, and the Inter-denominational Conference of Social Service Unions in Great Britain. The latter body, besides proclaiming Christian social principles, pointed out specific evils and remedies and was thus not open to the charge often fairly lodged against religious groups that their reform pronouncements "are abstract, platitudinous and usually harmless." The British Labor party program, as drawn up by the distinguished Sidney Webb, was "one of immediate radical reforms, leading ultimately to complete Socialism" — an outcome that Catholics could not approve. Turning to the program of the American Federation of Labor, the bishops feared that its proposal to tax land "into use" could "easily involve confiscation." More to be deplored was the AFL's opposition to legislation as a means of securing the eight-hour day and a living wage. Reliance on trade union action alone did not benefit "the weaker sections of the working class" and by implication denied that "the workers should ever aspire to become owners as well as users of the instruments of production."

The bishops were favorably impressed by the reconstruction measures of twenty Quaker employers in Great Britain, particularly their

[27] "The Bishops' Program," in Ryan, *Social Reconstruction*, Appendix, pp. 217–38.

assertion of the right of labor to organize, to bargain collectively with the employer, and to participate in the "industrial part" of business management. According to the Quaker employers, employees should be given their proper share of industrial management through the establishment of shop committees, working wherever possible with the trade unions. The bishops approved the Quaker plan and incorporated it in their own statement. "There can be no doubt," they asserted, "that a frank adoption of these means and ends by employers would not only promote the welfare of the workers, but vastly improve the relations between them and their employers, and increase the efficiency and productiveness of each establishment."

The bishops were sure that the continuance of many wartime economic policies would contribute greatly to social reconstruction. In behalf of demobilized soldiers and sailors, the federal government should not only continue and strengthen the United States Employment Service but also reclaim and colonize "millions of acres of arid, swamp and cut-over timber land. . . ." It was even more important and urgent that Congress transform the National War Labor Board into a peacetime agency "with all the power for effective action that it can possess under the Federal Constitution." The few guiding principles of the board — a family living wage for all male adult laborers, recognition of labor's right to organize and to deal with employers through its chosen representatives, and no coercion of non-union laborers by members of the union — had "prevented innumerable strikes, and raised wages to decent levels in many different industries throughout the country." The aims, methods, and results of "this institution," the bishops averred, "constitute a definite and far-reaching gain for social justice" — which should not be lost or given up in time of peace.

Nor should the general level of wartime wages be reduced. Only a few skilled workers had received wage increases in excess of the rise in the cost of living. For the overwhelming majority of workers, current wages barely sufficed, inasmuch as these workers were not receiving living wages when prices and wages began to rise in 1915. Even if the prices of goods should fall to the prewar level — an unlikely development within five years — "the average present rate of wages would not exceed the equivalent of a decent livelihood in the case of the vast majority." On the assumption, moreover, that workers currently received more than living wages, rates of pay should not be lowered on that account. For a living wage was not, as all Catholic authorities declared, the full measure of justice, only its minimum. And minimum justice in a country as rich as the United States "is not only of very questionable morality, but is unsound economically." At this point the bishops emphasized that "high rates of wages and high purchasing power by the masses"

is the surest guarantee of a continuous and general operation of industrial establishments. It is the most effective instrument of prosperity for labor and capital alike. The principal beneficiaries of a general reduction of wages would be the less efficient among the capitalists, and the more comfortable sections of the consumers. The wage-earners would lose more in remuneration than they would gain from whatever fall in prices occurred as a direct result of the fall in wages. On grounds both of justice and sound economics, we should give our hearty support to all legitimate efforts made by labor to resist general wage reductions.

The bishops believed that maintenance of current wage levels was not inconsistent with efforts to reduce the cost of living. In so far as high living costs stemmed from "monopolistic exertion," regulatory laws adequately enforced would ordinarily suffice to bring relief. It was noted that "government competition with monopolies that cannot be effectively restrained by the ordinary anti-trust laws deserves more serious consideration than it has yet received." Excessive middlemen charges, the main cause of high living costs, could be reduced by co-operative retail and wholesale stores on the Rochdale model. Once the American people took up consumers' co-operation in earnest, their "superior energy, initiative and commercial capacity" would enable them "to surpass what has been done in England and Scotland," and to "realize the folly of excessive selfishness and senseless individualism." Although the bishops were silent on the point, author Ryan expected American consumer co-operatives to build factories and other productive establishments and to share the ownership and profits with wage earners therein.

On the productive side, however, the bishops favored co-operative societies and co-partnership arrangements. In the former, as they explained, the workers own and manage the industries themselves; in the latter they own a substantial part of the corporate stock and exercise a reasonable share in the management. However slow the attainment of these ends, they will have to be reached before we can have a thoroughly efficient system of production, or an industrial and social order that will be secure from the danger of revolution. It is to be noted that this particular modification of the existing order, though far-reaching and involving to a great extent the abolition of the wage system, would not mean the abolition of private ownership. The instruments of production would still be owned by individuals, not by the State.

The Bishops' Program pleased the radically progressive elements in American society, including Catholics in the vanguard of the labor movement. "Nothing will do more to strengthen the cause of orderly but fundamental economic reform," wrote John Fitzpatrick, president of the Chicago Federation of Labor and sponsor of the city's Independent Labor party. Catholics in organized labor had denied the Socialist claim that the Catholic Church "is on the side of special privilege in the battle between privilege and democracy," and "today are rewarded with a pronouncement that . . . is undoubtedly the greatest ever put forth by any religious body." [28] Of like mind was Frank P. Walsh, co-chairman of the National War Labor Board, who saw in the Bishops' Program "proof that the leaders of organized Christianity" recognized and acclaimed an "identity of interest" between "true religion" and "economic democracy." Concerning the fear that labor's struggle for better wages, shorter hours, and self-mastery was a material struggle, the "four eminent bishops who sign this pronouncement do not consider it necessary to even discuss the point. They take for granted," he pointed out, "that the man who is physically brutalized by long hours of toil and a scant leisure spent amid squalid surroundings — the best that his wages will afford — is in no condition to respond to the spiritual appeals to which every healthy and normal man readily responds." Nor did the erstwhile chairman of the Commission on Industrial Relations fail to note that, in order to have pride in his work and eagerness to do his best, the worker "must have a voice in controlling the industrial processes and in the distribution of the product." [29]

[28] "The Bishops' Labor Programme," *N.C.W.C. Bulletin*, I (July 1919), 9–10.
[29] "The Significance of the Bishops' Labor Program," ibid. (August 1919), 18–19.

This was the conviction of the non-Catholic social liberals also. Among these was Raymond Swing, an industrial engineer by profession, who wrote in the *Nation* that the Bishops' Program in "substance" though not in "title" was one of "veritable social ownership." In its treatment of the ethics of remuneration and industrial management lay the "radical character" of the document. The philosophy of its carefully worded statements marked the leaders of the Catholic Church "as among our advanced labor thinkers." [30] Ecclesiastical leaders tended to play down the exceptional status of the document. Bishop Muldoon spoke for most Catholics when he pointed out that the program "is based upon the immutable principles of justice and charity which the Church holds, has held, and will ever hold." He disagreed with Swing's opinion that the document was "the product of astute calculation," stating that at the close of the war

> it appeared that the world, and in particular the United States, was willing to listen to representatives of the Church, which throughout all the ages has striven not only to protect the workman but to further his progress in all ways consistent with Christian morality. In this you have the reason why the Bishops have brought forth once again the old, old principles of justice which the Church is bound to preserve and to teach as best she may.[31]

Muldoon and his associates were in for bitter disappointment. Not a single remedial or transforming proposal in the Bishops' Program was adopted during the 1920s. Whereas in the idealistic afterglow of the war Catholic and other progressives confidently expected economic democracy to be the basis of the forthcoming peace and reconstruction, they were soon to find their country in the grip of a frenzied reaction which wiped out the recent gains of union labor and imperiled the whole structure of prewar social legislation. The clumsy preparation of Bolshevist zealots for a Communist revolution in America frightened many people who lent a ready ear to the clever propaganda of business and other conservative groups that all reformers were Bolsheviks in disguise or the naïve and witless abettors of violent revolution. Within a month after the Bishops' Program

[30] Quoted in Michael Williams, "The Catholic Programme of Reconstruction," *ibid.* (June 1919), 8–10.

[31] Quoted in Ryan, *Social Reconstruction*, pp. 10–11.

was issued, a campaign was launched against it by Ralph M. Easley, secretary of the National Civic Federation, who alleged that its authors were misled by the "near-Bolsheviki" and spoke only for themselves, not their fellow bishops. Easley marshaled "expert testimony" from anonymous Catholics whose "composite opinion" was that the Bishops' Program of Social Reconstruction wàs not within the province of the National Catholic War Council and was withal dangerously radical. One Catholic critic, for example, equated co-partnership and producers' co-operation with Bolshevism.[32]

This charge was repeated by the State of New York's Joint Legislative Committee Investigating Seditious Activities, or the "Lusk Report," as it is commonly called, published early in 1920. The signers of the Bishops' Program were referred to as a "certain group in the Catholic Church with leanings toward Socialism, under the leadership of the Rev. Dr. Ryan. . . . " The "socialistic" tendency of the War Council's document was "most clearly" shown in the statements under the heading of "Cooperation and Copartnership." [33] Meanwhile, the National Civic Federation had appointed, as part of its plan to crush the radicals, a Committee on the Study of Socialism in the Churches. One of its most active members was Condé B. Pallen, long a prominent Catholic journalist and scholar. In its report, early in 1921, the committee alluded to but did not name "certain priests" who while not avowed Marxists "sympathize with, foster and aid the groups represented by such philosophy" and "tend ignorantly to undermine and destroy the confidence of their hearers in the Government and institutions of this country." Some of these priests, the committee regretted to state, were "in important positions in Catholic organizations and speak with apparent authority on economic and social questions." [34]

In the view of social justice champions the charge that the Catholic Church abetted socialism was malicious and groundless. They

---

[32] "Anonymous Criticism of the Bishops' Reconstruction Program," *Catholic Charities Review*, III (June 1919), 163–65; John Hearley, "Plutocracy Ascends the Pulpit," ibid., V (April 1921), 116–18; "A Belated Complaint," ibid. (October 1921), 271–72; Ryan, *Social Doctrine in Action*, pp. 147–49; Marguerite Green, *The National Civic Federation and the American Labor Movement, 1900–1925* (Washington, D.C., 1956), pp. 362–427.

[33] Quoted in Ryan, *Social Doctrine in Action*, pp. 147–48.

[34] Green, op. cit., p. 412.

recognized, however, that the "unevidenced accusation" could have been plausibly put forth only because ignorance of economic matters was widespread. They were not all the more convinced of the dire need of a long-range program of systematic teaching and study. That the desired diffusion of knowledge would take place was assured when the bishops resolved early in 1919 to transform the National Catholic War Council into a permanent peacetime agency. The logic of the situation dictated this course. The bishops could not seriously expect the federal government to continue its wartime labor policies if they themselves intended to liquidate their war and postwar activities. Even if industrial reform had been checked off as a futile enterprise, other reforms already in progress required the Church's continued oversight. Thus the civic education campaign would most certainly collapse if central direction should be abandoned. Moreover, the social service workers, both volunteer and professional, who had been mobilized for war work, would suffer demoralization in some degree should organization along the lines of the National Catholic War Council be not attempted for peacetime ends.

Social service responsibilities, heavy in the past and not adequately met, showed few signs of lessening as the war ended. The expectation in 1919 was that urban religious problems would become even more difficult in the years ahead. For one thing, immigration regained its prewar momentum, and few surmised that exclusion would become public policy within half a decade. In addition, many believed that rural Catholicism deserved more attention than it had formerly received. After a brilliant prewar career in the minimum wage movement, Edwin V. O'Hara of Portland, Oregon, shifted his interest to the rural field in the course of his work as archdiocesan superintendent of schools. In preparation of a paper or report on "The Rural Problem in Its Bearing on Catholic Education" for the National Catholic Educational Association at its 1920 meeting, O'Hara studied the federal Census, the *Official Catholic Directory*, and the replies to his questionnaire to a thousand rural pastors. His investigation indicated that urban dwellers because of their restricted birth rate, "both from voluntary and involuntary causes," failed to reproduce themselves, the phenomenal growth of cities coming from immigration and the "prolific population" of American rural regions. Since the Catholic Church was over eighty per cent urban, its future prosperity would depend largely on the expansion and stability of its rural parishes whence came numbers, leaders, and religious vocations. He suggested special training for rural pastors, resort to religious vacation schools after the Lutheran example, and provision of religious instruction through correspondence. This latter "will require," he said, "national organization working through convents in every diocese which will set aside capable teachers to supervise the papers of the rural pupils." [35]

Organizationally speaking, O'Hara was to secure his main support, at least initially, from the recently formed National Catholic Welfare Council. In response to the general belief that a national organization was essential, the bishops had authorized the council and set up its basic framework in 1919. The task began in late February at a meeting in the national capital of seventy-seven bishops to celebrate the Golden Jubilee of Cardinal Gibbons' episcopacy. At the suggestion of the Pope's representative, Archbishop Bonaventura Cerretti, the bishops attending this meeting, in their desire to have "united action in all matters that relate to the welfare of the Catholic Church in the United States," [36] voted to have annual meetings of the hierarchy in the future and set up the Committee on General Catholic Interests and Affairs, its members to be named by Cardinal Gibbons. The cardinal thereupon designated the four bishops serving as the administrative committee of the National Catholic War Council to constitute the new committee also. The four bishops were to survey the situation with a view to more definitive action by the first annual meeting of the bishops later in the year.

In approving these tentative plans the Pope, Benedict XV, happily noted that the bishops intended to concentrate on social and educational work. So urgent is "the call to a zealous and persistent economic-social activity that we need not further exhort you in this matter. Be watchful, however," he warned, "lest your flocks, carried away by vain opinions and noisy agitation, abandon to their det-

[35] Raymond Philip Witte, S.M., *Twenty-five Years of Crusading. A History of the National Catholic Rural Life Conference* (Des Moines, 1948), pp. 45–57; J. G. Shaw, *Edwin Vincent O'Hara* (New York, 1957), pp. 63–71.

[36] "The September Meeting of the American Hierarchy," *Ecclesiastical Review*, LXI (July 1919), 1.

riment the Christian principles established by our predecessor of happy memory, Leo XIII, in his Encyclical Letter, *Rerum Novarum.*" Not less important was the Catholic education of children and youth. Although Catholic schools flourished in the United States, "we must not so far trust to present prosperity as to neglect provision for the time to come," he counseled, "since the weal of Church and State depends entirely on the good condition and discipline of the schools, and the Christians of the future will be those and those only whom you will have taught and trained." [37]

In a letter to Cardinal Cerretti, the venerable Baltimore prelate noted that, owing partly to "defective organization," the Catholic Church in America "is not exerting the influence which it ought to exert in proportion to our numbers and the individual prominence of many of our people." While the diocesan units "indeed are well organized," the Church in America as a whole "has been suffering from the lack of a united force that might be directed to the furtherance of those general policies which are vital to all." The newly designated Committee on General Catholic Interests and Affairs would correct this situation if it were entrusted with directive authority.[38] For the guidance of the committee Gibbons outlined a comprehensive plan for which he half apologized as furnishing "almost enough matter of thought for a Plenary Council." Since the letter embodied the opinions of numerous other bishops as well as his own, he was not prepared to endorse the whole of its content. For one thing, he did not share the confidence of some bishops in the ability of the Church to raise millions of dollars for common religio-social purposes. Nor was the plan he submitted all inclusive: it ignored the immigrants and made only passing reference to the industrial situation in connection with its comments on social and charitable work. Gibbons noted that in the social service field "most valuable pioneer work" had been done by the National Conference of Catholic Charities and the National Catholic War Council, and that three things were needed:

First, the presentation, definite, clear and forceful, of Catholic social principles. Second, more knowledge as to the best methods of Catholic social and charitable work. Third, a more general impulse to put our

[37] "Letter of Pope Benedict XV to the American Episcopate," *ibid.,* 4–7.
[38] "Letter to Cerretti, May 1, 1919," *ibid.,* 7–9.

social principles and methods into practice. Society never had greater need for guidance. It is turning for light to the Catholic Church. Too often, we must admit, our principles, the principles of the Gospel, have been hidden in our theologies, so much so that the recent pamphlet on Social Reconstruction appeared to many a complete novelty. The Church has a great work of social education and social welfare lying before it. Here, again, the Hierarchy must take the lead.[39]

If on other issues Gibbons was less positive, he insisted that the hierarchy formulate policies with respect to all of them. Inasmuch as the centralizing trend in public education which seemed to meet a real need would affect the Catholic schools, the committee should have "a careful treatment of this subject prepared and submitted to the judgment of the most expert." He suggested that a literary bureau under the patronage of the bishops would increase the output of good books and pamphlets with which "to enlighten inquirers or strengthen the faith and deepen the piety of our own people." Materials supplied the secular press by such a bureau would serve most effectively to repel attacks against the Church and better still secure a "sympathetic hearing" for Catholic thought and action. Although it bristled with difficulties, the problem of trying to prevent legislation hostile to the Church would have to be faced. Should the bishops, after the manner of Protestant churches and all other interests, appoint a Washington representative, the cry would be raised that the Church is in politics — a charge dating back to the Sanhedrin that condemned Christ. "It is a matter, however, which we must carefully consider," he observed, "and upon which the Hierarchy will desire a report." [40]

In three meetings during the spring and summer of 1919, the Committee on General Catholic Interests and Affairs translated Gibbons' comprehensive plan into an operational program, suggesting that the bishops become, for the purpose of deliberating on the realization of common Catholic objectives, the National Catholic Welfare Council with departments on missions, education, press and literature, social and charitable services, and societies and lay activities. At its second meeting, in July at the University of

---

[39] "Letter to Committee on General Catholic Interests and Affairs, May 5, 1919," ibid., 10–16.
[40] Ibid.

Notre Dame, the committee under prodding by Father Dietz and other clerical and lay partisans of labor decided to include industrial relations in the future council's work.[41] When the bishops — ninety-three of the 101 total — convened on September 24 for their first annual meeting, they accepted the committee's report in its main outlines after a clarifying discussion. In order that they might function continuously as the National Catholic Welfare Council, the bishops set up an Administrative Committee of seven members "to transact all business" and carry out their "wishes" between the annual sessions. By secret ballot the committee's personnel was chosen, the chairmanship going to Edward J. Hanna, Archbishop of San Francisco.

In early December the Administrative Committee, meeting at the Catholic University, addressed itself to the task of organizing the various departments. No steps were taken to set up a department of domestic and foreign missions, on which Gibbons had laid so much stress, but his warning to be on guard against unfriendly legislation was heeded by the committee's decision to create a Department of Laws and Legislation. Each department was to be chaired by a member of the Administrative Committee: that of Education by Austin J. Dowling, Archbishop of St. Paul; of Laws and Legislation by Denis J. Dougherty, Archbishop of Philadelphia; of Social Action by Peter J. Muldoon, Bishop of Rockford; of Lay Organizations by Joseph Schrembs, Bishop of Toledo; and of Press and Publicity by William T. Russell, Bishop of Charleston. To these familiar names was added another, the Reverend John J. Burke, who was named general secretary of the Administrative Committee and placed in charge of its Washington office, an "executive department" through which all N.C.W.C. activities were co-ordinated and day-to-day business carried forward. By mid-1920 the departments had largely completed their organizational work, the necessary funds being supplied by members of the hierarchy in proportion to their resources.

The Social Action Department began operations in February 1920. In setting up the department Bishop Muldoon was counseled by priests and laymen experienced in the field of social action. Some of these met with the bishop at the Loyola University School of Sociology in late December 1919. At this meeting an executive com-

[41] Fox, op. cit., p. 141.

mittee was chosen, consisting of five priests (M. J. Splaine, William J. Kerby, Frederic Seidenburg, William A. Bolger, and Edwin V. O'Hara) and four laymen (Charles P. Neill, James E. Hagerty, Frederick P. Kenkel and George J. Gillespie). Father Dietz had suggested that a labor leader — preferably Matthew Woll of the Executive Council of the AFL — be invited to the meeting. His advice on this as on other points was not followed. Dietz wanted to head the department's "sub-division for labor," but Muldoon refused to appoint him against the opposition of the executive committee. Ryan was made director of industrial relations while Lapp was placed in charge of citizenship and social service. Even if Dietz had not been personally obnoxious to some members of the executive committee, he was too closely identified with trade unionism to be acceptable. He considered co-partnership and producers' co-operation, as urged in the Bishops' Program, to be a delusion and a snare. "Co-operation is almost as lofty an ideal as the Communion of Saints," he had written, "but until the labor movement goes in for co-operation whole-heartedly, the other forces in that direction are worse than wasted; in that they delude, however well meaningly, those who believe them." [42]

Ryan, on the other hand, as the author of the Bishops' Program, was prepared vigorously to defend it. In their Pastoral Letter of 1919, the first since 1884, the bishops reaffirmed their conviction that industrial stability was contingent upon ownership being shared with workers "as rapidly as conditions will permit." While the trade union was still necessary, "in the struggle of the workers for fair wages and fair conditions of employment," it was "essentially a militant organization. The time seems to have arrived," the bishops thought, "when it should be, not supplanted, but supplemented by associations or conferences, composed jointly of employers and employees, which will place emphasis upon the common interests rather than the divergent aims of the two parties, upon cooperation rather than conflict." [43] The new department welcomed the postwar decision of the American Federation of Labor to base its future wage and hour demands on industrial productivity rather than on living costs as formerly. In striving to participate in the gains of

[42] Ibid., pp. 140–45.
[43] Peter Guilday, *The National Pastorals of the American Hierarchy* (*1792–1919*), pp. 322–23.

the improved technology, labor should not, however, aim wholly, or even mainly, at wage increases, but should claim a significant share in management, profits, and ownership.[44]

This seemed a counsel of perfection in the 1920s when the power of organized labor was steadily waning. It was unable to prevent wage cuts in the postwar depression (1920–23) and barely survived the concurrent open-shop drive which the general public in frenzied fear of alien radicals accepted as the "American Plan" of industrial relations. The Social Action Department courageously resisted the reactionary tide, denouncing the open-shop crusade in one of its earliest public statements.[45] The movement was "a hypocritical attempt," said Ryan, "to cripple the unions under the guise of promoting freedom of contract in industrial relations."[46] Ryan's assistant, the Reverend Raymond A. McGowan, heaped ridicule on the open-shop department of the National Association of Manufacturers which in a letter "To the Catholic Clergy" argued that Leo XIII had condemned the closed union shop as incompatible with Christianity.[47]

More disturbing in the view of the Social Action Department was the seemingly hostile attitude of government toward the labor movement. Repeatedly and pointedly, the department criticized decisions of the judiciary which allegedly abused its authority to issue injunctions in labor disputes and disallowed, generally by a close vote, protective labor laws, notably the federal statutes abolishing child labor and the minimum wage laws. Ryan was aroused to the point of anger by the Supreme Court's decision in *Atkins v. Children's Hospital* invalidating the District of Columbia's minimum wage law for women and minors.[48] This decision epitomized, he contended, the Court's false conception of economic freedom. The judges had read into the "due process" clauses of the Constitution the social and

[44] R. A. McGowan, "Trends in the Labor Movement . . . ," *N.C.W.C. Bulletin*, VII (November 1925), 28–29.

[45] John A. Ryan, "Criticisms of the Social Action Department," ibid., III (July 1921), 17–18.

[46] "Cooperation Between Capital and Labor," ibid. (May 1922), 13.

[47] "Garbling Pope Leo's Encyclical," ibid., V (September 1923), 27–28. See also Francis J. Haas, "Individualism and the Open Shop Campaign," *Salesianum*, XVI (April 1921), 2–15.

[48] "The Minimum Wage and the Constitution," *N.C.W.C. Bulletin*, IV (May 1923), 18–20; "The End of the Minimum Wage Laws," *Catholic Charities Review*, IX (November 1925), 339–40.

ethical philosophy of utilitarianism, that is, the freedom of individuals to do anything they like which does not interfere with the abstract legal freedom of others to do the same thing. But this was a negative view of liberty. Positive economic liberty, on the other hand, would guarantee to all "actual and effectual opportunity" to earn a decent income and to possess property.[49] So wedded were the courts to the negative form of economic liberty that Ryan urged an amendment to the Constitution empowering Congress to enact social and labor legislation.[50]

Only less than the industrial relations section the civic education program of the Social Action Department exerted a socially liberal influence. Inherited from the War Council, the program remained until 1927 under the vigorous direction of John A. Lapp. With headquarters in Chicago, Lapp labored tirelessly — and not without success — to introduce civics instruction among alien adults and parochial school children.[51] Always insisting that true Americanism was only another name for social justice, Lapp challenged the contrary view that patriotism meant nativism and the suppression of alien and other minorities.[52] He warned the Catholic minority to be on its guard against "clever and wicked propagandists" who often tried to pin an anti-Catholic label on welfare measures which were in fact in no sense detrimental to religion. "It is a tragedy," he wrote, "when men and women follow like sheep a false leader who deceives them in the belief that the Church or religion is in danger." Believing that Catholics erred in appearing before legislative hearings only when evil measures were under consideration, Lapp urged them to assist also "in the passage of legislation for human betterment." By giving up the negative role and working with others "for good things" we will have supporters "from the friends we have made," he reasoned, "to help us stand against those things which we consider evil." [53]

[49] *Declining Liberty and Other Papers* (New York, 1927), pp. 20–34.

[50] Ibid., 239–50; "A Constitutional Amendment for Labor Legislation," *N.C.W.C. Bulletin*, V (December 1923), 5–6; ibid. (January 1924), 5–6.

[51] See, for example, "Civic Education in the Diocese of Newark," ibid., VIII (June 1926), 27–28.

[52] "It was not known then, and perhaps it is not known now," wrote Lapp in 1936, "that this program of civic education was the most extensive program of civic education ever carried out in the history of this country." "Father Burke and Civic Education," *Catholic Action*, XVIII (December 15, 1936), 37–38.

[53] "Why We Organize," *N.C.W.C. Bulletin*, VIII (January 1927), 7–8, 26.

In its high resolve to familiarize the public generally with the social teachings of the Catholic Church, the Department of Social Action widely disseminated the written and spoken word. From time to time it published books, the first two being *The Church and Labor* (1920), a collection of letters and documents, edited by Ryan and Husslein, and *The Social Mission of Charity* (1921), by William J. Kerby, who viewed social service from a synthesized Christian-scientific point of view. More numerous were inexpensive pamphlets summarizing Catholic social teaching or dealing with some important problem in significant detail. The more useful ones constituted the department's "Half-Inch Labor Book Shelf." [54] One of these, *The Catechism of the Social Question* (1921), was designed primarily for the use of study clubs, which numbered over four hundred by 1927.[55] The department also sponsored hundreds of lectures in Catholic colleges and universities, especially during the early 1920s. It was hoped that the information conveyed by these lectures would inspire a large number of college men and women to prepare for careers in professional social service — the most pressing need of the Catholic Church in the postwar years.

In order further to personalize its teachings, the Department of Social Action initiated the Catholic Conference on Industrial Problems. At the department's call about a hundred persons interested in the wider diffusion of Catholic industrial ethics met on December 29, 1922, at the Loyola University School of Sociology in Chicago. The conference they formed proposed "to discuss and promote the study and understanding of industrial problems," mainly through periodic meetings, at which no vote was to be taken "on any question of industrial policy." David A. McCabe, professor of economics in Princeton University, was chosen president, the Reverend Raymond A. McGowan, assistant director of the Social Action Department, was made secretary-treasurer, while Patrick H. Callahan, Louisville industrialist, Ellis Searles, editor of the *United Mine Workers' Journal*, the Reverend Joseph Husslein, associate editor of *America*, Frederick P. Kenkel, director of the Central Verein's

[54] "A Half-Inch Labor Book Shelf," ibid., V (March 1924), 24–25; H. T. Henry, "Preaching on the Industrial Problem," *Ecclesiastical Review*, LXXI (July 1924), 23–37.

[55] Charles A. McMahon, "Study Clubs as a Help in Adult Education," *N.C.W.C. Bulletin*, VIII (December 1926), 12–13.

Central Bureau, and Miss Linna Bresette of the Social Action Department were named vice-presidents. On the invitation of Archbishop Messmer, the Catholic Conference on Industrial Problems held its first meeting in Milwaukee, June 27–28, 1923.[56]

In his opening address at the Milwaukee meeting McCabe announced a philosophy of action which was to guide the Catholic Conference on Industrial Problems during the quarter century of its history. "We shall, of course, stress," he said, "the binding force of ethical obligations in industrial relations."

> But we shall also seek to comprehend the practical problems that confront the several parties and interests in our complex industrial life and to appreciate the difficulties which must be overcome here and there if industry is to meet in full the high ideals of Christian justice. We have men and women here from all sections of our economic life and we look to them for this service of enlightenment. It is the need of viewing moral precepts in the setting of industrial facts and of viewing the facts in the light of these precepts that has brought us together.

A session each was given to "Wages," "Collective Bargaining," "The State and Industry," and "The Worker and Ownership," with both management and organized labor represented among the speakers on each topic, while in a luncheon forum "Women in Industry" was likewise discussed by employers, union officials, "and men learned in the principles of Catholic social teaching." A mass meeting concluded the Milwaukee conference, whose procedure was a model for succeeding conventions, national and regional, which numbered nearly a hundred by 1940.[57]

These meetings, which were well attended, were more instrumental than any other agency in acquainting the Catholic and non-Catholic public with the Church's social doctrine. During its first five years this "traveling school of social thought" had gone far, its second president, Frederick P. Kenkel, believed, "towards establishing a Catholic public opinion on questions pertaining to industry

[56] "Catholic Conference on Industrial Problems Established," *ibid.*, IV (February 1923), 14; "Catholic Conference on Industrial Problems," *Salesianum*, XVIII (April 1923), 70–72.

[57] R. A. McGowan, "The Catholic Conference on Industrial Problems," *N.C.W.C. Bulletin*, V (August 1923), 11–13; Ryan, *Social Doctrine in Action*, p. 156.

and labor." [58] Disappointingly, if not unexpectedly, the conference appealed less to employers than to employees, educators, and social workers. Reporting on the third meeting at Chicago in 1925, Callahan estimated that employers comprised not more than ten per cent of the attendants. Catholic employers, with few exceptions, did not take kindly to the three "programs" — *Rerum novarum*, the Bishops' Program of Social Reconstruction, and the Pastoral Letter. These men said frankly, "It is the business of the Church to save souls and not be like the Protestant churches, butting into everyone's business." One large employer had asked Callahan: "What did Leo XIII know about digging subways with steam shovels and handling 'Wops' and 'Hunkeys'?" With few businessmen in attendance, the Chicago meeting, though an open forum, overworked "the greed and avarice of the employers" theme, even the educators showing a "labor complex." [59] The weaknesses to which Callahan alluded could not be satisfactorily overcome in the years that followed.

Scarcely less than its industrial relations program, the social service outlook of the Social Action Department encountered opposition — from the many Catholics who continued to suspect that Christian and scientific charity were imcompatible. The department's main interest was the social survey with a view to the co-ordination of diocesan charities. After the example of the New York and Pittsburgh surveys made by the War Council, the Social Action Department employed the same personnel to canvass the welfare situation in several other dioceses — Toronto, Canada, in 1921; St. Cloud in 1922; Des Moines in 1924; Newark in 1925; Brooklyn in 1927; and Davenport in 1928. [60] Directed by Lapp and assistants, principally Rose J. McHugh, the department's chief authority on

[58] Quoted in *N.C.W.C. Bulletin*, X (June 1928), 27.

[59] "The Catholic Industrial Conference," *Fortnightly Review*, XXXII (August 15, 1925), 333–35.

[60] Lapp, "The Field of Social Work," *N.C.W.C. Bulletin*, IV (August 1922), 5–6; "Survey of the Field of Catholic Social Work," ibid. (September 1922), 3–5; Rose J. McHugh, "Social Problems in the Diocese of Des Moines," ibid., VI (May 1925), 20–21, 24; Lapp, "Social Survey of the Diocese of Newark," ibid., VII (February 1926), 18–19; McHugh, "Survey of the Diocese of Newark," ibid., VIII (March 1927), 13–14; "Social Survey of Davenport," ibid., X (November 1928), 31. For a discussion of these surveys from the point of view of child-welfare institutions, see McHugh, "Some Conclusions from a Series of Studies by the National Catholic Welfare Conference," National Conference of Social Work, *Proceedings*, 1929, pp. 125–34.

social case work, these social inventories were made with a view to enabling Catholics to meet more intelligently and more comprehensively their charitable responsibilities through united diocesan action. While the survey personnel suggested ways of improving the work of existing Catholic agencies, the chief interest was in discovering neglected fields where relief and rehabilitation were necessary to maintain or restore Catholic faith and practice. Catholics felt a definite responsibility, as Lapp explained, for doing those things that are "essential to the spiritual protection of Catholics from the cradle to the grave." But they did not feel that "in other matters, essentially material in character, or not involving spiritual care, Catholics should necessarily be limited to the helping of Catholics, nor that others should be absolved from helping Catholics as they do other members of the community in distress." [61] In order to determine from the Catholic angle the proper boundaries between public and non-sectarian agencies on the one hand and religious charities on the other, the survey, as all agreed, was necessary.

Social service as envisioned by the Social Action Department gained steadily in favor during the 1920s.[62] Over thirty representative dioceses — about one third of the total — established charitable bureaus, all of which involved some use of the social service survey.[63] The Social Action Department also conducted or helped finance special surveys, beginning with a rural survey in Lane County, Oregon. Impressed by Father Edwin V. O'Hara's views on rural Catholicism, Bishop Muldoon urged the priest to head a Rural Life Bureau to be set up in the department. O'Hara agreed on condition that he secure a rural parish for laboratory purposes. On Muldoon's entreaty Archbishop Christie transferred O'Hara, June 1, 1920, to Eugene, Oregon, a parish embracing nearly nine thousand square miles and about equally divided in membership between town and country. Here, on the basis of survey and experiment, O'Hara outlined a Catholic rural life program whose simplicity and scope appealed to a growing number of Catholics in the postwar era. Already aware of the need for religious education in rural areas, O'Hara at

---

[61] "Social Survey of the Diocese of Newark," loc. cit.

[62] John O'Grady, "The Future of Catholic Case Work," *Catholic Charities Review*, VI (March 1922), 93–95.

[63] O'Grady, "Training for Social Service," *N.C.W.C. Bulletin*, VII (May 1926), 12; same author, "New Perspectives in Charity," *Commonweal*, October 30, 1929.

once successfully experimented with vacation schools for children and correspondence study for both children and adults. Discovering that rural people lacked proper medical care, he persuaded Mercy Hospital and the medical department of the State University, both located in Eugene, to engage in systematic health extension work. Concerning social and economic betterment, he soon found that the first step was to bring Catholic farmers into touch with the multiplying public and private agencies for agricultural advancement. To this end, O'Hara organized the Catholic Agricultural Union of Lane County which, among other efforts, encouraged its members to affiliate with the farmers' co-operative movement which was beginning to flourish on the Pacific Coast.[64]

In this way was inaugurated the Rural Life Bureau. The National Catholic Welfare Council supplied a trained social worker as well as a part-time secretary. The priest's brothers, Frank and John, the one a professor of economics in the Catholic University of America and the other a journalist in Oregon, helped with research, publicity, and the preparation of the correspondence lessons, while the nun, Mary Basilla, a sister of Caroline Gleason, supervised the religious vacation schools. As the movement made headway, Monsignor Victor Day of Helena, Montana, became in 1921 supervisor of religious correspondence courses for the Rural Life Bureau, and O'Hara himself the following year launched *St. Isadore's Plow*, a four-page tabloid, as the bureau's official organ, the while writing, speaking, and making contacts with the personnel of the country's leading agricultural colleges and rural organizations. At the St. Louis convention of the American Country Life Association in 1923 O'Hara and like-minded ruralists formed the National Catholic Rural Life Conference, which in its field was comparable to the Catholic Conference on Industrial Problems in the area of industrial relations.[65]

As director of the Rural Life Bureau, O'Hara became the ex-

64 Shaw, op. cit., pp. 68–77; Witte, op. cit., pp. 57–59; "The Lane County, Oregon, Experiment in the Catholic Rural Program," *N.C.W.C. Bulletin*, II (December 1920), 6–7, 13; "Needs of Rural Catholic Parishes. Digest of Dr. O'Hara's Survey of Lane County, Oregon," ibid., III (September 1921), 4–5.

65 Shaw, op. cit., pp. 77–97; Witte, op. cit., pp. 59–69; "Religious Correspondence Courses Promoted by N.C.W.C. Rural Life Bureau," *N.C.W.C. Bulletin*, III (March 1922), 19; "Rural Problems of American Home," ibid., IV (December 1922), 23; "First National Catholic Rural Life Conference," ibid., V (December 1923), 16–17.

ecutive secretary of the conference while Bishop Muldoon, chairman of the Social Action Department, was honorary president of the new organization. At the suggestion of Monsignor Francis C. Kelley of the Church Extension Society, the Reverend Thomas Carey of Lapeer, Michigan, a successful church extensionist, was chosen first president of the conference. The incipient rural life crusade also enlisted support from Central Verein leaders, notably Frederick P. Kenkel, and from the American Board of Catholic Missions, successor to the prewar Americanist and rurally orientated American Catholic Missionary Union. After 1930 this mission board became the financial mainstay of the National Catholic Rural Life Conference. But during the 1920s the principal accomplishment of the conference, namely, the rapid increase in vacation schools, resulted from the efforts of the National Council of Catholic Women, which financed many of these schools and furnished them with health and recreational facilities.[66]

In supporting these schools, one of its many projects, the National Council of Catholic Women exemplified the procedural program of the National Catholic Welfare Council. From the outset the Welfare Council disclaimed any desire to impinge on the autonomy of other Catholic institutions, deeming its function to be one of service, encouragement, and co-ordination, not one of centralized domination. This attitude was clearly evident in the relations between the Welfare Council and the two councils of Catholic women and Catholic men which constituted the Department of Lay Organizations with Bishop Schrembs as chairman. These councils, formed in 1920, were designed to be channels of communications and influence between the National Catholic Welfare Council at the center and the Catholic people in all parts of the country. Through the councils the other departments of the Welfare Council were to be given a

[66] Shaw, op. cit., pp. 106–13; Witte, op. cit., pp. 69–88; "Second National Catholic Rural Life Conference," *N.C.W.C. Bulletin*, VI (October 1924), 24; Michael B. Schlitz, "St. Paul Meeting of Catholic Rural Life Conference," ibid., VII (November 1925), 30–31; "Religious Vacation School Movement Endorsed by N.C.W.C. Convention," ibid. (December 1925), 18; "Cincinnati Meeting of Catholic Rural Life Conference," ibid., VIII (November 1926), 27–28; "The Catholic Rural Life Problem. An Official Pronouncement of the Catholic Rural Life Conference," ibid. (January 1927); "Fifth Annual Rural Life Conference . . . ," ibid., IX (July 1927), 31; "Growing Influence of the Rural Life Conference," ibid. (September 1927), 22–23.

knowledge of the needs of the Catholic laity of the country, "and reciprocally, through them," as Charles A. McMahon so well stated, "there goes out to the laity the information, service, and experience which the N.C.W.C. departments supply, to be used by lay groups locally to broaden their knowledge, unify their action, and strengthen their efforts in behalf of Catholic interests." [67] Until 1924 the National Catholic Welfare Council met the operating expenses of both the men's and the women's organizations; thereafter each group derived its support from its affiliated individual and society members. But each council was expected to adjust its work to overall needs and opportunities.[68]

In its determination to meet this requirement, the National Council of Catholic Women scored an impressive record. Mrs. Michael Gavin (a daughter of railway king James J. Hill) served as first president, from 1920 to 1924, and Agnes G. Regan for a much longer period as executive secretary, both women of vision and untiring devotion to religion and society. On the ground that prevention was better than relief, the council urged Catholic women to support social legislation, including the Sheppard-Towner maternity bill to subsidize needy mothers and their infant children.[69] In the field of charity the council specialized — wisely, Carlton Hayes believed — in the training of social workers, the handling of immigrants, and protective care of women and girls.[70] In 1921 these organized women pledged their financial support to the National Catholic Social Service School for Women, successor to the War Council's similar institution. The National Council of Catholic Women not only met current expenses but liquidated over a ten-year period an indebtedness of three hundred fifty thousand dollars which had been incurred in the purchase of site, buildings, and equipment. Although its campaign for an endowment of six

[67] "The N.C.W.C. During 1927 — A Year's Review," ibid., IX (January 1928), 4–6, 28.

[68] Agnes G. Regan, "Financing a National Organization," ibid., V (December 1923), 24–26; Austin Dowling, "The National Catholic Welfare Conference," *Ecclesiastical Review*, LXXIX (October 1928), 344–45.

[69] *N.C.W.C. Bulletin*, II (January 1921), 13.

[70] "Professor Hayes Explains Nation's Need of Spiritual and Intellectual Leadership," ibid., III (November 1921), 23–25.

hundred thousand dollars did not succeed, the council met its obligations mainly from annual contributions of its membership.[71]

The school received forty-five thousand dollars from the Laura Spelman Rockefeller Memorial Foundation. Only a few students could meet their full expenses or even their tuition of five hundred dollars a year, which was paid by tuition scholarships established by diocesan councils or affiliated societies.[72] While the majority of enrollees in the school were college graduates, no young woman otherwise qualified to pursue social service study was denied admission. Students were privileged to take either the two-year or the one-year course; college graduates pursuing the two-year course were eligible for a master's degree at the Catholic University of America. The faculty of the school was drawn from professors at the university and the personnel of the National Catholic Welfare Council. The priests Kerby, Ryan, and Thomas Verner Moore taught sociology, industrial ethics, and child problems respectively, while Charles P. Neill, the first director of the school, Rose McHugh, and Helen Cronin supervised the courses in economics and social legislation, case work, and domestic economy. Attendance increased from sixteen in 1921 to forty-nine in 1930.[73]

[71] Rose Marie Moorman, "The First Annual Convention of the National Council of Catholic Women," *Catholic Charities Review*, V (November 1921), 302–3; same author, "The National Council of Catholic Women," ibid., VI (December 1922), 362–64; *Catholic Charities Review*, IX (December 1925), 397–98; ibid., XI (November 1927), 349; ibid., XII (December 1928), 334; "The So-Called National Catholic School of Social Service," *Fortnightly Review*, XXXIII (November 15, 1926), 513; *N.C.W.C. Bulletin*, IV (December 1922), 4–6, 15; ibid., V (October 1923), 25; ibid., VI (December 1924), 5; ibid., VII (December 1925), 20; ibid. (March 1926), 17; ibid. (May 1926), 9–27; ibid., VIII (June 1926), 17–19, 21; ibid. (July 1926), 27–28; ibid. (November 1926), 20; ibid. (February 1927), 30–31; ibid., IX (November 1927), 13–14; ibid., X (November 1928), 12; ibid. (January 1929), 12; ibid., XII (October 1930), 18, 31.

[72] Ibid., V (December 1923), 27; ibid. (February 1924), 27; ibid., VI (July 1924), 24, 27; ibid., VII (March 1926), 21; ibid., VIII (August 1926), 28; ibid. (September 1926), 24; Elizabeth R. Shirley, "The NCSSS — Retrospect and Prospect," ibid., VII (May 1926), 9.

[73] "The National Catholic Service School," ibid., III (November 1921), 8–9; John J. Burke, C.S.P., "The National Catholic Service School," ibid., V (June 1923), 3–5; Elizabeth R. Shirley, "Service School Holds First Commencement," ibid. (July 1923), 11, 32; ibid., VIII (October 1926), 26; ibid., XI (June 1929), 16–17; ibid., XII (December 1930), 10–11.

Although maintaining the National Catholic Social Service School was a heavy burden, it in no sense monopolized the women's council's efforts, even from the educational angle. Through careful planning and constant agitation the national council assisted in the formation by 1930 of local councils in forty-two dioceses — in two fifths of the total number.[74] Thus organized, Catholic laywomen were prepared to complete many projects dear to the heart of the National Catholic Welfare Council. Local women were particularly active in "follow-up" work in behalf of dwindling immigrants. At the ports of entry the oversight of Catholic newcomers after 1920 was supervised by the Bureau of Immigration set up in the "executive" department of the National Catholic Welfare Council. While the bureau could exercise some influence over the distribution and location of the new arrivals, it was not equipped to help solve their personal and social problems. To this task of immigrant aid and Americanization the diocesan councils of Catholic women devoted their major efforts in the early 1920s, helping immigrants through "home classes" in immigrant households, civics classes and club activities in community houses and elsewhere to make many new and painful adjustments. [75]

To the ever increasing need of homeless working girls for protective care the National Council of Catholic Women devoted special attention.[76] With a view to raising standards in this area the council employed the Social Action Department in 1924 to survey the girls' housing situation in American cities. The study was conducted by Dr. Lapp and Miss McHugh with the co-operation of ninety-one Catholic boarding homes, fifty-four of which were under the management of religious orders. This report urged Catholic protective agencies to become constituent parts of the National Travelers' Aid Society in order to provide shelter for transient women, and in like manner to utilize room registries to secure living accommodations in private homes and reputable board-

[74] Ibid., XII (December 1930), 10.

[75] Mrs. Michael Gavin, "Annual Report," ibid., III (December 1921), 24–26; Mary C. Delaney, "The Catholic Immigrant and Her Immigrant Neighbor," ibid., IV (July 1922), 2–3, 19.

[76] "N.C.C.W. Plans Girls' Welfare Bureau," *Catholic Charities Review*, VII (November 1923), 343; "Resolutions of the Convention, National Council of Catholic Women," *N.C.W.C. Bulletin*, V (October 1923), 15.

inghouses for working women and girls more or less permanently resident in cities and towns. As a general rule only girls and the younger women needed the protective care of existing and future Catholic boarding homes: middle-aged women should be excluded. Nor should the homes fix their rates so low as to encourage employers to pay less than living wages. The homes should be self-supporting, "including payment of taxes, interest and depreciation." These standards did not preclude social service to girls in need of rehabilitation or improved vocational status.[77]

Besides social work, the National Council of Catholic Women promoted social study. The council desired its members, as Mrs. Gavin put it, to "become thoroughly conversant with modern social conditions, understand the institution of government, and exercise intelligently and efficiently the right of suffrage." [78] Nearly all the early Catholic study clubs were formed under the auspices of the council. The council helped the Social Action Department prepare social study outlines and assumed the cost of their publication and distribution. In reply to a questionnaire sent out by the council's national office, the clubs indicated that working women were more widely interested than their leisured sisters in study and preferred social and civic information to purely cultural subjects.[79]

If the National Council of Catholic Women realized its objectives only in part, it was decidedly more successful than its masculine counterpart, the National Council of Catholic Men. At their first convention in September 1920 the men planned to establish a Catholic Bureau of Immigration, set up and conduct a Catholic Social Service School for Men, and push the formation of diocesan and parochial councils.[80] None of these ends was attained. While they encouraged miscellaneous activities, including the organizing

[77] "Social Action Department Reports on Girls' Welfare Survey. Summary of Findings in Study of Boarding Homes for Girls," ibid., VI (December 1924), 16–17; "Place of Room Registries in a Program of Girls' Welfare," ibid. (February 1925), 28–29; "Girls' Housing Committee Reports to N.C.C.W. Convention. Employed Working Women and Girls Present Problem for Catholic Organizations," ibid., VII (December 1925), 13.

[78] "Annual Report," loc. cit.

[79] Bishop Schrembs, "Work of National Council of Catholic Women During 1925–26," ibid., VIII (October 1926), 25.

[80] Charles A. McMahon, "The National Catholic Welfare Council Explained," ibid., III (January 1922), 27.

of Boy Scout troops, they were identified with no one thing until
they assumed responsibility for the Catholic Radio Hour in March
1930.[81] The men's council languished and became, as its critic
charged, a "paper organization" partly because it feared that the
Church was about to disown the National Catholic Welfare Council.[82]

The fear was not without justification. At the first annual meeting
of the bishops in 1919 Bishop Charles E. McDonnell of Brooklyn
had opposed the formation of the Welfare Council on the ground
that its work would uncanonically interfere with the authority of
bishops in their respective dioceses.[83] Several prelates shared
McDonnell's views, voiced them in Rome, and persuaded Pope
Benedict XV to withdraw his approval of the council. His decision
being confirmed by his successor, Pope Pius XI, the National Catholic
Welfare Council was in a state of suspended animation during the
first five months of 1922. In response to representations on the
council's behalf by Bishop Schrembs and others, Pius XI changed
his mind. On his order the Sacred Consistorial Congregation issued
a clarifying decree, June 22, 1922, permitting the council to continue. The decree reminded bishops with "misgivings about united
action" that attendance on yearly meetings was entirely voluntary
and that the decisions "have nothing in common with conciliar
legislation." From the beginning it had been clearly understood
that "the meetings are held merely for friendly conferences about
measures of a common public interest for the safeguarding of the
Church's work in the United States." Inasmuch as the name, the
National Catholic Welfare Council, "is open to some misunderstand-
ings, and in fact has not been acceptable to all," the decree suggested that the bishops choose some other name, for instance, the
National Catholic Welfare Committee. At their annual meeting in
1923 the bishops substituted "Conference" for "Council." [84]

[81] "National Council of Catholic Men," *Catholic Charities Review*, VIII
(November 1924), 329; "National Council of Catholic Men," *N.C.W.C. Review*, XII (December 1930), 11–12.

[82] Mark O. Shriver, "Catholic Lay Organization," *Commonweal*, November
4, 1925.

[83] John Tracy Ellis, *The Life of James Cardinal Gibbons*, II, 304.

[84] "New Decree of Sacred Consistorial Congregation Concerning National
Catholic Welfare Council," *N.C.W.C. Bulletin*, IV (September 1922), 2, 10;
"What the Bishops Did at Their Annual Meeting, September 26–27, 1923,"
ibid., V (October 1923), 4.

If the effort to safeguard the autonomy of bishops was a sincere one, it also served to camouflage opposition to the social program of the National Catholic Welfare Conference. Not many Catholics openly opposed the conference on this score. A few did, however, notably die-hard "Cahenslyites" in New England who saw in the National Catholic Welfare Conference a cruel conspiracy of "Irish" bishops to "Americanize" French-Canadian Catholics. In 1924 these extremists established at Woonsocket, Rhode Island, a newspaper, *La Sentinelle,* which directed at first a daily and then a weekly diatribe against the N.C.W.C.'s "assimilation" policies. The paper deplored the wide circulation of Lapp's Civics Catechism and of Father (later Bishop) James H. Ryan's *A Catechism of Catholic Education,* which affirmed, "The Catholic educational policy is to insist that all subjects be taught in English, not excepting religion." [85] Some Catholics, including the still influential Arthur Preuss of the *Fortnightly Review,* believed that irrespective of its policies the mere existence of the conference and the alleged claim of its agents to represent both the hierarchy and the laity increased the effectiveness of Ku Klux Klan attacks on the Church.

Actually the conference was a potent factor in the campaign against the Klan and its principal anti-Catholic objective, the destruction of the parochial school system. Claiming that private schools were divisive and un-American, the Klan inspired movements in about a dozen states to make attendance in public elementary schools compulsory for all children. By a small majority the electorate of Oregon in 1922 voted that elementary education would be confined to public schools beginning in 1926. Alarmed lest other states follow suit, the National Catholic Welfare Conference mobilized public opinion against the law and financed the legal battles against its constitutionality. Victory came in 1925 when the United States Supreme Court in *Pierce v. Society of the Sisters* disallowed the statute as "unreasonably" interfering "with the liberty of parents and guardians to direct the upbringing and education of children under their control." [86]

Indirectly this decision exerted a profound influence on Catholic social action in the 1920s. The Oregon school case convinced most

[85] J. Albert Foisy, *The Sentinellist Agitation in New England, 1925–1928* (Providence, 1930), pp. 30–32, 51–54.
[86] 268 US 510 (1925).

Catholics that in the judiciary lay the only sure defense of their minority rights and interests; consequently they opposed — often vehemently — any change in the existing constitutional framework. Yet as currently interpreted the federal Constitution drastically curbed the authority of government on all levels to legislate in the social justice field. Under the influence mainly of John A. Ryan, social justice enthusiasts among Catholics wished, by an amendment to the Constitution if necessary, to limit the power of the Supreme Court to declare acts of Congress or state legislatures unconstitutional. Some with Senator La Follette would have given Congress the authority to override a Supreme Court decision while others proposed that the Court be permitted to disallow social legislation only by a near-unanimous vote — not less than seven to two. This voting arrangement would have meant, according to Ryan, that the measures disallowed would be unconstitutional beyond "reasonable doubt." But "a priest-professor of ethics" whose opinion Ryan valued "very highly" objected that under the plan the obnoxious Oregon anti-parochial school law then in the courts would probably be upheld.[87]

Ryan preferred his horn of the dilemna. Refusing to state where lay the balance of justice as between the claims of labor and the Catholic schools of Oregon, he contended that the most expedient way to defend Catholic interests was to win friends among the labor and humanitarian elements of the country. Some opposition to Catholic interests was to be expected and served a good purpose in that it afforded Catholics an opportunity to explain and justify Catholic positions in the public forum. "It is not the bare fact but the magnitude and effectiveness of anti-Catholic political activities that are important," he pointed out in his rejoinder to John W. Cavanaugh, C.S.C., formerly president of the University of Notre Dame. In a public letter opposing La Follette for President in 1924 because of the senator's stand on the Supreme Court, Cavanaugh did not see "how Catholics can trust their future destinies to politicians or office holders" since "almost anything may happen in a state legislature or in Congress." Ryan denied the truth of these assertions: only one state by a relatively small majority had passed a hostile measure; persons "competent to judge" believed that the

[87] "The Supreme Court and Catholic Interests," *Catholic Charities Review*, VII (June 1923), 212–13.

Oregon proposal would have been defeated had the opposition been better organized and that the voters would have repealed it had it been submitted to the electorate in November 1924. More powerful and potentially more dangerous to Catholic interests were the social reform groups which would inevitably, he correctly predicted, bring the judiciary into line with their wishes. Should the Catholic minority "consistently and continuously" oppose judicial reform, it would become "an almost entirely isolated minority," alienated from the majority of the population and bereft of protection, even that of the Supreme Court. If, on the other hand, Catholics joined the social justice forces, "we shall be able to win for our religious and educational interests a sympathetic hearing," he reasoned, "and to prevent as effectively as a minority can ever hope to prevent legislation against our welfare." [88]

This advice was ignored by Catholics generally during the controversy over the proposed Twentieth Amendment empowering Congress "to limit, regulate and prohibit the labor of persons under eighteen years of age." While leading Catholic liberals urged ratification most Catholics were vehement opponents, co-operating with the National Association of Manufacturers and other conservative economic groups to prevent the amendment's adoption. Through the influence of Cardinal O'Connell the referendum vote in Massachusetts went against ratification. Here and in some other localities the opposition to the proposal took on a "Catholic aspect," observed ex-Congressman Edward Keating, joint author of the first of the two federal child labor laws declared unconstitutional by the Supreme Court.[89] Although Keating and Senator Thomas J. Walsh of Montana among Catholic social liberals pointed out that O'Connell's attitude aided the enemies of social justice, this consideration was without effect on opponents of the amendment, who insisted that its ratification would introduce "real Bolshevism" — a "Spartan and Russian State absolutism over our children." [90]

[88] "A Question of Tactics for Catholic Citizens," ibid., VIII (November 1924), 314–17; P. H. Callahan, "Tactics for Catholic Citizens," *Fortnightly Review*, XXXI (December 15, 1924), 481–83.

[89] "Child Labor Criticism," ibid., XXXII (February 15, 1925), 65–68.

[90] For the verbal duel between the Reverend Henry Loecker, an opponent, and the Reverend Francis J. Haas, a supporter of the amendment, see "The Child Labor Amendment," *Salesianum*, XX (January 1925), 53–61, and "The Child Labor Amendment Again," ibid. (April 1925), 29–36.

They assumed — without justification, the friends of ratification thought — that, given power over the "labor," Congress would also control the "education" and "activities" of youth, with injury to parochial schools and the exercise of parental rights. Even if Congress should keep within the bounds of moderation, the states would be free to invade the inner precincts of family life inasmuch as the United States Supreme Court would hesitate to prevent the states from exercising a power which the federal government possessed. In vain the social liberals protested that the Child Labor Amendment only remotely endangered private educational interests.[91]

By the mid-1920s the Catholic minority was an obstructionist influence so far as labor legislation was concerned.[92] When the Ku Klux Klan and allied groups attacked Catholicism on patriotic grounds the Church's leaders decided to forgo the benefits of social legislation lest it be used against Catholic interests. In effect, if not in so many words, Catholics shelved the Bishops' Program until a period more propitious for its application arrived. Other phases of postwar reconstruction continued, however, to manifest vitality and progress. This was particularly true of scientific social service, the main Catholic social interest during the 1920s. Social work enjoyed a marked growth during the war and its immediate aftermath — in response to a more vivid sense of human need and suffering. The numerous community houses established and financed by the National Catholic War Council gave a marked impetus to Catholic endeavor along social settlement lines. As in the prewar period Italian immigrants continued to be of much concern to Catholic social workers, who in 1922 formed a special organization, the Cyrenians, for the improvement and co-ordination of their activity.[93]

[91] "Child Labor Correspondence," *Fortnightly Review*, XXXII (April 15, 1925), 166–69; P. H. Callahan, ibid. (March 1, 1925), 95–98.

[92] Archbishop Dowling, "Holy Name Society Sermon, Cincinnati, 1925," quoted in P. H. Callahan, "Catholics and Community," *Fortnightly Review*, XXXIII (February 15, 1926), 70–71; "Insulated Catholics," *Commonweal*, August 19, 1925; "The Spell of Prosperity," ibid., September 15, 1926; "Justice and Society," ibid., May 25, 1927; J. W. R. McGuire, C.S.V., "Catholic Opinion and Social Reform," *Catholic World*, CXXIII (August 1926), 635–38.

[93] "The Cyrenians, a New Association for Immigrant Welfare Work," *Catholic Charities Review*, VI (October 1922), 277–80; "The Cyrenians," ibid. (December 1922), 364–66; ibid., VII (February 1923), 60–61; Anna C. Menogue, "Meeting the Italian Situation in Cincinnati," *N.C.W.C. Bulletin*, VIII (September 1926), 21.

After the war the sisterhoods no longer displayed their earlier indifference to the newer forms of social service. Symbolic of their changing attitude was the formation in 1920 of the Sisters' Conference in the National Conference of Catholic Charities. Some of the older sisterhoods increasingly participated in social settlement work, while for the same purpose new ones were organized along the lines of the Community of Catholic Social Workers in New York City, formed in 1920 by graduates of the Fordham School of Social Service. The entry of trained social workers into sisterhoods whether old or new was designed to circumvent the lingering prejudice against professional social service by lay people. But the combined efforts of the nuns, the lay volunteers, and the lay professionals were not extensive enough to bring about a marked expansion in settlement work during the 1920s.[94] An investigating committee appointed by the National Conference of Catholic Charities in 1927 found that there were only fifty-nine organizations under Catholic auspices in the United States "that merit the name settlement." Not only was the number of Catholic settlements "appallingly small," but their facilities in terms of buildings, staffs, and budgets were "pitifully inadequate to the task faced." As a substitute for "commercial recreation, all too often vile and degrading in type, the wholesome and unconsciously uplifting influence of the Catholic settlement," the committee insisted, is "more and more needed."[95]

Although its usefulness was admitted, the social settlement was in fact pushed to the periphery of Catholic interest during the 1920s. Attention centered rather on case work designed chiefly to rehabilitate and improve the home life of needy Catholic families. The widely felt desire for this type of social service partly prompted the formation during the decade of diocesan bureaus of Catholic charity in about thirty ecclesiastical jurisdictions, including nearly all the more populous ones. Through trained social workers the bureaus sought, as one of their prime objectives, to remove the causes of family disintegration, be they social or personal, or a

[94] For settlement and community house developments, see *N.C.W.C. Bulletin*, III (November 1921), 29; ibid. (March 1922), 11–15; ibid. (April 1922), 5–6; ibid., V (January 1924), 24–27; ibid. (May 1924), 5–6; ibid., IX (June 1927) 21–22; ibid. (July 1927), 17.

[95] Rev. Dr. Edward R. Moore, "Catholic Settlement Work," *Proceedings*, Fourteenth Session of the National Conference of Catholic Charities, 1928, p. 322.

combination of the two as was often true. Perhaps the principal evidence of family disorder was the inability or unwillingness of many Catholic parents to support and train their offspring. All too often children were hurtled into "orphanages" — misnamed institutions since more than four fifths of their "population" had either one or both parents living.

While the orphanages provided maintenance and religious training, they were in most other respects poor substitutes for the Christian home. Resort to the orphanage could be lessened if parents were encouraged and helped to shoulder ˙their responsibilities. Should careful investigation disclose, however, that a particular child should be temporarily separated from his parent or parents, his stay in the institution could be shortened if a fuller and more intensified training were provided and if in the meantime the child's home could be put on a sound footing. Reform along these lines, involving over five hundred and fifty Catholic child-caring institutions, would require careful study, constant supervision, and the closest co-operation among social agencies, non-Catholic as well as Catholic. However herculean the task, its accomplishment was the price Catholics must pay to stay in the child-caring field. The revulsion against institutional abuses and limitations was intense on the part of the non-Catholic public, which increasingly urged the state to place dependent children in foster homes irrespective of religious considerations.

Not until after World War I did Catholic child-caring experts seriously begin to meet this long-present challenge. In order to personalize child-care work and to create a more homelike atmosphere, cottage-plan institutions, beginning with the Angel Guardian Home in Chicago, were erected in several dioceses. In this arrangement a sister or two lived with not more than forty children in a separate building with its lawn and all other household essentials, the various cottages coming together only for school and chapel purposes.[96] The Diocese of Cleveland utilized the plan on a gigantic scale, caring for over two thousand children in a miniature village, a veritable "children's paradise." [97] While the costliness of the cottage plan

[96] John O'Grady, "A New Child-Caring Home," *Catholic Charities Review,* IX (January 1925), 26.

[97] Edwin L. Leonard, "The Future of Our Child-Caring Institutions," *Proceedings,* Eighth National Conference of Catholic Charities, 1922, p. 149.

precluded its wide adoption, its essential feature, the handling of children on a group as opposed to a mass basis, was applicable in traditional "congregate" institutions. So promisingly did several orphanages, mainly in the New York area, experiment with "the small group system" that its general adoption was urged by the National Conference of Catholic Charities. Its Committee on Standards, appointed in 1921 with the Reverend Bryan J. McEntegart of New York as chairman, endorsed the small group system in its report, "A Program for Child-Caring Homes," recommending also that policies with respect to the intake, discharge, and follow-up of children be formulated with a view to family rehabilitation.

The program, carefully studied by non-sectarian as well as by Catholic experts, was adopted by many Catholic child-caring institutions. "The general drift," wrote the Reverend John M. Cooper in 1931, "appears to be quite a decided one away from the congregate plan and in the direction of the cottage or group plans." [98] Increasingly, the child-caring homes welcomed the counsel of their respective diocesan bureaus of Catholic charities and thereby "kept together," asserted John O'Grady, "hundreds of families whose children would otherwise be scattered to the four winds." [99] O'Grady cited St. Paul's Orphan Asylum in Pittsburgh, which by adopting modern methods had reduced its population from 875 to 672 in an eight-year period. This institution admitted and discharged children only after investigation and approval by the Diocesan Conference of Catholic Charities. A trained social worker was employed to keep the orphanage in touch with the diocesan body and to carry on follow-up activities among children discharged to their own or foster homes. Professional personnel also met health and recreational needs. Adopting most features of the small group system, "St. Paul's is a good illustration," O'Grady thought, "of the possibility of developing a modern child program in an old congregate institution." [100]

The experience of many orphanages paralleled that of St. Paul's. That the vast majority might be induced to modernize their work,

[98] *Children's Institutions. A Study of Programs and Policies in Catholic Children's Institutions in the United States* (Philadelphia, 1931), p. 559.

[99] "Problems of Service to Children in Their Homes," *Proceedings*, Eleventh National Conference of Catholic Charities, 1925, p. 305; same author, "A Preliminary Survey of Catholic Child-Caring Work in the United States," *Catholic Charities Review*, VII (April 1923), 141–43.

[100] "St. Paul's Orphan Asylum," ibid., XI (June 1927), 221–24.

the National Conference of Catholic Charities sponsored the preparation of a manual for the guidance of child-caring administrators and teachers. Under the direction of the Reverend John M. Cooper, professor of anthropology at the Catholic University, a corps of field workers studied in minute detail nearly a hundred Catholic child-caring homes in order to discover and describe the methods and plans which had secured successful results. Financed by a grant of $16,500 from the Commonwealth Fund of New York City, the investigation was made in 1927–28 and its findings published in final form in 1931 in a meaty volume entitled, *Children's Institutions. A Study of Programs and Policies in Catholic Children's Institutions in the United States.* "The study was made of Catholic institutions by Catholics and for Catholics," as a representative of the Child Welfare League of America observed, "but 95% of the manual might well be taken to heart by all persons conducting children's institutions in all parts of the country." [101]

This appreciation of Catholic "standards" in child care suggested that Catholics were fruitfully participating in social service. At first followers in this comparatively new and uniquely American field, as Father O'Grady observed in 1925, they had in the previous decade been making up for lost time, "and now, at least in some sections, we are standing shoulder to shoulder with our fellow-citizens in the development of social work policies and programs." [102] Not only in child care but also in recreation, health, and various other areas Catholics during the 1920s formulated modern standards and in some degrees embodied them in practice. Much of the new social work was carried out under the guidance of diocesan bureaus of Catholic charities, which were set up in virtually all great urban centers. These co-ordinating bodies brought to the local level the national outlook fostered by the National Conference of Catholic Charities, the National Catholic War Council, and its successor, the National Catholic Welfare Conference, whose departments of social action and lay organizations (especially the National Council of Catholic Women) were of primary importance. Within a decade

[101] Louise McGuire, "Catholic Participation in the Social Work Conferences," *N.C.W.C. Review*, XII (July 1930), 28–29.

[102] "Catholic Leadership in Social and Civic Work," ibid., IX (February 1925), 74–75.

the Welfare Conference had begun to realize, notably in social service, many of the objectives envisaged by Cardinal Gibbons in 1919. Although the "dollar decade" minimized the importance of industrial ethics, the Social Action Department repeatedly warned that economic conditions were unsound "so long as productivity was high and the income of the masses, including that of the farmers, low." [103] When the Great Depression began in 1929 the department was prepared to do its part in making this idea — the purchasing power theory — basic in public policy.

[103] R. A. McGowan, "Catholic Work in the United States for Social Justice," *Catholic Action*, XVIII (May 1936), 5–11.

CHAPTER VII

The Depression Decade and Catholic Action:
Social Justice to the Forefront

During the Great Depression of the 1930s the Catholic social movement seemingly flourished. All the immediate measures set forth in the Bishops' Program of 1919 were adopted in whole or in part.[1] This may have meant, to be sure, little more than that the framers of the program had anticipated the general direction likely to be taken by any reform movement which in the presence of an economic collapse wished only to repair, not to tear down and rebuild the existing structure of society. The desire to restore rather than to uproot informed the New Deal, whose inception and growth registered victory — a permanent one, it would seem — for the positive state, that is, for the theory that government must guarantee to its citizens a substantial minimum of economic security and welfare. Although not unaffected by Catholic and other ideal formulations of social justice, the New Deal was essentially a political procedure seeking simultaneously to satisfy the frantic demands of savagely conflicting interests and to re-establish a workable economic order. On this secular level most Catholics, like Americans generally, supported or opposed the Rooseveltian "revolution." Some Catholics, however, insisted that the movement needed aid, criticism, and moral guidance.

In their eagerness to help rout depression and to restore the economy on a sound basis, Catholic social leaders were not obliged to devise new plans, only to revive and amplify earlier formulations of social justice. In every depression since the Civil War segments of Catholic opinion had insisted that government was duty bound to provide for the needs of the unemployed poor, preferably through

[1] John A. Ryan, "The Bishops' Program of Social Reconstruction," *American Catholic Sociological Review*, V (March 1944), 25–33.

public works.[2] From the 1880s, if not earlier, the partisans of state aid invoked the authority of the early Church Fathers who had warned the rich that their superfluous goods "in justice as well as charity" belonged to the poor[3] — a central item in patriotic radicalism. As restated in the early 1930s, most fully by the *Catholic World*, this truly "hard saying" was widely acclaimed and helped to discredit irresponsible wealth.[4] By the same token the doctrine strengthened the arguments of the Social Action Department and the diocesan directors of Catholic charities in behalf of a liberal federal relief and public works program.

The Hoover Administration opposed federal aid to the unemployed, maintaining that the relief of human distress devolved on private charity and local governments. Increasingly dubious of the Hoover formula, Catholic leaders in close touch with the mounting unemployed deemed it unjust and inopportune to throw the whole burden on financially hard-pressed cities and towns. One incensed priest, James R. Cox of Pittsburgh, led a "hunger march" on Washington early in 1932, and on his return home enrolled some fifty thousand unemployed workers in an organization which threatened independent political action if the old parties failed to bring relief. "A Catholic priest such as Father Cox," observed the *Christian Century*, "lives very close to a large portion of the public that is actually suffering. Leadership from such a source is not academic nor doctrinaire." [5] The likelihood of Hoover's defeat in the fall election forestalled, no doubt, the fruition of the priest's plans.

The call for a generous federal relief and works program was in keeping with the theory that the depression stemmed from underconsumption and would end only as mass purchasing power was restored and vastly extended. In a remarkable series of articles following the 1929 crash, John A. Ryan "traced unemployment to the gap between output and buying power" and "advocated higher wages and shorter hours" [6] along with a five-billion-dollar federal works program as against President Hoover's attempt to dispel de-

---

[2] Supra, p. 48.

[3] Ibid., p. 63.

[4] "Editorial Comment," CXXXIII (May 1931), 225–34.

[5] "A Portent from Pittsburgh," February 3, 1932.

[6] McGowan, "Catholic Work in the United States for Social Justice," loc. cit.

pression by making more credit available to business.[7] In the fall of 1930 the Social Action Department released its study of unemployment in which employers were urged to pay high wages (on the basis of living needs and worker productivity), to shorten hours, and to deal with employees through labor unions and collective bargaining. The study favored unemployment insurance, preferably through the joint action of management and workers, but this failing, through the state governments. An extensive program of public works (to include housing) and co-ordinated employment bureaus was also endorsed.[8] In more general terms the bishops, meeting in November 1930, attributed unemployment to the lack of justice in the economic field, pointing out that what was most needed was a change of heart which would so "organize and distribute our wealth that no one need lack, for any long time, the security of being able to earn an adequate living for himself and those dependent on him." The assembled prelates quoted from the Bishops' Program of 1919 to the effect that "high purchasing power" was "the surest guarantee of a continuous and general operation of industrial establishments" and opined that, had this truth been adhered to during the 1920s, it would "have gone far to prevent the calamity we now undergo." [9]

Nearly all Catholic social actionists deplored the weakness of unionism, none more strongly than the Reverend Francis J. Haas of St. Francis Seminary. "It is not too much to say," he argued before the National Conference of Catholic Charities in 1931, that if four fifths of American wage earners "had been organized during the past forty years . . . the present tragic condition of unemployment and business stagnation could not exist. A proper share of the

---

[7] "The Senate Looks at Unemployment," *Commonweal*, October 2, 1929; "The Experts Look at Unemployment," ibid., October 16, 23, 1929; "Unemployment: Causes and Remedies," *Catholic World*, CXXVIII (February 1929), 535–42; "Unemployment: A Failure in Leadership," ibid., CXXXI (July 1930), 385–93.

[8] McGowan, "Catholic Work in the United States for Social Justice," loc. cit.

[9] National Catholic Welfare Conference, *Our Bishops Speak. National Pastorals and Annual Statements of the Hierarchy of the United States, 1919–1951* (Milwaukee, 1952), pp. 191–93; for the hierarchy's 1931 statement see ibid., pp. 194–96; "U.S. Bishops Issue Statement on Economic Crises," *N.C.W.C. Review*, XIII (December 1931), 8; "Roman Catholic Bishops Defend Rights of Labor," *Christian Century*, December 2, 1931.

national product would have been consumed by workers, and savings made available for old age and emergencies. . . ." There would be no permanent recovery, predicted this future bishop, "unless wage earners are frankly accorded the right to organize and bargain collectively for wages and working conditions." Intelligently led union organization "is the only effective method of securing an adequate share of the national wealth for workers and their families."[10] Haas's view was sanctioned, at least by implication, in leading official statements of Catholic social doctrine, including Pope Pius XI's encyclical on reconstructing the social order, issued in May 1931, on the fortieth anniversary of *Rerum novarum.*

In *Quadragesimo anno,* as his encyclical was generally called, the erstwhile librarian and mountain climber declared that workingmen were in justice entitled to wages of "ample sufficiency." He recommended that where possible co-partnerships be introduced so that wage earners might become "sharers in some sort in the ownership or the management or the profits."[11] In the event that industrial depression undermined the ability of businessmen to pay living wages, the situation should be corrected through the joint action of employers and employees, aided by the public authority. Similarly, the causes of unemployment, one of which was "a scale of wages too low, no less than a scale excessively high," should be removed. In these ways Pius XI lent his sanction to the movement for economic planning which in this country was being popularized by some segments of labor and business and by numerous intellectuals of whom Stuart Chase and Charles A. Beard were the most vocal.[12]

In order the better to promote social justice and its great objective, namely, the common good, Pius XI urged that the direction of economic life be assigned to vocational groups, one for each trade,

[10] "Catholic Doctrine and Industrial Practice," Seventeenth National Conference of Catholic Charities, *Proceedings,* 1931, p. 248; reprinted in *Salesianum,* XXVII (January 1932), 1–9.

[11] "Quadragesimo Anno," in Appendix, Joseph Husslein, *The Christian Social Manifesto* (Milwaukee, 1931), pp. 284–323.

[12] John A. Ryan, "The New Things in the New Encyclical," *Ecclesiastical Review,* LXXXXV (July 1931), 7–8; A. I. Abell, "Labor Legislation in the United States: The Background and Growth of the Newer Trends," *Review of Politics,* X (January 1948), 51; L. L. Lorwin, "The American Front," *Survey,* LXVII (March 1, 1932), 569–71; ibid., "The Encyclicals of Leo XIII and Pius XI," *Current History,* XXXIV (July 1931), 486–87.

profession, or industry, in which employers and employees should "join forces to produce goods and give service." These groups ought to be "in a true sense autonomous," that is, self-governing bodies, with power to set prices, determine wage scales, and in general to control and regulate industrial conditions. The state would assist, not dominate the process, imposing restraints only when necessary to adjust unresolved differences or to safeguard the interest of consumers and the public generally. Bringing employers and employees into the same organization would put an end to class conflict and bind men together "not according to the position they occupy in the labor market, but according to the diverse functions which they exercise in society." The Pope strongly endorsed "unions" of a "private character," that is, trade unions, employer associations, and the like. He counseled these "free associations" which had produced so many "salutary fruits" to "prepare the way and do their part toward the realization of those still more ideal guilds or occupational groups which we have previously mentioned." [13]

As with *Rerum novarum* on its appearance in 1891, divergent groups were able to find in *Quadragesimo anno* support, in some degree, for their ideas and aspirations. While businessmen as a class were not impressed,[14] reformers, non-Catholic as well as Catholic, thought highly of the pronouncement. The non-denominational Protestant *Christian Century* esteemed the encyclical "a weighty deliverance which may in time become a notable landmark in social history." The document stated "with the clarity of genius the situation out of which grow all the economic problems that distress our modern world." In his eagerness to identify social progress with theological conservatism, the Pope wrongly, the journal asserted, attributed the evils of *laissez faire* to "liberalism." "As a matter of fact," the paper was quick to point out, "sweatshops and child labor have no relation to anything that has been called liberalism for many years." [15] The *Nation* [16] and the *New Republic*, which sympathized with socialism as expounded by the British Labor party, feared that the encyclical would deepen the attachment of American

[13] "Quadragesimo Anno," loc. cit., pp. 304–6.

[14] "The Pope Is Attacked as Socialistic!" *Christian Century*, June 24, 1931; "Needed Counsel," *Columbia*, X (July 1935), 18.

[15] "The Pope's Encyclical," June 3, 1931.

[16] June 3, 1931.

Catholics to conservative unionism — a synonym, in their opinion, for social futility. The latter journal predicted that the changes desired by Catholics could not "be brought about by the good will of those who are now economically powerful, balanced by trade unionism, 'pure and simple.' " [17]

To Catholics, however, the encyclical was more than a trade union document even if its main effect in the 1930s was to advance the interests of union labor. Some expected the encyclical to transform the present economic system into a "classless" society of property-holding workers — a guild order adjusted to modern mass production and technological progress. Others expected only a more equitable division of wealth and income among existing classes.[18] All agreed that the encyclical extolled the ideal of social justice and greatly enriched its meaning and significance. The Pope identified "social justice" with the "common good," by which he meant not merely the good of society viewed collectively or as a unified entity but the good or welfare of all persons and classes within the community.[19] Only as these goals were measurably realized could the Catholic people, for the most part poor and insecure, obtain the income with which to support the Church and its many projects and to resist the powerful birth control propaganda of many nonsectarian liberals and Protestant Christians.[20] The Catholic Church,

[17] "The Pope and Labor," May 27, 1931.

[18] For various opinions, see "The Prospects of Succeeding," *Guildsman*, I (December 1932), 11–13; "Why a New System?" ibid. (January 1933), 4–5; "Essentials of the New System," ibid. (February 1933), 8–10; "The Meaning of Capitalism," ibid., V (October 1936), 10; Dr. Franz Mueller, "What Is Capitalism?" ibid., VI (July 1938), 4–7; ibid. (August 1938), 2–5; Louis J. A. Mercier, "Capitalism and the Facts," *Commonweal*, January 8, 1937; Virgil Michel, "Facts about Capitalism," ibid., March 12, 1937; same author, "What Is Capitalism?" ibid., April 29, 1938; Philip Burnham, "Sniping at Capitalism," ibid., June 3, 1938.

[19] John A. Ryan, "The Concept of Social Justice," *Catholic Charities Review*, XVIII (December 1934), 313–15.

[20] Paul Kiniery, "Catholics and the New Deal," *Catholic World*, CXLI (April 1935), 10–20; Constantine McGuire, "Population and Prosperity," *Columbia*, X (August 1930), 5–6, 37; same author, "Mankind Alone Is Wealth," ibid., XVIII (June 1939), 3–4, 20; "Another Surrender," ibid., X (May 1931), 19; "Dr. Little Performs," ibid., XI (November 1931), 19; "The Sweet Get Low," ibid., XI (March 1932), 17; "Memo for Mrs. Sanger," ibid., XIV (January 1935); D. A. Saunders, "Liberals and Catholic Action," *Christian Century*, October 20, 1937.

as wrote the religious news editor of the National Conference of Christian and Jews, must "commit itself to a new social order if it wishes to cling to its traditional teaching on the birth control question." [21]

Not only the bishops and the "official" Church but various auxiliary groups saw in *Quadragesimo anno* the social justice norm and sought out ways to attain its realization. Most widely known was the "radio priest," Charles E. Coughlin of Royal Oak, Michigan, whose eloquent microphonic oratory was principally concerned after 1930 with the social justice issue.[22] As one keen observer wrote, Father Coughlin possessed an "uncanny ability to make himself the articulate voice for the manifold and deep discontents of the age." [23] Unrivaled in his power to expose abuses, he unsparingly attacked by name the alleged instigators and beneficiaries of injustice and fraud. His dealing in personalities, along with his partisan political and legislative commitments, made him a highly controversial figure. Indirectly, however, he publicized Catholic social teachings more widely than any contemporary, not only on radio, but on the public platform and after 1934 through the propaganda of the Union for Social Justice and its weekly journal, *Social Justice*.[24]

Coughlin did not envisage social justice as the function or product of integrated occupations.[25] He wrongly restricted the vocational group plan or the guild system to labor unions and relied on compulsory arbitration to secure peace and justice in the industrial field. He suggested that organized labor — which he strongly favored — be placed under the protective tutelage of the Department of Labor.[26] If this indicated a Fascist approach, as many of his enemies and critics alleged, the tendency owed less to Mussolini

[21] Louis Minsky, "Catholicism's Social Awakening," ibid., June 10, 1936.

[22] Ruth Mugglebee, *Father Coughlin of the Shrine of the Little Flower* (Boston, 1933), pp. 156–321.

[23] Wilfrid Parsons, S.J., "Father Coughlin and Social Justice," *America*, LIII (May 18, 1935), 129–31.

[24] "Father Coughlin: Whither?" *Guildsman*, III (January 1935), 9; ibid., V (October 1936), 10–11.

[25] "The Coughlin Controversy," ibid., III (July 1935), 10; "Provocatives," ibid., IV (May 1936), 12; "Father Coughlin's Recent Program," ibid., V (November 1936), 2–4.

[26] Charles E. Coughlin, *Eight Lectures on Labor, Capital and Justice* (Royal Oak, Mich., 1934), pp. 115–32; Parsons, op. cit.

or Hitler than to the tradition represented by the late nineteenth-century single taxers and Populists. Like these earlier reformers, Father Coughlin did not believe that the heart of the trouble lay primarily in conflict between employers and employees but rather in profound disturbances, chiefly of a financial and monetary character. In his view public ownership was the only cure for these maladies. "I believe in nationalizing those public necessities which by their very nature are too important to be held in the control of private individuals. By these I mean," he enumerated, "banking, credit and currency, power, light, oil and natural gas and our God given natural resources." He stressed the nationalization of banking and currency with a view to keeping prices on an even keel and liquidating "unbearable and unpayable debts." [27]

On a platform mainly of monetary reform, this "shepherd of the air" gained a wide following during the early 1930s, but for various reasons was unable to hold it intact. In behalf of labor, he demanded that every worker be guaranteed a minimum annual wage of eighteen hundred dollars. This tended to alienate small employers and other middle-class backers, many of whom made considerably less than this sum. Moreover, the clergy shunned their confrere, either out of envy or distrust, or because he did not invite or welcome their co-operation. They may well have concluded that the priest's movement was more personal and political than religious in character. They were repelled by his ambition to be a "religious Walter Winchell" and to put "the universal credo into Christianity." Aiming "to extend American ideals," the Union for Social Justice lacked a definitely Christian basis and gradually drifted into the anti-Semitic camp.

By way of reaction to the errors and limitations of the Coughlin movement many Catholics sensed the need, no doubt, to champion social justice along more approved lines. To the delight of his steadfast followers, chiefly lower middle-class German and Irish Catholics, Coughlin tongue-lashed clerical opponents, including the imperious Cardinal O'Connell. Coughlin's conduct recalled that of the single-tax rebel, Father Edward McGlynn, and must entail, many feared, equally bad results. That no schism and few defections occurred was owing partly to the fact that, unlike McGlynn, Coughlin had

[27] *Ibid.*, "The Coughlin Sixteen Points," *Guildsman*, III (April 1935), 10–11.

the backing of his ecclesiastical superior and was not given the opportunity therefore to pose as the martyr to a misunderstood cause even if he had wished to play the role of the prophet spurned. More important, perhaps, he was no match for Roosevelt in the political arena. The priest was popular so long as he preached "Roosevelt or Ruin"; he was all but ignored when he turned against the President and placed his own party — the Union party — in the field against him.[28] In this election of 1936 John A. Ryan asserted, in a spectacular radio speech, "Roosevelt Safeguards America," "that Father Coughlin's explanation of our economic maladies is at least 50 per cent wrong, and that his monetary remedies are at least 90 per cent wrong" — remedies, moreover, that found no support, he believed, in the encyclicals of either Pope Leo XIII or Pope Pius XI.[29]

Coughlin's program made little appeal to Catholics of education and substance. Some of these — scholars, publicists, and men of affairs generally — mobilized to bring influence on the business community, heretofore impervious to Catholic social teachings. Under the auspices of the National Catholic Converts' League, scores of the "best-known leaders in finance and industry, many non-Catholics as well as Catholics," met in New York City early in 1932 "with Catholic economists and teachers of ethics." The main speakers, John Moody, the noted business statistician, and the Apostolic Delegate, the Most Reverend Pietro Furnasoni-Biondi, attributed the current social chaos to the divorce in practice between business and ethics. Announcement was made at this meeting that steps were being taken by the Calvert Associates, publishers of the *Commonweal*, to form a nationwide League of Social Justice for the study and application of the economic teachings of Pope Pius XI.[30] The guiding light in this endeavor was Michael O'Shaughnessy, oil executive and industrial publicist.[31] "Several Catholic laymen, businessmen of substantial means," he reported later in the year to *America*, the Jesuit weekly, "have reached the conclusion that

[28] James P. Shenton, "The Coughlin Movement and the New Deal," *Political Science Quarterly*, LXXIII (September 1958).

[29] Quoted in A. I. Abell, "Monsignor John A. Ryan: An Historical Appreciation," *Review of Politics*, VIII (January 1946), 133.

[30] "A League of Social Justice," *Commonweal*, January 27, 1932.

[31] O'Shaughnessy refers briefly to his business career in "An Open Letter," *Social Justice Bulletin*, IV (August 1941), 2–3.

the social, financial and industrial dislocation that has overwhelmed the world demands that we conform our human relations to our spiritual ideals, that the value and security of all property and the material happiness of all the people of the United States depends on the attainment in this country of social justice as propounded by Our Holy Father, Pope Pius XI, in his inspired Encyclical, 'Quadragesimo Anno.' " [32]

No success was possible, he stressed, without "Divine assistance," so "overwhelmingly great" were the obstacles to be overcome. For this reason the league a-forming would exact of each member a pledge to attend holy mass daily and receive Holy Communion weekly, so far as possible, "and to do everything in his power — in his family and religious life and in his social and business contacts — to promote the principles of social justice as defined by our Holy Father." [33] Under the new technological conditions men's greed, as O'Shaughnessy patiently and graphically explained, induced an endless production of goods and services without providing the consuming masses with sufficient income to satisfy even their basic needs.[34] The redistribution of wealth, the special responsibility of the privileged few, called for a curb in the desire for excessive gain. All too many, having lost faith in their ability to curb their greed and to be fair to one another in the conduct of the world's business, "seek laws to force them to do what they can only do for themselves." Citizens devoid of moral responsibility would not obey laws, be they ever so reasonable and necessary.[35]

The remedy lay in human beings "practicing self-restraint and doing to others as they would be done by." It was easier to change human nature "to the extent of making men fair and honest in business than it is to force them to be so by law." The duty of Catholic laymen, leaders in finance and industry, was to use their brains and resources to curb avarice and "to establish Christian principles in the conduct of the world's business. If a baker's dozen of outstanding Catholic industrial and financial leaders could be induced to organize and finance such a movement," he confidently

[32] "Communications: Praying for Social Justice," September 24, 1932.
[33] Ibid.
[34] "How Strong Is the World's Industrial Arch?" *America*, January 30, 1932.
[35] "Greed Is the Witch," *Commonweal*, November 4, 1931.

asserted, "they might easily be the lump that would leaven the whole mass and do the country a service of inestimable value." [36] Great numbers need not at once join the Catholic League for Social Justice. Only thirty-one leading colonial citizens in the Declaration of Independence, he reminded the hesitant, "defied the most powerful monarch on earth and made possible the United States of America." A comparatively few Catholics, similarly dedicated, "can start a movement to bring the blessings of social justice to all the people of our country." [37]

O'Shaughnessy did not fail to correlate the attitudes of his group with the movement for economic planning which was popular with liberal intellectuals, trade unionists, and progressive businessmen during the early 1930s. He elaborated a plan of his own in a carefully written pamphlet, *Men or Money?* published in the summer of 1932.[38] Prudently omitting mention of *Quadragesimo anno*, he set out to show how the central idea in that encyclical could "be applied to American economic life." [39] Believing that state capitalism, as well as communism, meant slavery to government, O'Shaughnessy called for the reform of the capitalistic social order. "The profits urge, prostituted by greed, must be controlled," he argued, "by forcing industry to co-operate and not compete destructively in the conduct of the nation's business. Industry, through legalized monopolies, must be forced to conduct its affairs in the interests of the various units which constitute it and in the interest of labor and the public with a minimum of Federal Government supervision." He warned that the corporations could not be destroyed without destroying the country. "But they must be controlled in a manner to preserve," he insisted, "as great a degree of individualism to the citizen as is consistent with the changed conditions of our national life." [40] O'Shaughnessy proposed that trade associations be formed in all major industries for the purpose of insuring equal partition of available work among workers entitled to work in the industry; to maintain production on a profitable basis; to fix maximum and

[36] Ibid.
[37] "Communications: Praying for Social Justice," loc. cit.
[38] "The O'Shaughnessy Plan," *Commonweal*, April 20, 1932.
[39] Aloysius J. Hogan, S.J., "The Catholic Church and the Social Order," *Proceedings*, National Conference of Catholic Charities, 1933, p. 52.
[40] *Men or Money?* (New York, 1932), pp. 20–21.

minimum prices; to keep employed in each industry the average number of employees engaged in the industry over the period of the preceding ten years at wages large enough to support decently their families; and to set aside reserve funds to provide for fair and stabilized wages for workers and owners, based on the operations of the industry in the preceding decade.

In O'Shaughnessy's plan the trade associations would be controlled by nine directors, three each from and by management, labor, and the consuming public. The plan also provided for a federal agency with power to settle disputes and to veto decisions, chiefly price-fixing ones, the veto to be subject to court review.[41] O'Shaughnessy's proposals were circulated among people of influence, including every Cabinet member of the incoming Roosevelt Administration.

Meanwhile, the Catholic League for Social Justice gained momentum, having been publicly approved by Cardinal Hayes of New York on the Feast of Christ the King in October 1932.[42] In the course of the following year sixty-five bishops in the United States, along with several in Canada and Mexico, extended similar sanctions.[43] Although the league had "no formal organization, officers, initiation fees or dues," it enjoyed active support in twenty-four dioceses of the United States (about one fourth of the total) in the way of diocesan recorders, who circulated membership pledges, and organization committees, which sponsored study clubs and discussion groups. Impelled, as he claimed "by an uncontrollable urge to do something for God and my country in the most serious crisis in our history," O'Shaughnessy edited and published, largely at his own expense, the *Social Justice Bulletin,* a monthly review of current events in their relation to the social justice crusade.[44]

Not unexpectedly, enrollment in the league was small, not more than ten thousand. Yet, indirectly, through the press and various

[41] Ibid., 26–27.

[42] "In Retrospect," *Social Justice Bulletin,* I (September 1937) 2–3.

[43] "Here's Your Resolution," *Columbia,* XII (January 1933), 17; "A League for Social Justice," *America,* March 18, 1933; "The Crusade for Social Justice," ibid., May 27, 1933; "New Social Justice Bulletin," ibid. (September 30, 1933), 605; "Report for the Year 1933," *Social Justice Bulletin,* I December 1933), 1–2.

[44] Ibid. (November 1933), 1–2. The *Social Justice Bulletin* was published monthly at New Canaan, Connecticut, from January 1933 until June 1934 (in mimeographed form from January to August 1933; from June 1934 until November 1943 the journal appeared about four times a year at irregular intervals).

Catholic organizations, it seems to have exerted a persuasive influence.[45] In the Archdiocese of Chicago, for example, the Holy Name Society, at the suggestion of Bishop Bernard J. Sheil, director of the highly successful Catholic Youth Organization, urged its members to sign the league's pledge, while the National Council of Catholic Men endorsed "as worthy of universal support the object of the Catholic League for Social Justice and will cooperate in advocating adoption of its simple but most efficacious requirement." [46]

The league was to find its strongest echo in the National Catholic Alumni Federation, which from its formation in the mid-1920s displayed a growing interest in social questions. Through its regional and national meetings the federation in the early 1930s worked out "a definite and specific program" which in the interests of economic stability called for a better ordering of industrial relations, to be secured by trade associations in partnership with labor and government. "This is a far cry indeed," one commentator thought, "from the negative protests against Marxian socialism and the all too feeble pleas for greater justice to labor which characterized Catholic action just prior to the war." [47]

The third major agitation begun in the early 1930s was the Catholic Worker movement headed by Dorothy Day, journalist, social worker, and erstwhile Communist.[48] Aroused by the taunts of the Communists that Catholics had no love for the poor, she resolved late in 1932 to devise ways to personalize Catholic sympathy for the harassed victims of depression, especially the homeless and unemployed worker. Early the next year, with the help of Peter Maurin, a French-born itinerant social philosopher, she opened in lower New York a house of hospitality which combined the functions of soup kitchen, discussion club, and reform center. Similar houses — thirty of them by 1940 — were established in cities from coast to

[45] John Corbett, S.J., "The Crusade for Social Justice," *Social Justice Bulletin*, I (November 1938), 2–3; "Youth and Social Justice," ibid., II (May 1939), 2–4.

[46] *Social Justice Bulletin*, I (December 1933), 2; see also "Significant Activities," ibid. (February 1934), 2.

[47] "National Catholic Alumni Federation," *Catholic World*, CXXXVI (December 1932), 367; Richard Dana Skinner, "Social Justice — a Program," *Commonweal*, July 28, 1933; "Radical Catholic Action," *Christian Front*, II (April 1937), 51.

[48] Dorothy Day, *From Union Square to Rome* (Silver Spring, Maryland, 1938).

coast.[49] A monthly paper, the *Catholic Worker*, also begun in the spring of 1933, pinpointed Catholic social doctrine and attained within a short time a circulation well in excess of a hundred thousand. Its phenomenal success inspired similar ventures elsewhere in the field of Catholic social journalism.

Like the Communists, the Catholic workers engaged in tireless indoctrination of the poor, the "ambassadors of God." The better to influence them, Miss Day and her co-workers practiced voluntary poverty, combined manual and intellectual labor, and performed works of mercy in a highly personalized manner. Their zeal and self-sacrificing spirit recalled, in fact continued in more intense form, the work of the early college social settlements. Like these precursors, the Catholic Workers actively supported the labor movement. While they did not deny that social legislation was needed, they stressed "personal responsibility before state responsibility." [50] More to their liking, therefore, was their participation in strikes and union organizational activities which afforded them excellent opportunities to counteract Communist influences and to expound the Christian philosophy of labor.

But the Christian handling of unemployment, the Catholic Workers contended, was the gravest problem the country faced — a more immediate problem than the unionizing of workers. "In fact the unionizing of workers," wrote Miss Day, "cannot get on while thirteen million men are unemployed and those employed are hanging on to their jobs like grim death and not willing to make any forward steps which could jeopardize those jobs." American unemployment was as horrifying as leprosy in medieval France, and as France had two thousand leper houses run by religious orders, so this country needed a comparable number of houses of hospitality to lessen hunger, cold, and sickness. For the shelter afforded by city and state to the unattached unemployed "is liable to make them leprous in soul and utterly incapable of working for sustenance or salvation." [51] Through houses of hospitality "in the shadow of the Church" men would be recalled to Christ "and to the job of rebuild-

[49] Dorothy Day, *House of Hospitality* (London, 1939), V–XXXVI, pp. 257–75; Will Woods, "And Hospitality Do Not Forget," *Social Justice Review*, XXXIII (September 1940), 152–53.

[50] Day, *House of Hospitality*, p. 60.

[51] Day, "Houses of Hospitality," *Commonweal*, August 15, 1938.

ing the social order." [52] By their mission-field approach to reform, the Catholic Workers furnished a sense of direction to the enlarging corps of Catholics anxious to crusade for social justice. "Sometimes," as Jesuit Albert Muntsch wrote, "neither clergy nor laity know exactly what to do in order to follow out the so-called 'Catholic Program.'" The *Catholic Worker* "tells what to do and how to do it," he observed. "It comes down to the level of the people." [53]

As Catholic leaders mobilized for social justice they were in a position to evaluate the New Deal recovery and reform measures. Few denied that the New Deal's grandiose plan, the National Industrial Recovery Act, resembled, superficially at least, the vocational group system outlined in the Pope's recent encyclical.[54] Through industrial codes — 731 in all — the act sought "to induce and maintain united action of labor and management under adequate governmental sanction and supervision." By relaxing the anti-trust laws, the code authorities, manned by business leaders, were empowered to check overproduction and ruinously low prices, the result, it was held, of excessive and unfair competition, low wages, long hours, and child labor. The codes, therefore, provided for a minimum wage of from twelve to fifteen dollars a week, reduced the work week to forty hours, and abolished child labor. These features were designed to stimulate re-employment, increase purchasing power, and improve working conditions.

The act expressly affirmed labor's right to self-organization, declaring in Section 7 (a) that "no employee and no one seeking employment shall be required as a condition of employment to join any company union, or to refrain from joining, organizing, or assisting a labor organization of his own choosing." This provision, along with its other guarantees, led O'Shaughnessy to write that the NIRA ended "industrial slavery" in the United States and aimed to establish a nationwide "partnership status" between employers and employees for "the orderly conduct of industry." [55] Actually, labor

[52] Day, "The House on Mott Street," ibid., May 6, 1938.

[53] "A Promising Journalistic Venture," *Guildsman*, III (April 1935), 6–7.

[54] "Recovery or State Socialism," *America*, July 22, 1933; F. J. Eble, "Bankrupt Economic Individualism," *Guildsman*, II (October 1933), 4–7; "Which Way, Leader Roosevelt," ibid., I (March 1933), 11–12; "Betraying the True Alternative," ibid., III (November 1934), 5–6.

[55] "The N.I.R.A.," *Social Justice Bulletin*, I (September 1933), 3–4.

had no direct voice in the new arrangement, not being represented in the code authorities at policy-determining levels. Labor's exclusion was deplored by virtually all Catholic social leaders.[56] The more optimistic, including John A. Ryan, now a monsignor, hoped for a speedy correction of the defect. In that event the code authorities, he wrote, "would become substantially the same as the occupational groups recommended by Pope Pius XI." [57]

Some feared that the new legislation unduly magnified the powers of government. Pius XI's encyclical "does not contemplate the extent of intervention on the part of the State that is now in evidence," argued the Central Verein.[58] The Verein's sociological representative, Frederick P. Kenkel, doubted if anything was to be gained by "the exchange of Individualistic Capitalism for a planned economy politically controlled by a central government — i.e., State Socialism." [59] Speaking mainly for small businessmen and farming families, Kenkel wished government to be divorced from corporate enterprise rather than used, as the economic planners desired, to incorporate labor and agriculture into the monopoly structure. In his view low wages, even low farm prices, would be in the public interest provided relief was afforded the people from high tariffs, unfair taxes, intolerable debts, and the excessive prices exacted, often for inferior wares, by trustified industries.[60] The Kenkel groups favored anti-monopoly measures designed to reverse the trend

[56] R. A. McGowan, "Testing the N.I.R.A. by Catholic Teaching — III," *Catholic Action*, XVI (January 1934), 11–12, 31; "Is the N.I.R.A. 'Ideal'?" *America*, December 23, 1933; "Employers and the Government," ibid., March 10, 1934; "New or Old Deal?" ibid., March 24, 1934; "Labor Revolts," ibid., July 28, 1934; Clarence J. Enzler, "The N.I.R.A. and the Future," *Columbia*, XIII (October 1933), 12–13, 15, 20; "Dictating Industrial Recovery," *Guildsman*, I (July 1933), 8–10; "When Labor Is Bought and Sold," ibid. (August 1933), 11–12; "A Critique of the N.I.R.A.," ibid., II (February 1934), 19; "Organization and Organic Structure," ibid., III (October 1934), 3–5; "The Exit of the N.I.R.A.," ibid. (June 1935), 5–6.

[57] "Shall the N.I.R.A. Be Scrapped?" *Proceedings*, National Conference of Catholic Charities, 1934, p. 57.

[58] "Resolutions of the CV Convention," *Guildsman*, I (September 1933), 14–15.

[59] Quoted in "Views on the Recovery Act," ibid. (August 1933), 14–15.

[60] "The Farmer and Economic Planning," *Proceedings*, National Conference of Catholic Charities, 1932, pp. 200–4; "The Irrepressible Agrarian Conflict," *Central-Blatt and Social Justice*, XXIII (March 1931), 412–13; "What the Farmer Needs Most," ibid., XXIX (June 1936), 84; see also "On the Eve of State Branch Conventions," ibid., XXV (April 1932), 22; "Catholic Farmers State Their Position Towards Farm Problems," ibid., XXVI (June 1933), 99.

toward business concentration. In an anti-monopoly and minimal government context, Christian forces could the more successfully combat the profit-making craze, the root of the prevalent social disorganization. The New Deal recovery and social security measures, on the other hand, by providing temporary relief, tended to perpetuate the existing system and to divert attention from the pressing task of building up Christian attitudes toward industry and property.

The Catholic planners admitted that the insatiable desire for gain endangered the success of the New Deal program. The New Deal Administration had exercised its vast powers "wisely and justly . . . in the interests of all the people," O'Shaughnessy claimed, "but human greed and selfishness are intervening to nullify its efforts." [61] After interviewing representative persons in many parts of the country — corporation managers, labor leaders, workers, farmers, and consumers — he concluded that "all were considering this program from a standpoint of personal self-interest." [62] No person or group seemed willing to make sacrifices for the common good. Most at fault were the business leaders who thwarted the efforts of the government to restore the purchasing power of workers and farmers and unjustly passed on the costs of recovery to the consuming public. O'Shaughnessy regretfully noted that the leaders of both capital and labor sought domination, not partnership. By herding workers into company unions employers aimed to defeat the effectiveness of the collective bargaining principle on which the Recovery Act was based. Equally wrong was the attempt of an "over-lordship of labor organizers" to represent all workers rather than to encourage their organization, as the law intended, on a nationwide scale industry by industry. He recalled that the act conferred privileges of organization on both corporations and workers "to enable them to cooperate, as a partnership, each upon terms of full equality, to serve consumers efficiently and justly, to stabilize property values and to promote social security." [63]

The crux of the difficulty, as O'Shaughnessy lamented, was that too few realized that recovery was impossible without reform. He

[61] "The A.A.A. and the N.R.A.," "Revolution and the New Deal," *Social Justice Bulletin*, I (October 1933), 3–4.

[62] "Public Opinion and the 'New Deal,' " ibid. (November 1933), 3–4.

[63] "Section VII (a)," ibid. (September 1933), 4.

warned the privileged classes not to block the "social revolution," lest they "force the Government to collect, through excessive taxes, the larger part of capital required to finance all industry, agriculture and commerce." [64] Monsignor Ryan also believed that should the NIRA fail the people in all probability "will turn to government operation of the essential industries." [65] Sharing this belief and fear, most thinking Catholics urged that the National Recovery Administration be retained and perfected. When the Supreme Court invalidated the measure in the spring of 1935, one hundred thirty-one distinguished leaders of Catholic thought and action affixed their signatures to *Organized Social Justice*, a pamphlet published by the N.C.W.C.'s Social Action Department, urging an amendment to the federal Constitution which would empower Congress to re-establish the NRA along genuine vocational group lines.[66] The project largely of Monsignor John J. Burke, *Organized Social Justice* was pronounced by John A. Ryan "the most fundamental, the most comprehensive and the most progressive publication that has come from a Catholic body since the appearance of the Bishops' Program of Social Reconstruction." [67]

Among the obstacles to the establishment of an occupational group system, *Organized Social Justice* listed first "the inadequate organization of some of the most important social classes." Thus labor unions comprised "only a small minority of the wage earners"; farmers' co-operatives were "relatively few and feeble"; consumers' co-operatives "even fewer and feebler"; and "the quasi-independent middle classes in the cities" were also "for the most part ineffectively organized." As a group the signers of *Organized Social Justice* believed that adequate group organization would come slowly and "to a large extent" would "have to wait upon the creation of the framework of the new economic order." [68] Privately, some of

[64] "Public Opinion and the 'New Deal,'" loc. cit.

[65] "Shall the N.R.A. Be Scrapped?" loc. cit., p. 62.

[66] John A. Ryan, "Organized Social Justice," *Commonweal*, December 13, 1935; "Catholic Plan for Organized Social Justice," *Catholic World*, CXLII (January 1936), 488–90.

[67] "Monsignor Burke and Social Justice," *Catholic Action*, XVIII (December 15, 1936), 19–20.

[68] National Catholic Welfare Conference, *Organized Social Justice. An Economic Program for the United States Applying Pius XI's Great Encyclical on Social Life* (New York, 1935), pp. 14–15.

the signers evidently thought that labor organization must precede rather than follow the inauguration of a vocational group plan. As Father Haas observed, the Pope, in proposing integrated occupations with the government acting as mediator between and over the component parts, demanded more than labor unions as they existed in the United States. But his plan "assumes that workers are almost, if not entirely unionized." Haas believed that "we are wasting our time and our energy if in promoting the Catholic industrial program, we neglect, or what is worse, try to dodge this important fact." Only by helping workers to form free unions "can we hope ultimately," he opined, "to make the social program of the Holy Father a reality." [69]

On the other hand, a coterie of Catholic leaders, partly as a result of observing the NRA experiment, denied that partnership in industry involved a substantial increase in union membership. Brilliantly representative of this viewpoint was Aloysius J. Muench, successively professor of sociology in St. Francis Seminary, its rector, Bishop of Fargo, North Dakota, and Papal Nuncio to West Germany. Not solidarity but intense conflict, he pointed out, had marked and continued to mark the relations between capital and labor in this country. In their attempt to wrest from plutocratic capitalism the right to a living wage, the right to collective bargaining, shorter hours, and better working conditions, the trade and industrial unions had become aggressively militant organizations. [70] Precisely for this reason "they do not appear to offer the right approach," he felt, "to a cordial and harmonious understanding between capital and labor, and therefore to the corporate reconstruction of the social order according to the ideas of Pope Pius XI." In like manner, capital, fearing domination by organized labor, was "wary of a corporate reorganization of business in which both the employers and employees own and manage on a basis of mutuality." Overtures from labor to this effect were viewed with suspicion and distrust by most employers. [71]

[69] "Competition and Social Justice," *Salesianum,* XXX (October 1935), 17–24.
[70] "Self-Government in Industry," ibid., XXIX (April 1934), 33–40; "Strikes and Recognition of Unions," ibid. (July 1934), 1–7; "Labor's Struggle for Collective Bargaining," ibid. (October 1934), 8–15.
[71] "A New Alignment of Capital and Labor," ibid., XXX (January 1935), 1–5.

Muench did not think the situation a hopeless one — far from it. A foundation on which to build a corporative industrial order had been laid, he believed, by the "few ideally constructed employee representation plans." Just as some independent unions were radical or venal, so also some company unions were in the workers' interest. He listed the William S. Filene Sons Company, Dutchess Bleacheries, the Boston Consolidated Gas Company, and Callahan's Louisville Paint and Varnish Company as firms which had made a tender of business fellowship to their employees. The Philadelphia Rapid Transit Company and the Columbia Conserve Company permitted employees, he pointed out, "to acquire common stock, own it as a group, vote it as a block, elect their representatives to the Board of Directors, and, if desired, ultimately to obtain control." The better employee representation plans had given employees a degree of control and ownership not ordinarily obtainable through the collective bargaining process. While organized labor should maintain its defensive power, it should also withdraw its opposition to the good employee representation plans and join with well-disposed industrialists to extend them over as wide a field as possible. Otherwise, the idea of the corporative reconstruction of the economic order "will never be achieved." [72]

For good or ill, little heed was paid Muench's suggestions. After the passage of the National Labor Relations Act (the Wagner Act) and the formation of the Committee on Industrial Organizations (the CIO), both in 1935, the attention of mass-production workers centered on unionism, the rapid progress of which entailed no end of violence and bitterness. If the vocational group plan provided the truly sane and just solution, neither side was in a mood to accept it. Discussing the subject with John L. Lewis, Bishop R. E. Lucey complained that industrial unionism did not "go far enough. The Holy Father wants the workers to join the employers in the management of industries." "I realize that," Lewis replied, "I have read the encyclicals and I use them, too, but I don't dare advocate workers' sharing in management just now. It would mean a great furor, and I would surely be put down as a Communist." [73] The failure of the guild idea to catch on encouraged many Catholics, no

[72] *Ibid.*, 5–9.
[73] "Labor in the Recession," *Commonweal*, May 6, 1938.

doubt, to seek alternative solutions, notably consumers' co-operation along the lines of the Rochdale system. Editor Edward Koch, uncompromising guildsman, regretfully reported in 1936 that the Catholic people were "predominantly devoted to the Cooperative and Coughlin programs." [74]

The success of co-operatives among Catholics, mainly fisherfolk, in Antigonish, Nova Scotia, and in lesser degree in St. Mary's County, Maryland, was widely publicized.[75] About fifty thousand Catholics participated in parish credit unions, some two hundred in number.[76] While most of the credit unions were formed in urban parishes, Catholic rural leaders devoted no little attention to the co-operative movement in general. The National Catholic Rural Life Conference kept in close touch with American and Canadian developments and in 1937 set up a special committee to study and promote co-operatives among rural Catholics.[77] The movement derived its strongest support from the Central Verein, whose conventions and publications, particularly the *Central-Blatt and Social Justice*, were increasingly preoccupied with the study of the subject in all its aspects. Kenkel's opinion that "Cooperators are the guildsmen of the 20th century" was shared by many without as well as within the Central Verein. Kenkel believed that if consumers' co-operation became widespread in the American economy, it would serve as a "yardstick" against monopoly and help to rehabilitate the concept of the "just price."

The great majority of Catholic co-operators sought only the ends mentioned in the Bishops' Program, namely, lower middlemen's costs and the socialization of worker and consumer attitudes. Some wished to go further and bring the whole economy — production as well as distribution — under consumer sway. The steps in this direction successfully taken by the co-operatives of Great Britain suggested the possibility of making consumer control universal — of

[74] "Promote the New Order!" *Guildsman*, IV (September 1936), 9.

[75] Virgil Michel, O.S.B., *Christian Social Reconstruction* (Milwaukee, 1937); Edward Hugh Dineen, S.J., "Beyond the Cooperatives," *Columbia*, XIX (November 1939), 6; same author, "The Limits of Cooperation," ibid. (May 1940), 6, 23; George Boyle, "Down to Earth," ibid. (January 1940), 6, 20; same author, "Co-ops Are Concrete," ibid., XX (December 1940), 5, 23.

[76] Gerald M. Schnepp, S.M., "Credit Unions," *Christian Front*, II (July, August 1937), 113–15.

[77] Witte, *Twenty-five Years of Crusading*, p. 107.

ushering in a consumers' commonwealth.[78] Among Catholics who proposed in this manner to overcome the evils of the capitalist system, the strongest voice was that of J. Elliot Ross, veteran Paulist writer. Admittedly influenced by Kenkel, Ross became a co-operative enthusiast, and in his book, *Cooperative Plenty* (St. Louis, 1941), a distillation of his many magazine articles,[79] he argued that if they wished the American people could establish "a cooperative economy" and thereby secure a more equitable division of wealth and a satisfactory balance between production and distribution. With James P. Warbasse of the Cooperative League of the United States, Ross made much of the alleged fact that in a consumers' commonwealth only a bare minimum of state intervention in industry would be necessary.

But to the editor of the *Guildsman* the proposed commonwealth would "be a sort of socialistic state," for it mattered little, he thought, "whether the means of production and distribution and the professional establishments be owned and controlled by the people as citizens or as consumers." [80] Partly to meet the charge that consumers' co-operation was "a dangerous slippery incline toward Socialism," [81] leading co-operators pointed out that their movement could accomplish its purpose without gaining control of all economic life. It was only necessary for co-operatives to do from ten to twenty per cent of the business in any field to break the power of monopoly and effectively checkmate extortion and profit-piling.[82]

Even partial consumer control was anathema to the more rigid guildsmen, who were sure that social justice was concerned mainly with producers, chiefly the conflicting interests of employers and employees. Some ardent co-operators, on the other hand, con-

[78] For bitter opposition to consumer control, see Edward Koch, "Merits of the Co-operative Movement," *Guildsman*, I (November 1932), 6–9, and similar comments in nearly every succeeding issue, I–IX (December 1932–September 1941).

[79] Notably "Toward a Consumers' Economy," *Central-Blatt and Social Justice*, XXXII (June–November 1939), 75–78, 113–14, 154–56, 190–92, 229–31.

[80] "Is Consumers' Co-operation the Remedy?" IV (December 1935), 4–6.

[81] "Fallacious Propaganda for Co-operation," *Guildsman*, VI (May 1938), 8–9.

[82] L. S. Herron, "Co-operation Cures without Destroying Economic Liberty or Human Values," *Central-Blatt and Social Justice*, XXXI (September 1938), 147–49, and "Co-operation the Way to Plenty with Freedom," *Social Justice Review*, XXXIV (January 1942), 299–301, a review of Ross's *Cooperative Plenty*.

tended that their movement marked the emergence of corporative society in harmony with or superior to the plan outlined in *Quadragesimo anno*. More profoundly, others viewed the consumer cooperative as a first step in the evolution of a corporative society whose ultimate organization could not be precisely anticipated. "Contrary to what some may think," wrote Virgil Michel, Benedictine liturgical leader, "there is not extant anywhere a completely worked out scheme, much less *the* true scheme or plan, of a corporately organized society. Least of all," he thought, "does the *Quadragesimo anno* pretend to furnish such a plan." [83] Most Catholic thinkers hoped, with the Central Verein, that consumers' co-operation would "eventually lead" to the guild or occupational group system. In so doing it would simultaneously exert a corrective influence. "In the guild system and in the steps toward it," wrote Father McGowan, the co-operative system would check "the perfectly possible wrongdoing of guildsmen." [84]

The opinion of the more ardent guild advocates to the contrary, the enthusiasm with which many Catholics supported consumers' co-operation is best viewed as further indication of American Catholicism's social awakening. The increasing output of social literature also suggested a renaissance in Catholic social interest. In 1940 Kenkel alluded to the "tremendous" number of references contained in recently compiled Catholic social study lists "as compared with those of a quarter-century ago." He explained that American Catholics were "apparently attempting to make up for lost time and by a desperate burst of energy to acquire at least a talking knowledge of the social question." [85] As the decade of the 1930s neared its end, the Catholic leadership realized that the Church's safety and progress now rested in large part on social gains. What with unemployment continuing, the birth control movement making inroads on the Catholic population, and Communists infiltrating the new industrial unions, the Church's hold on her membership would be jeopardized unless a large measure of social justice could be speedily secured. [86]

Danger unmistakably lurked on the new industrial front. Timid

[83] *Christian Social Reconstruction*, p. 91.
[84] *New Guilds: A Conversation* (New York, 1937), pp. 15–16.
[85] "The Social Question to the Fore," *Central-Blatt and Social Justice*, XXXII (February 1940), 348–49.
[86] Louis Minsky, "Catholicism's Social Awakening," loc. cit.

Catholics not in close touch or sympathy with the labor movement were sorely perplexed by the "sitdown" strikes and displays
of violence which accompanied the organizational drives in the
mass-production industries. With a naïveté compounded of fear
and ignorance, these Catholics ascribed the rise of the CIO, as well
as its obnoxious activities, to Communist influence alone. In some
parts of the country Knights of Columbus (possibly members of
the American Federation of Labor) circulated pamphlets to the
effect that John Brophy was really a "red" who on orders from Mos-
cow had organized the CIO to overthrow the United States Government! [87] This aggressively negative attitude, rejoined Brophy, was
"very poor policy," putting "our Church on the side of the industrialists and against the workers," who are led to believe that "the
Catholic press is insincere about Social Justice." The few Communists in the CIO were dangerous only because of the apathy
of Catholic leaders and Catholics who were "the largest creedal
body" in the new unions. One Communist, "not afraid to speak,"
Brophy sadly reported, "draws as much attention as one hundred
or so Catholics." [88]

Worse still, some Catholics, taking their cue from Father
Coughlin's later speeches, held Jews responsible for the world's
ills.[89] By their turbulent, even brutal anti-Semitism, these "Christian fronters" not only antagonized labor unionists but also deepened
the apprehensions of many non-sectarian liberals that out of hatred
of communism the Catholic Church planned to betray democracy
to fascism. In order to give the lie to these charges and fears, social
justice Catholics resolved to support the labor movement in an
active, not merely verbal, manner. "If it is necessary to march on
the picket line and speak at strike meetings in order to reach
the workers, then the priests belong there," asserted Monsignor Joseph
Smith of Cleveland, who practiced what he preached.[90]

---

[87] Monsignor Joseph Smith, St. John's Cathedral, Cleveland, quoted in Richard
Deverall, "Crusading Monsignor," *Christian Front*, III (September 1938),
103–4.

[88] Richard Deverall, "John Brophy Speaks," ibid., II (September 1937), 125–
26, 135.

[89] " 'Christian American' Jew Baiting," by the editors and staff of *Christian
Social Action*, IV, (September 1939), 101–15, is an excellent "factual" account
of the economic origins and purposes of Catholic anti-Semitism.

[90] Deverall, "Crusading Monsignor," loc. cit.

The coterie of priests and laymen for whom Monsignor Smith spoke had acquired a knowledge of "realistic economics" and urged all Catholics to follow their example. "Our schools, our press, and our seminaries," John Brophy thought, "must fortify themselves with a clear knowledge of economics and ethics, and their inter-relations, thus yielding a deep understanding of the Labor Encyclicals and their applications." [91] The Bishop of Amarillo, Texas, Robert E. Lucey, presented this viewpoint with great force and clarity. Lest the Church's reputation among the working poor be further compromised, he suggested that orators and editors uninformed on labor matters speak cautiously or better still remain silent. Only Catholics properly instructed could speak and act wisely and effectively; their number must be vastly augmented if the broken social order was to be rebuilt. The time had come, wrote Lucey in 1938, for the Church to take a new forward step in social education. A half century ago, he recalled, nursing was the work of amateurs, and charity two decades back was in the hands of volunteers, religious and lay. But today "our schools of nursing education are among the best in the land," the trained social worker is indispensable, "and standardized Catholic Welfare Bureaus are functioning everywhere." Still to be met was the industrial crisis, brought to the fore by two incomparable popes, two depressions, and two economic phenomena, namely, militant communism and a virile labor movement. "Now at last it becomes apparent," the bishop remarked, "that labor colleges and schools of economics are essential if we wish to find any intelligent solution for the problems of industry and agriculture." Going to the workingmen, as Pope Pius XI exhorted his priests, meant more than writing "academic editorials in defense of his rights. I think we ought to get into the parade and go down the road with labor. We should be with them, for them, of them. They belong to us and we belong to them." [92]

This idea that the Church should identify itself with the labor movement gained wide currency in the closing years of the depression decade. In some degree the new attitude stemmed from the two National Catholic Social Action Conferences, the first one meeting in Milwaukee in May 1938, and the other in Cleveland in June of

[91] Ibid., "John Brophy Speaks," loc. cit.
[92] "Are We Fair to the Church?" *Commonweal*, September 16, 1938.

the following year.[93] Sponsored and organized by the Social Action Department, these two gatherings utilized the seasoned procedures of the Catholic Conference on Industrial Problems whereby employers, employees, and social encyclical experts participated on equal terms in the speaking and discussion. With "A Christian Social Order" and "A Christian Democracy" as their respective themes, the conferences analyzed the current economic scene with special attention paid the mass-production industries then in the course of rapid unionization. "Little time," wrote Father McGowan, "was spent in outlining evils except to emphasize the methods of their correction," namely, the development of self-governing industries and professions along occupational group lines. The proceedings of the Milwaukee meeting indicated, he thought, "that we can move gradually from our present position by practical steps into the whole Encyclical program." [94] The editor of the *Guildsman,* generally critical of Catholic social trends, noted happily "that such a theme has come to engage the minds of our people and that it replaces apathy on the part of some and, on the part of others, exclusive interest in union labor or cooperatives" which were of limited merit.[95]

Although laymen were present in sizable numbers, the relatively high proportion of bishops and priests attending was one of the highlights of the conferences. Their participation as teachers and learners not only "gave the lie to the Communists that the hierarchy and clergy are reactionary," one lay observer wrote, but demonstrated once again "that the real trouble with social action in America is not clerical indifference, but rather lay apathy." [96] In special sessions of their own, the clergy thoroughly canvassed the work to be done by priests in social action. They decided to become better acquainted with employers and trade unionists. Carping criticism of either group was to be avoided. When correction of union practices was morally necessary, it should be given in a sympathetic and constructive

[93] *Catholic Action,* XX (March 1938), 3; ibid. (April 1938), 3; John A. Ryan, "Program of the Milwaukee Catholic Social Action Conference," ibid., 9–10; ibid., XXI (May 1939), 13; George J. Olejnyik, " 'Christian Democracy' Theme of Social Action Congress," ibid. (June 1939), 7–8.
[94] "Social Justice Makes Its Claim," ibid. (June 1938), 9–11.
[95] "Marks of a Christian Social Order," VI (June 1938), 1–2.
[96] Charles J. Cooke, "Don't Quote Me," *Christian Front,* IV (June 1939), 84.

spirit. The suggestions were made that priests should attend labor conventions regularly, speak at organizing meetings, and prepare themselves to mediate and arbitrate industrial disputes. A paper on "Catholic Action and Social Action" by Bishops Edwin V. O'Hara and Karl J. Alter urged the formation of diocesan priests' committees whose task would be, in association with zealous lay folk, to develop effective social action groups on the local level.[97]

The priests at the Milwaukee and Cleveland meetings also took note of the social action schools for the clergy and the rapidly multiplying schools for union labor leaders.[98] The first social action schools were conducted in the summer of 1937 at Toledo, Milwaukee, San Francisco, and Los Angeles with a total attendance of nearly three hundred priests from twenty-four dioceses.[99] Similar schools were held in Chicago, Pittsburgh, New York, Brooklyn, Baltimore, and Washington, D.C., during the following two years. Over a four-week period these schools studied the industrial situation in the light of the social encyclicals, devoting a week each to "The Moral Standards of Economic Life," "Organization as a Partial Remedy," "Legislation as a Partial Remedy," and "The Social Order as a Full Remedy." The subject matter was dealt with in three or four one-hour courses which met five times each week. The first course, involving theory and doctrine, was in charge of visiting priests who were recognized authorities on the encyclicals in general and the particular phase under consideration. The second course, taught generally by local priests, applied encyclical teachings to current situations and problems, both local and national. The third course tended to be clinical or workshop in nature with its instructors drawn from employers, labor leaders, and public servants. Two periods a week were given to a survey of what priests had done, were doing, and should do in social action. The priests who studied in these schools

[97] "Summary of the Priests' Meeting," *Proceedings*, First National Catholic Social Action Conference (Milwaukee, 1938), pp. 402–8.

[98] Wilfrid Parsons, S.J., "The Congress at Cleveland," *Columbia*, XIX (August 1939), 2, 22.

[99] Edwin V. O'Hara, "Catholic Action and Social Action," *Proceedings*, First National Catholic Social Action Conference., p. 384; R. A. McGowan, "Clergy Hails Schools of Social Action," *Catholic Action*, XIX (August 1937), 16–17.

were prepared in some measure to initiate, as Pope Pius XI enjoined, the apostolate of workingmen to workingmen.[100]

For socially informed priests the Association of Catholic Trade Unionists furnished an arena of continuous usefulness. Formed in February 1937 by a handful of Catholic Workers in New York City, ACTU, as the association was called, took seriously the admonition in *Quadragesimo anno* that "side by side with . . . trade unions there must always be associations which aim at giving their members a thorough religious and moral training, that these in turn may impart to the labor unions to which they belong the upright spirit which should direct their entire conduct." This meant, in terms of the current labor situation, that ACTU aimed to remove a prime cause of Communist and criminal influences in the labor movement, namely, the widespread apathy and ineptitude of Catholic union members. But its attitudes and methods were positive, not negative: ACTU favored the expansion of unionism and endorsed all strikes which upon investigation were found to be just, its members taking their place on picket lines and participating in various other demonstrations of worker militancy.[101]

As it faced its herculean task, ACTU had the approval of Cardinal Hayes and the encouragement and counsel of its chaplain, the Reverend Dr. John P. Monaghan, who soon "gathered about him as assistants a score or more of the diocesan and regular clergy." Also at an early date ACTU opened a night school for workers, with courses in the ethics of labor relations, in labor law, labor history, parliamentary law, and union procedure. The Association of Catholic Trade Unionists supplemented its labor school with educational meetings, mass rallies in working-class parishes, and a newspaper, the *Labor Leader*. The ACTU program was expanded geographi-

---

[100] "Clergy Social Action in Buffalo and Chicago," ibid., XX (September 1938), 20; McGowan, "Social Action Schools for the Clergy," ibid., XXI (September 1939), 21.

[101] Neil O'Connor, "Priests and Labor," *Christian Front*, III (October 1938), 122–23; Paul Weber, "A.C.T.U.," ibid. (December 1938), 153–55; Norman McKenna, "Catholics and Labor Unions," *Columbia*, XVIII (May 1939), 6, 24; Sebastian Erbacher, O.F.M., "The A.C.T.U.," *Christian Social Action*, V (December 1940), 330–37; "Archbishop Mooney Explains A.C.T.U.," *Catholic Action*, XXII (June 1940), 12; Philip Taft, "The Association of Catholic Trade Unionists," *Industrial and Labor Relations Review*, II (January 1949), 210–18.

cally through the formation of branch chapters in Pittsburgh, Detroit, Chicago, Cleveland, San Francisco, and other industrial centers — fifteen in all by 1940.[102] The Pittsburgh chapter was an outgrowth, in 1938, of a Catholic Worker group, the Catholic Radical Alliance, formed the previous year by labor priests Charles Owen Rice and Carl P. Hensler.[103] Here and elsewhere the ACTU chapters were formed, often during strikes, to give a Christian social direction to the organizational campaigns of working people.

Understandably, Detroit Catholics were exceptionally active on the labor front under the direction of their first Archbishop, Edward, later Cardinal, Mooney (1937–58). Besides a chapter of ACTU, organized by the Reverend Sebastian Erbacher, about forty parish labor schools were opened as parts of an Archdiocesan Labor Institute. Restricted to union members, these schools taught by priests and Catholic attorneys stressed industrial ethics, public speaking, and parliamentary law. The Archdiocesan Labor Institute taught Catholic principles to its students and trained them to be articulate while leaving to ACTU the formulation of policies in particular situations.[104] In addition to the schools in Detroit, New York, and Pittsburgh, twenty similar ones were opened by 1940 in a dozen cities, among them Brooklyn, Buffalo, Rochester, Philadelphia, Chicago, and St. Paul.[105] In Washington, D.C., the Social Service School, still under the direction of the National Council of Catholic Women, promoted labor education through its annual institutes of industry. The teaching and administrative personnel of the labor schools — professors, lawyers, and industrial experts — were recruited from men and women in close touch with the Catholic Worker movement, the Catholic League for Social Justice, the National

[102] Norman McKenna, "Catholic and American Labour," *Month*, CLXXIII (February 1939), 142–48; same author, "Catholic Trade Unionists in America," ibid., CLXXVI (November 1940), 303–7.

[103] Richard Deverall, "Catholic Radical Alliance," *Christian Front*, II (October 1937), 141–43; Charles O. Rice, "A Priest on Labor," ibid., III (September 1938), 105–6; same author, "Policy and Action," *Commonweal*, July 29, 1938.

[104] Raymond S. Clancy, "Detroit ALI," *Christian Social Action*, IV (December 1939), 210–16.

[105] Linna E. Bresette, "Labor Schools Promote Catholic Teaching," *Catholic Action*, XXII (March 1940), 8–9. See also William J. Smith, *The Catholic Labor School* (New York, 1941), and John F. Cronin, *Catholic Social Action* (Milwaukee, 1948), pp. 229–35.

Conference of Catholic Charities, and the various departments of the National Catholic Welfare Conference.

The labor schools climaxed the effort which made Catholic social action "second to none" in the decades after World War I.[106] Earlier, in the late nineteenth century, the social justice ideal was associated with non-Catholic reformers — ministers, social workers, and professional scholars. Gradually leadership (outside the political field) passed into Catholic hands as immigrants Americanized, as social experts — Ryans, Dietzes, and Kenkels — appeared on the scene, and as the hierarchy itself assumed collective responsibility for social progress by setting up the National Catholic Welfare Conference. In the wake of the Great Depression the postwar Bishops' Program of Social Reconstruction was translated into public policy, excepting only the proposals to modify or supplement the wage system through producers' co-operation and co-partnership. Although neither capital nor labor showed any real interest in industrial partnership, Catholic social thinkers continued to insist on its adoption, fortified as they were after 1931 with *Quadragesimo anno* and its plan to invest the co-partnership principle with public authority. The vocational group plan was not adopted — in fact it was sharply criticized — but it provided an ideal in the light of which Catholics estimate the strength and shortcomings of all reform measures in the industrial field.

[106] James Hastings Nichols, *Democracy and the Churches* (Philadelphia, 1951), pp. 131, 251.

CHAPTER VIII

Catholics and Contemporary Unionism:
A New Version of an Old Story

In the last two decades Catholic social action has been primarily concerned with the problem of establishing satisfactory relationships with the powerful labor unionism which emerged under the New Deal during the depression and World War II. By the end of the war the unions, some independent but most of them either AFL or CIO affiliates, numbered about fifteen million members, which included from a fourth to a third of all production and clerical workers. The new unionism wielded substantial economic power. In the words of a Twentieth Century Fund report the war "enabled unionism to draw on collective bargaining to cover in a single stride many intermediary steps in its evolution from hired help to something akin to partnership in United States industry." [1] In the new even more than in the older unionism Catholic workers were numerous, in some unions, large and small, comprising the overwhelming majority. On the policies and conduct of these unions depended not only the economic but also the moral and spiritual welfare of a large part of the Catholic population. Not since the heyday of the Knights of Labor in the mid–1880s had the Catholic Church in America faced so fateful a crisis in the labor field.

The two situations differed in that in the recent period Catholic social action has functioned in the context of America's new and changing role in world affairs. The failure of isolationist policy to prevent the nation's involvement in World War II induced the great majority of the electorate, reluctantly but resolutely, to assume the onerous burdens of international leadership. Even before World War II many Americans, including the more alert social action Catholics, realized that the maintenance of peace and freedom is contingent on the extension of economic welfare to all peoples.

[1] *Trends in Collective Bargaining* (New York, 1945), p. 186.

As long ago as 1919 the authors of the Bishops' Program of Social Reconstruction averred in their foreword that "the only safeguard of peace is social justice and a contented people." [2] In 1927 persons closely connected with the Social Action Department of the N.C.W.C. formed the Catholic Association for International Peace, which in the years that followed thoroughly explored the bearing of movements for social betterment on the cause of peace and on efforts for a juridically directed system of world organization. Through its pamphlets, reports, and yearly meetings the association labored to steer Catholics away from ultra-pacifist organizations and to combat the fierce isolationist sentiment which prevailed among Catholics and the people generally. [3]

As the nation abandoned isolationism for world leadership after Pearl Harbor, it faced the problem of convincing the international community that it intended to bring its practice more fully into harmony with its democratic traditions and aspirations. The contrast was most glaring in race relations, notably the brutal discrimination against the Negro. Previous to Pearl Harbor a few Catholics had endeavored to mitigate racial strife. After 1933 an Interracial Council in New York, formed under the direction of the Jesuit priest John La Farge, and its journal, the *Interracial Review*, campaigned against segregation in Catholic churches and schools outside the South. [4] When war came, the movement picked up strength: new councils were formed and support given to Negro leaders who demanded an end to discrimination in the armed forces and in war production plants. When in 1943 President Roosevelt set up the Fair Employment Practices Committee, Monsignor Francis J. Haas served as its chairman several months until appointed Bishop of Grand Rapids. [5] After the war the desegregation of Catholic in-

[2] A. I. Abell, "The Catholic Church and the American Social Question," in Waldemar Gurian and M. A. Fitzsimons, editors, *The Catholic Church in World Affairs* (Notre Dame, Ind., 1954), p. 377.

[3] Abell, "The Religious Aspect," in Stephen D. Kertesz and M. A. Fitzsimons, editors, *What America Stands For* (Notre Dame, Ind., 1959), pp. 202–6; see same author, "La Situation Religieuse," in Yves Simon, *La Civilisation Américaine* (Paris, 1950), esp. pp. 231–36.

[4] See La Farge's books, especially *Interracial Justice. A Study of the Catholic Doctrine of Race Relations* (New York, 1937); *No Postponement* (New York, 1950), pp. 141–239; and *The Catholic Viewpoint on Race Relations* (Garden City, 1956), pp. 51–74.

[5] Sister Marie Josephine, "The Work of FEPC," *America*, October 27, 1945.

stitutions progressed steadily, in the South as elsewhere, despite some opposition, notably in New Orleans where a portion of the Catholic people successfully resisted the interracial policies of their archbishop, Joseph F. Rummel.

Basic, however, to progress in racial and social justice was the maintenance of full employment and ever higher levels of productivity. On the success of this effort rested hopes of Allied victory against the Axis Powers and of world peace and freedom thereafter. During the defense and war years (1919-45) Catholic as well as other champions of social justice doubted the likelihood of success in this respect. They feared that when hostilities ceased massive unemployment with all its ghastly horrors would return. Only if the wartime co-operation of management, labor, and government should be continued into the peace years would this dire calamity be averted.[6] "The basic causes that produced the depression," as a Benedictine priest reminded a Western meeting of the Catholic Conference on Industrial Problems, "will not only *not* have been removed by the war, but will have been enormously complicated by such factors," he enumerated, "as the discharge of soldiers, the release of millions from war work, the ending of war production and trade, extraordinary tax burdens, accelerated mechanization of industry and agriculture, and the vast increase in the ability to produce." [7] Inasmuch as this was the viewpoint of most thoughtful Americans, planning for peace assumed the character of a major activity: by 1943 more than a hundred organizations and agencies were engaged in studying the nation's postwar economic needs. "Unfortunately this laudable effort to look ahead," commented the National Catholic Welfare Conference, "has not won sufficient popular understanding and support to guarantee anything more than a 'muddling through' policy when postwar issues shall confront us in the flesh." [8]

From a social justice point of view many of the proposed plans were patently defective, either overstressing the role of government in economic life or relying almost wholly on private enterprise. Monsignor John A. Ryan, who assumed that an extensive public

---

[6] "Bulwarks of Democracy," *Catholic Action*, XXIV (April 1942), 11-14; see also "We Face the Future," ibid., XXVII (April 1945), 8-10.

[7] Thomas R. Handley, "A Sound Social Order," ibid., XXVI (June 1944), 9.

[8] "Preparing for Post-War Life," ibid., XXV (April 1943), 7.

works program would be necessary to maintain full employment after the war, feared that the government would fall into the hands of the "free enterprisers," who would provide only temporary relief for the returning soldiers. "When I reflect upon the insidious and enormous power of American plutocracy and its retainers and satellites in politics, in journalism and in the professions," he opined in 1943, "I am inclined to be pessimistic." Only in the event "the white collar classes" informed themselves on economic issues would there be grounds for hope that the people in 1944 would "choose for their rulers men who believe in labor organization and social justice." [9]

Other social justice advocates among Catholics were less openly apprehensive if scarcely more hopeful. They complained, as they had in years past, that, while popular welfare as a goal in economic life was increasingly accepted, popular control in this sphere, aside possibly from collective bargaining, did not command genuine enthusiasm. They were fairly well pleased, however, with the Murray Industry Council plan. In the hope of speeding up defense production Philip Murray, the new president of the CIO, proposed in December 1940 that in each defense industry an Industry Council be set up with authority to introduce more efficient methods of production and to encourage, to this end, union-management co-operation. In each Industry Council decisions would be made by a board having equal representation from labor and management and one impartial person representing the government. No provision was made for a government representative on local Industry Councils whose functions in the plant or plants were similar to the industry-wide councils. The inevitable tasks of co-ordination were to be handled by a top National Board of Review with equal representation of management, labor, and government.[10]

The Industry Council system was not adopted. Designed to meet defense needs in the twilight period between armed peace and total war, this interval of only a year was too short to permit an adequate presentation of the plan's merits. The plan lacked sufficient power

9 "Labor after the War," *Catholic Digest*, VII (April 1943), 22–24.
10 John C. Cort, "Are We Missing a Bus? Why Not Support the Murray Industry Council Plan?" *Commonweal*, August 14, 1942; Brother Robert L. Shannon, F.S.C., "The Industry Council Plan as an Instrument of Reconstruction," *Review of Social Economy*, II (January 1944), 87–99.

and scope to insure total industrial mobilization following Pearl Harbor. In the unexpected prosperity which continued after the war, neither management nor labor saw any advantage in integrated industry, being able to pass on the cost of increased profits and wages to the public through higher prices. In the public interest, in behalf of social justice and the common good, Catholics, that is, the Catholics who really favored a guild social order, lined up behind the Industry Council plan as containing the essential ingredients of the "vocational group system" outlined in *Quadragesimo anno*.[11] Murray himself, in frequent speeches before the Association of Catholic Trade Unionists and other Catholic groups, asserted that his plan "follows the encyclical almost completely." [12]

Actually, the Industry Council plan was little more than an expanded form of union-management co-operation. In respect to structure the Industry Councils did not possess, as in their encyclical counterpart, any inherent legal or compulsive authority. They were in essence the agents of the unions and managements which between them retained the plenitude of power. In *Quadragesimo anno*, on the other hand, employer and employee associations were viewed as causes or expressions of dangerous class conflict and were permitted therefore to play only a subordinate role, chiefly by way of advice and protest. To say nothing of managements, the powerful unions presented a most difficult structural problem. Either the Industry Councils "must be limited," as Karl J. Alter, Cincinnati's archbishop, emphasized, "or else the unions must be limited. They cannot both be the determining authority." [13]

Not all persons recognized that a rightly organized Industry Council involved more than a device for union-management co-operation. Viewing the Murray plan in this essentially incorrect sense, the majority of non-Catholic industrial sociologists opposed it, out of fear that it conferred dangerous power on either government or private groups.[14] Also alive to the inordinate influence of private groups

[11] Wilfrid Parsons, S.J., "What Are Vocational Groups?" *Thought*, XVII (September 1942), 464–76.

[12] Cort, "Are We Missing a Bus?" loc. cit.

[13] "Industry Councils," *Sign*, XXIX (May 1950), 53.

[14] G. J. Schnepp, "A Survey of Opinions on the Industry Council Plan," *American Catholic Sociological Review*, XII (June 1951), 75–83.

was Father Leo Brown, S.J., director of the Institute of Social Order at St. Louis Univeristy, who pertinently commented:

> I find it hard to see where these principles (the principle of subsidiarity of function and the principles of social justice and social charity) compel us to throw the weight of Catholic thought behind a socio-economic structure, basically composed of organized labor and organized capital, fused together in some way at a second or higher stage of the economic hierarchy. I do not think that such a fusion corresponds to the integration built around the community of action and interest which the encyclicals have in mind. Merely joining a large labor union to a large trade association does not, by the fact of juxtaposition, knit them together. It is entirely conceivable that such a structure would point up class warfare in a much more violent fashion.[15]

If from the encyclical viewpoint the Murray plan as generally interpreted was structurally defective, it fared little better on the functional level. Many Catholics would deny to Industry Councils the authority to control major economic functions. Summarizing Catholic thought on this subject by 1952, Archbishop Alter noted that all interested persons wished to see councils established to deal with personnel and social security issues such as pensions, sick benefits, unemployment compensation, and vacations. But many Catholic authorities, perhaps a majority, he pointed out, would exempt wages, profits, and prices from the jurisdiction of the projected councils, leaving these questions to the determination of the free market, subject of course to the current social controls.[16] This narrow interpretation reflected the popular revulsion after World War II against totalitarian tendencies in government and industry.

It mirrored too the impatience with economic planning in a period of unexampled prosperity. Postwar Catholic conservatism was personified by the Reverend Edward A. Keller, C.S.C., a professor of economics in the University of Notre Dame. Contending that the ratio of the national income assigned to profits was low and declining, Keller argued that the instability and injustice in the economy

---

[15] Quoted in Karl J. Alter, "The Industry Council System and the Church's Program of Social Order," *Review of Social Economy*, X (September 1952), 106.

[16] Ibid., 97–100; John F. Cronin, S.S., "Implementing the Social Encyclicals in American Economic Life," ibid., V (June 1947), 1–18.

stemmed from disparities between low agricultural income (especially in the South) and high urban income, on the one hand, and between the highly organized, highly paid workers and the unorganized, lower-paid workers on the other. On the dangers of this situation he quoted from the American bishops' statement of 1940 on *The Church and the Social Order*, to the effect that if "skilled laborers, who through rigid organization have a monopoly of their craft raise the rate of hourly wages too high, they do not gain their advantage exclusively from the wealthy but from the poor also, in terms of excessive prices." This quotation was based, in turn, on a passage in *Quadragesimo anno* in which Pope Pius XI had warned that unemployment resulted from a wage scale excessively high or excessively low.

Father Keller did not ask that the wages of the highly paid workers be lowered but that their productivity be increased and "passed on to the consumer in the form of lower prices," in this manner enabling "the lower-paid worker to buy more of the products of the higher-paid workers and thus bringing the two groups into better balance." The money wage of the highly paid workers should not be further increased, he insisted, for their gains would be "obtained at the expense of all the other workers of the nation," and the economic maladjustment would be intensified.[17] Keller professed interest in the Industry Council plan, but asserted its introduction must await the development of employers' associations comparable in strength to the labor unions. He also insisted that the plan could successfully function only to the extent the current materialism of capitalists and workers should be overcome.[18]

With the view that Christian social reconstruction presupposed moral renovation the "labor priests" were in full agreement. But they thought Father Keller unduly simplified the economic problem, that he ignored the unsocial policies of many corporate managements, that, in short, he was not alive to economic realities.[19] Even more

[17] "The Church and Our Economic System," *Ave Maria*, XLV (March 15, 1947), 338–41.

[18] *The Case for Right-to-Work Laws. A Defense of Voluntary Unionism* (Chicago 1956), pp. 60–65.

[19] See C. P. Hensler, "Does the Church Approve the American Economic System? A Reply to Rev. Edward A. Keller," *Catholic Educator*, XVIII (January 1948), 239–43.

strongly than Keller, Bishop Haas urged employers to organize, not primarily to fight the unions, but to sustain fair wages under conditions of expanding production and full employment. Denying that either "big business" or government could justifiably determine wages, prices, and profits, Haas and his sympathizers believed that in time the public would insist that these issues be settled by labor and management through the collective-bargaining process, assisted and watched over by government in the interest of the general welfare.[20] "While this decision is pending," wrote Jesuit Benjamin L. Masse in early 1946,

> organized labor will move, as it is now moving, more or less unconsciously, to gain for workers greater economic security than they have known in the past. Unless interrupted by force, the process will involve a continual encroachment on prerogatives of management as generally understood, an evolution toward a new relationship between workers and employers, a relationship in which workers and employers, while remaining workers and employers, will become partners in a sense not yet understood or appreciated by either labor or management.[21]

The evolving partnership would terminate, Catholic social theorists believed, in a genuine system of Industry Councils. As the hierarchy stated in 1948, "American Catholic students of the Social Encyclicals have expressed their preference for the name 'Industry Councils' to designate the basic organs of a Christian and American type of economic democracy into which they would like to see our economic system progressively evolve. . . ." [22] The successive directors of the Social Action Department after Ryan's death in 1945, Fathers Raymond A. McGowan and George G. Higgins, featured Industry Councils as "the over-all program which gives meaning and direction," it was said, "to the short-range objectives of the Department and

[20] "Three Economic Needs of the 1880's and of the 1940's," *Ecclesiastical Review*, CXVII (December 1947), 406–20; for the employee's similar duty, see Martin E. Schirber, O.S.B., "The Christian Obligation of Employees to Reach and Maintain Maximum Production," *Review of Social Economy*, VII (March 1949), 55–60.

[21] "Labor's Finger in Management's Pie," *America*, February 2, 1946; same author, "The Wage-Price Dilemma," ibid., October 20, 1945.

[22] Quoted in George G. Higgins, "Social Action Program of the National Catholic Welfare Conference," *Review of Social Economy*, VII (September 1949), 34.

against which these short-range objectives are measured and appraised." [23] Early in 1951 the more zealous friends of the program incorporated the Industry Council Association with Monsignor John P. Boland of Buffalo, formerly chairman of the New York Labor Relations Board, as president. The basic purpose of the organization was "to bring labor, management, and the public into councils of co-operation in each industry on local, regional, and national levels." [24]

The need by this date for the proposed councils seemed more imperative than ever. Apart from considerations of social justice, the mounting inflation of the postwar years pointed to the desirability of some agency to maintain "a balance between wages, prices and profits." [25] While the Industry Council system was ideally suited to perform this task, as John C. Cort observed, it would be most difficult to establish and would not properly function until the so-called experts arrived at truly scientific definitions of "just" wages, prices, and profits. However well disposed, Catholics would not contribute much to the erection of a new social structure so long as they disagreed among themselves — so spectacularly, in fact, that Father Keller presented a view basically at variance with that of the bishops and the Social Action Department. Cort called for "more and better economists." With all due respect to the late Monsignor Ryan and contemporary Catholic economists, "it may be," he intimated, "that we have not yet produced an economist who has the Christian sense of 'social justice and social charity' and at the same time a brilliant over-powering grasp of the technical problems that his authority stands up as a beacon and a landmark that cannot be denied." Before deciding to support the Industry Council plan, Catholic labor leaders, businessmen, journalists, and teachers demanded, not unreasonably, "a little more light, a little more detail, and a little more unanimity." [26]

The Industry Council system was obviously an eventuality of the future. In the meantime, reforming Catholics would sanction the extension of unionism, the formation of employers' organizations,

[23] Ibid., 34–38.

[24] "Industry Council Association, Inc.," *Sign*, XXX (January 1951), 6.

[25] W. J. Smith, S. J., "Catholic Viewpoint on Industrial Councils," *Ecclesiastical Review*, CXXII (February 1950), 107–20.

[26] "A Plea for Economists," *Commonweal*, March 19, 1948.

piecemeal measures in line with the New Deal and the Bishops' Program of Social Reconstruction, including profit-sharing and other types of co-partnership,[27] and, above all, the eradication of abuses in existing labor organizations.[28]

In some sectors organized labor had become venal, subversive, and socially exclusive. By the end of World War II these abuses, some of recent appearance, others hoary with age, were obvious to all informed people, to the friends as well as the enemies of the labor movement, to outside observers and students as well as increasingly to the rank-and-file union membership. The abuses chiefly complained of stemmed from the ability and willingness of some union leaders to fleece and otherwise exploit the membership of their respective bodies. In numerous instances whole unions were at fault: some unions, notably in the building trades, restricted membership — unduly, it was alleged — through rigid apprenticeship rules or inordinately high initiation fees while the railway brotherhoods and many locals in virtually every industry excluded Negroes. Whether at the expense of outsiders or insiders the manifest exploitation was intolerable in a period when unions were becoming powerful and influential.[29]

In boss-controlled unions the membership was exploited either by racketeers or by Communists. In the former the members often suffered from "sweetheart" contracts in which union leaders at their own suggestion were bribed to accept only nominal wage increases and other worker demands. If work was scarce, union leaders in the industry affected were in a position to demand a kickback on the wages of the favored workers. If a member protested this discrimination he faced the likelihood of expulsion for "insubordination."

[27] Higgins, op. cit., 35–37.

[28] "Clean up the Unions," *America*, August 17, 1940; Masse, "Labor Lessons from Local 75; Obligation to See That Union Is Managed Honestly," ibid., February 21, 1942; "Democracy in Labor Unions," *Sign*, XIX (February 1940), 390; H. M. Wright, ibid. (May 1940), 596–98; "Communists in Labor Unions," ibid., XX (July 1941), 709; J. D. Connors, "What's Wrong with the Unions?" ibid., XXV (May 1946), 7–9; W. T. Smith, "Trade Unionism on Trial," *Social Justice Review*, XXXVI (April 1943), 8–11; W. J. Smith, S.J., *Spotlight on Labor Unions* (New York, 1946).

[29] See American Civil Liberties Union, *Democracy in Trade Unions* (New York, 1943), discussed in Cort, "Labor on Trial," *Commonweal*, January 7, 1944.

Racketeering was most likely to occur in highly competitive service industries whose employers resorted to bribery in order to stay in business. The unions, mostly locals, under the control of the various rackets were almost invariably affiliates of the American Federation of Labor.

The Communist-controlled unions, on the other hand, were affiliated with the Congress of Industrial Organizations.[30] Somewhat reluctantly, first John L. Lewis and then Philip Murray welcomed Communists as organizers in the new federation. Zealous for the war effort because of our alliance with the Soviet Union, Communists were able deeply to penetrate the CIO unions. By the end of the war they controlled sixteen international unions comprising perhaps twenty-five per cent of the total CIO membership.[31] This show of strength imperiled the future independence of the American labor movement; more immediately it suggested that Communists were about to acquire the balance of power in American politics. The danger on this score was revealed by the manner in which Sidney Hillman, chairman of the CIO Political Action Committee, supported the Communist-dominated American Labor party in the presidential election of 1944.[32] If Communists did not in many cases negotiate "sweetheart" contracts, their presence in the labor movement indirectly perpetuated the rackets game. Thus in 1945 the powerful "rank-and-file" strike in the International Longshoremen's Association against the corrupt leadership of President Joseph Patrick Ryan lost public support and collapsed when Communists tried to capitalize on the situation.[33]

In no union, not even in locals, were racketeers or Communists a majority of the membership. While racketeers often gained and maintained control through violence and murder, the Communists relied for domination upon disciplined planning and skillful parlia-

[30] Cort, "Catholics, Communists, and Unions," *Sign*, XXVIII (November 1948), 12–15, 70.

[31] Max. M. Kampelman, *The Communist Party vs. the CIO* (New York, 1957), pp. 45–46.

[32] Masse, "Communism and the CIO–PAC," *America*, November 18, 1944; same author, "Showdown in CIO," ibid., February 24, 1945.

[33] "Labor's Dirty Wash," ibid., October 27, 1945; Masse, "Story of a Strike," ibid., November 10, 1945; ibid., November 17, 1945.

mentary tactics. Both types of minority rule rested on the ignorance, indifference, and apathy of the rank-and-file membership. Catholic workers were as irresponsible as others in these respects. They had failed most conspicuously in the Transport Workers' Union. Formed in 1935, this union represented the omnibus and subway workers in New York City. Although more than four-fifths Catholic in membership, its leadership was consistently Communist until near the end of the 1940s. If its president, Michael J. Quill, was not a card-carrying Communist, he "fronted" for the party and its henchmen in his union until 1948.[34] In the United Electrical, Radio and Machine Workers, the third largest affiliate of the CIO, Communists through deception and secretive methods gained control and then, in 1940, deposed the "religiously motivated Catholic" president, James B. Carey, replacing him with a Communist "fronter" of Catholic faith, Albert J. Fitzgerald. While Catholics constituted a large part of this union's half-million membership, they seemed powerless to influence policy or leadership. The intense factionalism which characterized the first years of the United Automobile Workers played into the hands of Communists, who controlled that union until Walter Reuther's definite triumph in 1947.

So long as the United States and the Soviet Union fought side by side against the Axis Powers Communist influence in the labor movement was of only peripheral concern. The speedy rift between the two Powers almost immediately following the war brought an equally rapid change in public opinion. The nation's wrath descended on the variously intrenched Communist subversives, including the ones in the labor unions. Catholics by 1945 were in fair measure prepared to participate fruitfully in the anti-Communist campaign. They worked chiefly through their labor schools, which numbered nearly a hundred at the time of the Communist crisis. A sizable number of the attendants and "graduates" of these schools, over seven thousand yearly, entered unions in order to reform them or, if already trade unionists, joined the democratizing movement. Twenty-four schools were directed by Jesuits, thirty-two by diocesan authorities, and the rest by Catholic fraternal organizations, colleges,

---

[34] Kampelman, op. cit., pp. 148–51.

and the Association of Catholic Trade Unionists.[35] Besides conducting several schools of its own, this association exerted no little influence on the formation and activities of the others.[36]

The Association of Catholic Trade Unionists aimed at more than education and propaganda: it aided trade unionists to maintain their rights and to perform their duties. When necessary, the members of the ACTU participated in strikes which upon investigation were found to be just, and furnished, free of charge, legal aid to union members harassed by Communist or criminal leadership. In their meeting halls the ACTU sponsored "conferences" in which groups of workers drawn from all races and creeds discussed abuses in their unions and planned the strategy to bring about their removal. A relatively small group, chiefly active in New York, Pittsburgh, and Detroit, the ACTU was nevertheless a highly effective organization within the labor movement.[37] Much of its influence derived from its widely circulated newspapers, the *Labor Leader* and the *Wage Earner*, published under the auspices of the New York and Detroit chapters respectively. The first journal, a fortnightly, was edited by John C. Cort, a founder of the ACTU, while the second, a weekly, was under the direction of Paul Weber, an experienced Detroit journalist. Norman McKenna, who had been a co-founder of the *Christian Front* in the mid–1930s, assisted, at intervals, both the *Labor Leader* and the *Wage Earner*. These men bore the imprint of the Catholic Worker movement, as did also Edward Marciniak, who headed the Chicago Labor Alliance, which, in its origins a part of the ACTU movement, preferred to work independently along undenominational lines. The alliance published *Work*, a monthly journal.[38]

Alongside their labor news coverage, these papers directed a withering fire at union corruptionists, be they racketeers, gang-

[35] Ibid., p. 153.

[36] Cort, "Teaching the Workers; What Labor Schools Can and Cannot Do," *Commonweal*, April 7, 1944.

[37] Cort, "Nine Years of ACTU," *America*, April 6, 1946.

[38] Cort, "The Labor Movement, Ten Years," *Commonweal*, May 23, 1947; Norman McKenna, "Story of ACTU," *Catholic World*, CLXVIII (March 1949), 452–59; Philip Taft, "The Association of Catholic Trade Unionists," *Industrial and Labor Relations Review*, II (January 1949), 210–18.

sters, or Communists. The individuals or groups attacked fought back. In several New York teamster locals the rank and file, influenced by members in attendance on the ACTU schools, demanded reforms, whereupon Daniel J. Tobin, teamster boss, ordered his membership to boycott the ACTU and the labor schools. Equally vexed, Communist James Matles, organizational director of the Electrical Workers, circulated a lengthly pamphlet against "clerical domination." In reply to the Tobin and Matles charges the ACTU argued cogently that it was a reforming, not a religiously divisive, influence in the labor movement. That it was able to make its weight felt few denied.[39] In the opinion of *Fortune* magazine the Detroit ACTU was the major factor in the defeat of the Communists in the UAW elections of 1946.[40]

Some of the non-ACTU labor schools were also notably active. Among these was the Xavier Labor School, at the Church of St. Francis Xavier in New York, directed by Father Philip A. Carey, a Jesuit. The school appealed strongly to many clerical workers in the New York Omnibus Company. On graduation these men followed two of their fellow students, John Brooks and Raymond Westcott, into the red-tinged Transport Workers' Union. These reformers spearheaded the successful drive against Communist control in the locals of the Omnibus Company — a rank-and-file revolt which influenced President Quill to break with the Communists.[41] Several labor schools in various parts of the country joined the ACTU in a similar effort to rid the Electrical Workers of Communist domination. Conspicuous among Catholic leaders was the chaplain of the Pittsburgh chapter of the ACTU, Charles Owen Rice, past master in the arts of Communist exposure.[42] But he and his associates were unable to defeat the entrenched Stalinists notwithstanding the mounting

[39] McKenna, op. cit.; A. Juntunen, "Leaven in the Unions," *Catholic Digest*, XI (November 1946), 56–60; J. F. Burns, "ACTU Bores from Within," ibid., XIII (April 1949), 50–53; G. A. Kelly, "ACTU and Its Critics," *Commonweal*, December 31, 1948; J. Oxton, "ACTU Was There," *America*, March 11, 1950.

[40] McKenna, op. cit.; T. Le-Berthon, "Detroit and the Nation," *Catholic Digest*, IX (September 1945), 37–42; Kampelman, op. cit., p. 74.

[41] Kampelman, op. cit., pp. 151–55.

[42] Ibid., pp. 135–36; Rev. Thomas J. Darby, *Thirteen Years in a Labor School. The History of the New Rochelle Labor School* (New York, 1953), pp. 29–50.

dissatisfaction of the rank and file. As more and more electrical, radio, or machine workers grew restive under Communist subjection they withdrew into rival unions, chiefly the International Brotherhood of Electrical Workers — a secession that took on mass proportions when the parent group was expelled from the CIO in 1949.

By this date the Communist threat to the labor movement had been largely overcome either through victories of anti-Communists in existing unions or by their desertion to new unions. The Catholic labor schools and the ACTU were now free to put pressure on union racketeering amd allied abuses. Attention centered on the waterfronts where dock workers as a condition of employment were forced to pay tribute to vicious, irresponsible exploiters in the guise of union leaders. The "waterfront priest" echoed the cry for reform, for clean and effective unionism. Of these priests the most effective, perhaps, was John M. Corridan, S.J., associate director of the Xavier Labor School in New York, who defended, if he did not inspire, the great postwar strikes on the New York docks to break up the collusion between employers and the union bosses, headed by Joseph P. Ryan of the International Longshoremen's Association.[43] Becoming after 1945 thoroughly familiar with the situation, Corridan in speech and print urged the workers to reject Ryan's "sweetheart" contracts. In 1948 when Ryan settled with employers for a ten-cent hourly increase, the priest's article, "The Longshoremen's Case," published in *America* and circulated in thousands of reprints on the waterfront, helped the men successfully to hold out for a welfare fund and improved vacation terms. When the men walked off the docks again in 1951, Corridan insisted that the "real issue in the strike is Ryan's leadership. Those who stayed at work are mob controlled. The strike is just another symptom," he thought, "of the bitterness of the men over their exploitation." [44]

The reform of unions did not, of course, monopolize the activity of the labor priests, not even the ones on the waterfronts. Thus Edward D. Head of New York, Dennis J. Comey of Philadelphia,

[43] Allen Raymond, *Water-front Priest* (New York, 1955).
[44] Malcolm Johnson, "Father Gangbuster of the Docks. John M. Corridan, S.J., Leads a Winning Fight to Clean Up the World's Largest Port," *Catholic Digest*, XVI (May 1952), 26–33.

and John T. Powers of Boston gained distinction as mediators and arbitrators between longshoremen and their employers. "There is no corruption, kickbacks or racketeering on this waterfront," reported Father Powers, who in a two-year period, 1952–54, settled thirty-five disputes between the Boston Shipping Association and seventeen local unions. "Relations between labor and management . . . are most amicable," he happily observed.[45] Although the labor priests helped unions to get rid of Communist and racketeer leadership, they also believed that unions of the approved type should be extended to include practically all workers, contending, to this end, that ordinarily every Catholic worker was morally obligated to join a union in his industry or craft. Thus viewing the industrial picture, the labor priests did not approve the postwar drive to put legal restrictions on the power and influence of unionism. While they recognized that the Taft-Hartley Act of 1947 weakened Communist-led unions by denying them the protection of the National Labor Relations Board, these priests felt that the underlying purpose of the measure was not to equalize labor and management at the bargaining table but rather to harass labor and to check the onward march of unionization.[46]

They were more disturbed by the turn of events in the states. Under the Taft-Hartley Act every worker was obliged to become a dues-paying union member provided the majority employed in any particular bargaining unit voted to this effect. Overwhelmingly, the workers in government-supervised elections supported union security, or compulsory unionism, as its opponents dubbed it. So unnecessary did these elections prove to be that by amendment the law discontinued them in 1951. But the Taft-Hartley Act in Section 14(b) expressly permitted the states to deny union security, that is, to put unionism on a substantially voluntary basis. Although a few states, beginning with Florida in 1944, had outlawed union security before Taft-Hartley, the passage of the act undoubtedly encouraged other states, chiefly in the South and the trans-Mississippi West, to pass so-called right-to-work laws. Only Indiana, the last of the eighteen

---

[45] *Social Action Notes for Priests*, March 1955.
[46] Masse, "Moral Aspects of the Taft-Hartley Act," *Review of Social Economy*, VI (May 1948), 29–51; Charles W. Anrod, "Philosophy and Analysis of Recent Union-Control Legislation," ibid., 52–79.

states to enact this legislation, in 1957, was a predominantly industrial and urban community.[47]

By and large priests and bishops vigorously opposed the right-to-work movement, voicing their convictions in the press and before legislative committees in state after state. They were not impressed by the arguments of the few priests who backed the movement — John E. Coogan, S.J., of Detroit University,[48] Francis Connell, C.SS.R., dean of the school of theology at the Catholic University,[49] and above all Edward A. Keller, C.S.C., of Notre Dame, whose book, *The Case for Right-to-Work Laws*, already cited, attracted wide attention. Keller stated that in the interests of freedom the states should fully guarantee the right of the worker to join or not to join a union just as he saw fit. He contended that in the presence of the current powerful and aggressive labor movement compulsory unionism was unnecessary, a threat to the worker's liberty, political and otherwise, and therefore not a requirement of the moral law. "Nowhere in the social encyclicals," he said,

> is compulsory unionism specifically or implicitly demanded, nor do the social encyclicals state that workers have a moral obligation to belong to a union to exercise the right-to-work. In fact, Pope Pius XI, quoting Pope Leo, states that each individual "is quite free to join or not" private associations.[50]

The Notre Dame priest regretfully conceded, however, that the clergy and Catholic press were all but unanimously against him. Without denying that unionism was powerful in some segments of the economy, Keller's critics pointed to its weakness in most right-to-work states, in which the wage earners were often poorly paid and sometimes cruelly exploited. In effect Father Keller agreed with his Notre Dame colleague, Professor John H. Sheehan, that voluntary unionism was virtually impossible in plants or industries with a high and continuous labor turnover. As impatient of right-

[47] John V. Spielmans, "State Rights in Union Security Legislation," ibid., IX (September 1951), 111–23; John H. Sheehan, "What About 'Right-to-Work' Laws?" *Ave Maria*, April 23, 1955.

[48] "Can Nothing Be Said for State Right to Work Laws?" *Ecclesiastical Review*, CXXXIII (December 1955), 370–76, and "Protest: Case for Right to Work Laws," *Social Order*, VII (January 1957), 47.

[49] Connell to Monsignor Philip M. Hannan, May 31, 1955, quoted in Keller, *The Case for Right-to-Work Laws*, pp. 27–28.

[50] Ibid., p. 59.

to-work laws as of segregated schools, Archbishop Rummel of New Orleans pronounced the Louisiana measure of 1954 "unfair and unsocial class legislation contrary to the common good." [51] Although the measure, with the backing of sixty-six Catholic businessmen who defied the archbishop, was enacted, it was repealed for urban labor two years later. In other states — for example, Washington, Connecticut, and Ohio — the opinions of bishops may have turned the tide against right-to-work proposals. In a statement on March 22, 1955, before a joint House-Senate Labor Committee of the Connecticut General Assembly, the Archbishop of Hartford, Henry J. O'Brien, disputed the claim "that a fundamental right of the individual is invaded if he must join a union." It was neither immoral nor unethical, he said, "to require union membership for the greater common good of the group." He pointed out that in "our modern and complex society, every one is subject to prohibitions and restraints. . . ." [52]

Others spoke in much the same vein, with stress on the undesirability — and impossibility — of unlimited freedom in the economic sphere. The Reverend William J. Smith, Jesuit director of St. Peter's Institute of Industrial Relations in Jersey City, insisted that the "so called right-to-work type of legislation, based as it is on a principle of exaggerated individualism, is completely contrary to the basic concepts of a social philosophy." This kind of legislation was "a direct denial of the social aspect of labor" and "the end result of its universal application could be nothing short of anarchy." [53] Less bluntly but to the same effect reasoned the bishops of Ohio in urging defeat of a right-to-work constitutional amendment which was up for consideration by the voters in 1958. These bishops believed that the state should enforce union maintenance only when it was mutually accepted by management and labor through collective bargaining. Failure to do so under these conditions would, they feared, precipitate new causes of strife and bitterness.[54] This factor was stressed, to no avail, by the Reverend Thomas J. McDon-

[51] Masse, "Right-to-Work Laws," *America*, September 1, 1956.
[52] Masse, "What's Happening to Right-to-Work Laws?" ibid., May 7, 1955.
[53] *What's Wrong with Right-to-Work Laws* (Washington, D.C., 1958), pp. 6–7.
[54] "Statement on 'Right-to-Work' Amendment," *News Release*, March 20–21, 1958. Copy in Collection on Right-to-Work Laws, Department of Economics, University of Notre Dame.

ough, C.S.C., head of the department of economics at Notre Dame, and his colleagues (excepting Father Keller) in their telegram opposing passage of Indiana's right-to-work bill.[55] Father Benjamin L. Masse best summarized Catholic attitudes toward right-to-work legislation. Father Keller was correct, he said,

> in insisting that the state has a right in certain circumstances to limit the freedom of private groups, including the freedom of unions and employers to agree to union-shop contracts. Where most Catholic authorities in this country dissent from Father Keller is on the question of fact, namely, whether circumstances today justify the kind of state intervention represented by right-to-work laws. Almost all Catholic authorities who have spoken out on the issue regard right-to-work laws as an unnecessary and harmful restriction on union-management freedom — a restriction calculated to weaken unions, obstruct collective bargaining and embitter industrial relations. It is very doubtful whether anything Father Keller says to the contrary will change their minds.[56]

At the height of the right-to-work controversy an article in *Fortune* magazine dubbed the Catholic Church a pro-labor religious body — a widely held view in recent years, especially in conservative non-Catholic circles. Catholics generally, even zealous friends of social justice, resent the pro-labor tag as a caricature of their true position. In taking exception to the *Fortune* article the Reverend Neil O'Connor stated that the reason the Church "has been outstanding in this country in defending the rights of the working class is that, at times, their rights have been trampled on or ignored." In actual fact the Church stood for justice "and for the defense and promotion of the rights of all groups, be they workers or be they members of management or stock-holders or farmers." If in the future the reunited AFL — CIO should misuse its power, the leaders of the Church will "be speaking out in favor of the rights of management in a very sound and striking way." [57]

This attitude of Father O'Connor in the 1950s will recall to readers of this volume the precisely similar approach Catholics earlier had made to the labor movement. During the labor uprising of the

---

[55] "Indiana Curbs Unions," *America*, March 16, 1957; "The Reverend Thomas J. McDonough, C.S.C., Correspondence," Department of Economics, University of Notre Dame.

[56] "Right-to-Work Laws," loc. cit.

[57] "Church Pro-Labor," *Social Action Notes for Priests*, May 1955, p. 4.

1880s the Catholic leadership decided to support the workers on the assumption that their just demands could be met without injury to other groups or the public welfare. This positive conviction forthwith guided the successful efforts of Cardinal Gibbons in behalf of the Knights of Labor and later gave strength and persistence to the Catholic crusade against the rising tide of socialism in the labor movement. The most effective crusader had been Father Dietz, whose Militia of Christ, organized in 1910 to mobilize Catholic trade unionists for social justice, and his short-lived labor college a decade later, presumably foreshadowed the Association of Catholic Trade Unionists and the labor schools which have figured so prominently in Catholic social history in the last two decades. Although the founders of the ACTU did not acknowledge dependence on Dietz, many latter-day Catholic labor leaders, including Philip Murray, knew personally the pioneer priest and approved his program.[58]

Even more than the ACTU and the labor schools, the Industry Council plan mirrored past as well as contemporary Catholic aspirations and efforts in the field of industrial relations. As Murray and his friends among the clergy contended, the plan aimed to domesticate papal social teachings, particularly the occupational or vocational group system outlined in Pope Pius XI's *Quadragesimo anno* of 1931. Actually the roots of the plan penetrate far deeper into the soil of the Catholic social past. In some measure, at least, the plan was a final version of the late nineteenth-century Catholic stress on the arbitration process. While some journals, notably the *Pilot* of Boston, relied for labor's emancipation on strikes and boycotts, most leading Catholic publications urged peace with justice through arbitral tribunals armed with compulsory powers — a program sanctioned by implication in Pope Leo XIII's labor encyclical of 1891. In some respects this Catholic view of compulsory arbitration featured ideas and techniques of the mature social justice movement and its culminating agency, the Industry Council system.

Catholic concern with labor, from first to last, rested on the Church's manifold charities and benevolent associations. These in the first days were deemed a sufficient solution to social problems, and for a time, in the late 1870s and early 1880s, were offered as sub-

[58] Mary Harrita Fox, *Peter E. Dietz*, pp. 213–15, 279–81.

stitutes for labor unions. When, presently, the Church accepted the labor movement, the charitable organizations, sure now that prevention was better than cure, lent powerful support to trade unionism and labor legislation. This was especially true as social settlements and related adjuncts of scientific charity appeared on the social landscape after 1900. No group after 1910 championed, more firmly and wisely, the Church's full program, namely social justice and social charity, than the National Conference of Catholic Charities.

As Catholic social action began to make headway, it won encouragement from three successive movements of more or less representative character: the Catholic Congresses, the American Federation of Catholic Societies, and the National Catholic Welfare Conference. With the two Catholic Congresses — at Baltimore in 1889 and Chicago four years later — the "Americanist" or socially liberal bishops were closely associated. Inasmuch as the congresses were primarily concerned with showing "the compatibility of the patriotic profession with the religious one," they studied social questions in the broad context of Americanization. The American Federation of Catholic Societies (1901–18) was less insistent on speedy Americanization, being more tolerant and respectful of the cultural autonomy of the many immigrant groups in the Church's membership. The federation's successors, the National Catholic War Council (1917–20) and the National Catholic Welfare Council (Conference since 1923), launched a most impressive campaign for good citizenship in which immigrants were helped to learn English and acquire naturalization, and children were required to study civics in the parochial schools. The immigrant's main need, the N.C.W.C. insisted, was a socially just social order. To the cause of social justice, the N.C. W.C.'s Social Action Department, under the direction first of the brilliant John A. Ryan, and more recently of Raymond A. McGowan and George G. Higgins, has devoted four decades of unremitting effort, chiefly in the area of industrial relations, but with no little attention to social service, international peace, and interracial justice.

Undeniably, the Social Action Department has been important in its field. A competent religio-social historian has written that its influence has been "second to none in America" and that largely through its efforts "the Catholic record for social democracy probably outweighed the Protestant." [59] In recent years, particularly since 1933, Catholic social action has been extensive and richly varied, a response chiefly to the irresistible demands of the people in an era of depression and war for a greater measure of economic security, social justice, and democratic rights. Yet from its formative years American Catholicism had participated in reform movements: in the humanitarian crusade for urban welfare following the Civil War, in the labor crisis of the 1880s and 1890s, in the Socialist-social reform battles of the Progressive era, and in the organized social service of the World War I period. In affiliation with these movements, Catholic social action was prepared for its culmination in the impressive record of the last two decades.

[59] Nichols, *Democracy and the Churches*, pp. 131, 251.

BIBLIOGRAPHICAL NOTE

The materials on which this study is based have been utilized by the author in a series of articles and surveys published in the course of the last decade and a half: "The Reception of Leo XIII's Labor Encyclical in America, 1891–1919," *Review of Politics*, VII (October 1945), 464–95; "Monsignor John A. Ryan: An Historical Appreciation," ibid., VIII (January 1946), 128–34; "Origins of Catholic Social Reform in the United States: Ideological Aspects," ibid., XI (July 1949), 294–309; "The Catholic Factor in Urban Welfare: The Early Period, 1850–1880," ibid., XIV (July 1952), 289–324; "The Catholic Church and Social Problems in the World War I Era," *Mid-America*, XXX (July 1948), 139–51; "American Catholic Reaction to Industrial Conflict: The Arbitral Process, 1885–1900," *Catholic Historical Review*, XLI (January 1956), 385–407; "Preparing for Social Action, 1880–1920," in Leo R. Ward, C.S.C., editor, *The American Apostolate* (Westminster, Md., 1952), pp. 11–28; "The Catholic Church and the American Social Question," in Waldemar Gurian and M. A. Fitzsimons, editors, *The Catholic Church in World Affairs* (Notre Dame, 1954), pp. 377–99; and "The Catholic Factor in the Social Justice Movement," in Thomas T. McAvoy, C.S.C., editor, *Roman Catholicism and the American Way of Life* (Notre Dame, 1959), pp. 70–98. In this last article the writer stresses Catholic social action in the 1930s. The Yale scholar James E. Roohan has published a survey interpretative article, "American Catholics and the Social Question, 1865–1900," in United States Catholic Historical Society, *Historical Records and Studies*, XLIII (1954), 3–26, based on his doctoral dissertation of the same title. Much of the spadework in American Catholic social history was begun three or four decades ago by distinguished biographers, notably Allen S. Will, *Life of Cardinal Gibbons, Archbishop of Baltimore* (2 vols.; New York, 1922), and Frederick J. Zwierlein, *Life and Letters of Bishop McQuaid* (3 vols.; Rochester, 1925–27). More recently, specifically labor phases have been studied: J. W. Coleman, *Labor Disturbances in Pennsylvania, 1850–1880* (Washington, D.C., 1936); Henry J. Browne, *The Catholic Church and the Knights of Labor* (Washington, D.C., 1949); and Mary Harrita Fox, B.V.M., *Peter E. Dietz, Labor Priest* (Notre Dame, 1953). These books are exhaustive and illuminating. The foremost American Catholic champion of social justice, the late Monsignor John A. Ryan, detailed his "apologia" in his frank and vividly written autobiography, *Social Doctrine in Action. A Personal History* (New York, 1941). Ryan's social ethics is analyzed by Patrick W. Gearty, *The Economic Thought of Monsignor John A. Ryan* (Washington, D.C., 1953). Francis L. Broderick is preparing a biography of Ryan.

The Catholic crusade for social justice cannot be understood apart from the "Americanist" atmosphere which enveloped its genesis. Study of the Americanist movement has been at once the preoccupation and the glory of Catholic historical scholarship since World War II. In *The Great Crisis in American Catholic History, 1895–1900* (Chicago, 1957), Thomas T. McAvoy, C.S.C., has presented the first full story of the movement, not confining his penetrating analysis to America alone but exhibiting the impact of the "phantom heresy" on Catholics in Europe as well. Robert D. Cross, *The Emergence of Liberal Catholicism in America* (Cambridge, 1958), well treats the same subject from a present-day orientated point of view. The part played by German-American Catholics in the controversy is brought out by Colman J. Barry, O.S.B., *The Catholic Church and German Americans* (Milwaukee, 1953). Several superb biographies of Americanist leaders have recently appeared: Vincent F. Holden, C.S.P., *The Yankee Paul: Isaac Thomas Hecker,* (Vol. I; Milwaukee, 1958); John Tracy Ellis, *The Life of James Cardinal Gibbons, Archbishop of Baltimore* (2 vols.; Milwaukee, 1952); James H. Moynihan, *The Life of Archbishop John Ireland* (New York, 1953); and Patrick Henry Ahern, *The Life of John J. Keane, Educator and Archbishop* (Milwaukee, 1955).

In each of the foregoing books, with an exception or two, substantial quantities of personal papers and strictly archival materials have been utilized. In a study such as the present one, a generalized account of Catholic social action over a period of seventy-five years, newspapers and periodicals are indispensable for information and changing trends. This is especially true of the newspapers and periodicals which are devoted to some one special social interest as, for example, the *St. Vincent de Paul Quarterly,* I–XXI (1895–1916). Although not intended as a guide, Apollinaris W. Baumgartner, *Catholic Journalism, A Study of Its Development in the United States, 1789–1930* (New York, 1931), lists, dates, and locates (pp. 93–99) the 118 Catholic newspapers in existence in 1930, many of which had long histories. A few Catholic universities, notably the Catholic University of America and the University of Notre Dame, have extensive, if generally incomplete, files of several important Catholic newspapers. By far the best collection is owned by the American Catholic Historical Society of Philadelphia and housed at St. Charles Borromeo Seminary at Overbrook, Pennsylvania. Easily accessible here are the generous files, often coming down into the 1930s, of two hundred newspapers.

If one of the Catholic editors, Father David S. Phelan, of the *Western Watchman* of St. Louis, is to be believed, many Catholic papers "will compare favorably with the best Europe can produce." Their editorials, he wrote in 1905, "are read by all classes of Catholics from the heads of the hierarchy to the girl in the kitchen; and they really form the basis of Catholic public opinion." Their value to the religio-social historian is beyond question. On the genesis of the social justice movement in the last decades of the nineteenth century the *Pilot* of Boston is indispensable for fact and opinion, while the *Connecticut Catholic* of Hartford, the *Catholic Review* of New York, the *Catholic Advocate* of Louisville, and the *Catholic Record* of Indianapolis comment freely, often penetratingly, on the leading issues. The *Church Progress and Catholic World* of St. Louis ably voiced the conservative views of its editor, Condé B. Pallen. The *Catholic Herald* of New York, under the editorship of Dr. Michael Walsh, proudly championed the cause of workingmen along the lines of Leo XIII's labor encyclical. On the early twentieth-century Progressive movement the *New World* of Chicago, the Pittsburgh *Observer*, and the *Catholic Columbian-Record* of Columbus and Indianapolis are informative. Most important for pertinent comment are the major journals in Humphrey J. Desmond's newspaper chain, the *Catholic Citizen* of Milwaukee, the *Northwestern Chronicle* of St. Paul, and the *New Century* of Washington, D.C. For revealing details on Catholic-Socialist relationships, the scholar should consult the *Christian Socialist* (1903–21), edited by the Reverend Edward Ellis Carr for the (Protestant) Christian Socialist Fellowship. Arthur Preuss's *Catholic Fortnightly Review* of St. Louis urged the Church to organize itself for social service as did also the Jesuit weekly, *America*, from 1909, which with the *Commonweal*, since 1924, assumed a commanding position in Catholic journalism.

Throughout this study the author relied heavily on pertinent periodical material. The monthly magazine of the Paulists, the *Catholic World*, dating from 1865, devoted to labor and social problems hundreds of articles which were, for the most part, Americanist in viewpoint. The *American Catholic Quarterly Review*, I–XLIX (1876–1924), minimized Americanization while carrying many learned articles on charity, labor, and social theory as well as on literary and theological issues. The *Ecclesiastical Review* (*American Ecclesiastical Review*, I–XXXIII) from 1889 commented on new social needs and trends in short, well-written accounts. This magazine sponsored the *Dolphin*, "an ecclesiastical review for educated Catholics," I–VIII (1902–5). *Donohoe's Magazine*, I–LX (1879–1908), bore a somewhat similar relation to the *Pilot* through their common founder, Patrick Donohoe. Only a small portion of Catholic periodical literature has been systematically indexed: the *Catholic Magazine Index*, I–III (July 1937–December 1938), and the *Catholic Periodical Index*, 1930–33, 1939– , initiated by Paul J. Foik, C.S.C. Earnest Cushing Richardson, *Periodical Articles on Religion, 1890–1899* (2 vols.; New York, 1907, 1911), is an excellent subject and author index.

Many Catholic magazines and newspapers were official organs of societies and associations. The *I.C.B.U. Journal*, Philadelphia, 1873–1900, with historian and reformer Martin I. J. Griffin as its editor, and *Central-Blatt and Social Justice*, St. Louis, 1908 to the present (*Social Justice Review* since 1940), edited by the late Frederick P. Kenkel for more than four decades, detailed the religio-social work of the two great benevolent societies, the Irish Catholic Benevolent Union and the Central Verein. The *Bulletin*, 1880–1909, and the *C.T.A. News*, 1886–97, along with several papers of only local appeal, dealt with the Catholic Total Abstinence Union of America and the Catholic temperance movement in their heyday. The *St. Vincent de Paul Quarterly*, mentioned earlier, recorded Catholic charity trends, as reflected in Frederic Ozanam's great society, while the *Missionary*, after 1896, "devoted to the conversion of America" and published by the American Catholic Missionary Union, assigned two enlarged issues, IX (October 1904) and XI (October 1906), to the social question. Similarly, *Extension* magazine, the organ from 1906 of the Church Extension Society, surveyed the pre-World War I scene in a "Social Service Number," XI (October 1916). In *Columbia*, a monthly journal dating from 1921, the Knights of Columbus contributed substantially to later Catholic sociological literature.

The *Bulletin*, I–XII (1906–17), was published by the American Federation of Catholic Societies to advance general Catholic interests and the special social ends of the Social Service Commission. Under the same title the federation's successors, the National Catholic War Council and the National Catholic Welfare Conference (Council until late 1923), published a monthly journal (1919–29) and continued it, first as the *N.C.W.C. Review* (1930–31) and then as *Catholic Action* (1932–53), yearly indexed after 1933. Although informative, *Catholic Action* was decidedly less critical than the *Catholic Charities Review* which in 1917 replaced the *St. Vincent de Paul Quarterly*, becoming the common organ of the St. Vincent de Paul Society and the National Conference of Catholic Charities. On these journals Monsignor John O'Grady, secretary of the National Conference of Catholic Charities, after 1920, drew heavily in his *Catholic Charities in the United States. History and Problems* (Washington, D.C., 1930). No similar studies have been made of the American Federation of Catholic Societies and the National Catholic

Welfare Conference. But see, for a convention-by-convention account, Anthony Matre, K.S.G., "The American Federation of Catholic Societies," *Illinois Catholic Historical Review*, IX (January 1927), 247–59; ibid., X (July 1927), 38–47; ibid. (January 1928), 261–72; ibid., XI (July 1928), 56–65; ibid. (October 1928), 156–65; ibid. (January 1929), 251–63; ibid. (April 1929), 349–63; *Mid-America*, I (July 1929), 82–97; ibid., II (October 1930), 169–82; ibid. (January 1931), 269–87.

Some Catholic organizations have received adequate treatment: Sr. Joan Bland, *Hibernian Crusade. The Story of the Catholic Total Abstinence Union of America* (Washington, D.C., 1951); Joan Marie Donohoe, S.N.D., *The Irish Catholic Benevolent Union* (Washington, D.C., 1953), a superior study; Daniel T. McColgan, *A Century of Charity. The First One Hundred Years of the Society of St. Vincent de Paul in the United States* (2 vols.; Milwaukee, 1951); and Marguerite T. Boyland, *Social Welfare in the Catholic Church. Organization and Planning Through Diocesan Bureaus* (New York, 1941). M. Liguori Brophy, B.V.M., *The Social Thought of the German Roman Catholic Verein* (Washington, D.C., 1941), is somewhat lacking in historical orientation. Rural Catholicism is well treated in Mary Gilbert Kelly, O.P., *Catholic Immigrant Colonization Projects in the United States, 1815–1860* (New York, 1939); Mary Evangela Henthorne, B.V.M., *The Irish Catholic Colonization Association of the United States* (Champaign, 1932); James P. Shannon, *Catholic Colonization on the Western Frontier* (New Haven, 1957); and Raymond Philip Witte, S.M., *Twenty-five Years of Crusading. A History of the National Catholic Rural Life Conference* (Des Moines, 1948). Besides newspapers, these various books and monographs utilize available official records and personal material, mostly published. A good part of the William J. Onahan Papers at the University of Notre Dame, chiefly the ones concerned with the Catholic Congresses of 1889 and 1893, have been published: William H. Hughes, publisher, *Souvenir Volume Illustrated. Three Great Events in the History of the Catholic Church in the United States* (Detroit, 1889); and J. S. Hyland and Co., compilers, *Progress of the Catholic Church in America and the Great Columbian Catholic Congress of 1893* (4th ed.; Chicago, 1897). While the congresses did not have a journalistic organ, newspaper comment is well represented in the Onahan Papers. The two Missionary Congresses are covered in Francis C. Kelley, editor, *The First American Catholic Missionary Congress, 1908* (Chicago, 1909) and ibid., The Second American Catholic Missionary Congress, *Official Report, 1913* (Chicago, 1914).

Some of the books and journals mentioned earlier treat of the depression and early New Deal years. Among the books inspired by the crisis of the 1930s mention should be made of John A. Ryan, *A Better Economic Order* (New York, 1935), "the outcome of a course of lectures delivered at the 1934 summer session of the University of Wisconsin," and Virgil Michel, O.S.B., *Christian Social Reconstruction. Some Fundamentals of the Quadragesimo Anno* (Milwaukee, 1937). In the *Social Justice Bulletin*, January 1933–November 1943, Michael O'Shaughnessy, industrial journalist, opposed the enemies of the New Deal, chiefly greedy pressure groups, while Edward Koch of Germantown, Illinois, edited the *Guildsman*, I–IX (October 1932–September 1941), to combat wage-conscious unionism, consumer co-operation, and other alleged deviations from the guild or vocational group ideal. During the 1930s (and since) the *Catholic Worker*, from 1933, exerted a seminal influence. Two of its devotees among college graduates, Richard Deverall and Norman McKenna of Villanova College, launched the *Christian Front*, I–IV (January 1936–June 1939), "a monthly magazine of social reconstruction published and edited by Catholic laymen." When fascists and Jew-baiters appropriated its title, the journal continued as *Christian Social Reconstruction*, IV–VII (September 1939–June 1942). For the origins and tribulations of the journal, see "Over the Dam," by a Catholic editor, VII (November 1941), 267–72.

Much of the periodical material on Catholic social action since the beginning of World War II is reproduced in condensed form in the *Catholic Digest*, from 1936. Of special importance are the papers and discussions in the learned societies, the American Catholic Sociological Society, from 1938, and the Catholic Economic Association, from 1941, and in their journals, the *American Catholic Sociological Review*, from March 1940, and the *Review of Social Economy*, from December 1942. Also of use is *Social Order*, from 1947, published by the Institute of Social Order at St. Louis University, the most scholarly of numerous recently established Jesuit institutes or schools on social and industrial relations.

INDEX